# OXFORD HISTORICAL MONOGRAPHS

*Editors*

# GLADSTONE

## CHURCH, STATE, AND TRACTARIANISM

A study of his religious
ideas and attitudes,
1809–1859

BY
PERRY BUTLER

CLARENDON PRESS · OXFORD
1982

*Oxford University Press, Walton Street, Oxford OX2 6DP*

*London Glasgow New York Toronto*
*Delhi Bombay Calcutta Madras Karachi*
*Kuala Lumpur Singapore Hong Kong Tokyo*
*Nairobi Dar es Salaam Cape Town*
*Melbourne Auckland*

*and associate companies in*
*Beirut Berlin Ibadan Mexico City*

*Published in the United States by*
*Oxford University Press, New York*

*British Library Cataloguing in Publication Data*
*Butler, Perry*
  *Gladstone: church, state, and Tractarianism. –*
  *(Oxford historical monographs)*
  *1. Gladstone, W.E. – Religion*
  *I. Title*
  *941.081'092          DA563.5*

*ISBN 0-19-821890-7*

*Typeset by Servis Typesetting Ltd. (Manchester)*
*Printed in Great Britain*
*at the University Press, Oxford,*
*by Eric Buckley*
*Printer to the University*

To my Mother and Father
with love and gratitude.

And 'Hail the hour', they cried, 'when each high morn
England, at one, shall stand at the church gate,
And vesper bells o'er all the land be borne,
And Newman mould the Church, and Gladstone stamp the
State.'

William Alexander
*The New Atlantis*

# PREFACE

This monograph is a slightly modified version of the doctoral thesis I submitted to the University of Oxford in October 1977.

During the research and writing I have incurred many debts. I would like to thank the staffs of all the libraries and archives I have used: the National Library of Scotland; Oriel College, Oxford; Keble College, Oxford; Trinity College, Cambridge; Belvoir Castle, Leicestershire, and especially the staff of Bodley's Upper Reading Room and the staff of Duke Humphrey's Library; the Manuscript Room of the British Library and the archivist and staff of the Clwyd Record Office. Thanks are also due to Sir William Gladstone and the Warden and staff of St. Deiniol's Library, Hawarden; Miss Irene Wilberforce for allowing me to see the letters of Gladstone to R. I. Wilberforce, and the Principal and Librarians of Pusey House, Oxford.

Many friends have helped in various ways and also deserve my grateful thanks: Susan Bennett, Clive Burgess, Claire Cross, Sheridan Gilley, Brendan Keith, David Nicholls, Gladys Nixey, Geoffrey Rowell, Victoria Spencer-Ellis, Alan Warren and not least my pupils at Bromsgrove School.

My most enduring debt of gratitude must, however, be reserved for Dr John Walsh and Dr Colin Matthew. Dr Walsh suggested this subject, supervized the thesis, and has been a constant source of help, encouragement and wise counsel. Dr Matthew has generously shared with me his vast knowledge of Mr Gladstone and I am particularly grateful to him for helping me prepare the thesis for publication and for the sustained interest, encouragement and friendship of both him and his family.

Special thanks are due to my friend Leonard Marsh who helped with the proofs. A debt of another kind is acknowledged in the dedication.

Chiswick                                                    Perry Butler
September 1980

# CONTENTS

# ABBREVIATIONS

| | |
|---|---|
| *Autobiographica* | John Brooke and Mary Sorensen (eds.), *The Prime Ministers' Papers: W. E. Gladstone I: Autobiographica* (1971–2) |
| *BL* | British Library |
| *Diary* | M. R. D. Foot and H. C. G. Matthew (eds.), *The Gladstone Diaries 1825–1868,* 6v. (1968–78) |
| *Hawn. P.* | Hawarden Papers (deposited in St. Deiniol's Library, Hawarden) |
| *Lathbury* | D. C. Lathbury (ed.), *Correspondence on Church and Religion of W. E. Gladstone,* 2v. (1910) |
| *Memoranda* | John Brooke and Mary Sorensen (eds.), *The Prime Ministers' Papers: W. E. Gladstone II: Autobiographical Memoranda* (1971–2) |
| *Morley* | J. Morley, *Life of William Ewart Gladstone,* 3v. (1903) |

# INTRODUCTION

In one sense Gladstone had no religious development: he was what Tertullian called *anima naturaliter Christiana*. Although his long life spanned a century which saw the gradual loosening of the ties of orthodoxy and the growth of doubt and disbelief, Gladstone's personal faith remained unshaken. Although his mind was restless and his opinions altered on many matters, the overriding sense of God's Providence, the certainty of Judgement, the divine rule and governance of life that was his from childhood, never left him. He held to a conservative and dogmatic Christianity, never wavering in his commitment to it, nor tiring in his defence of it, nor attempting to modify or dilute it when it conflicted with the temper of the age. In his will he commended himself 'to the infinite mercies of God in the Incarnate Son as my only and sufficient hope'[1] with conviction and resignation more reminiscent of a medieval monk than a busy nineteenth-century politician.

Yet in another sense Gladstone had a religious development both complex and fascinating. Throughout his life he was constantly involved in religious controversy. He numbered among his friends some of the most important and influential religious figures of the age. Born into an evangelical home, he became a High-Churchman. An apologist for religious establishment, he abandoned his ideas as impractical, and came to believe that the Church could no longer rely upon State support to fulfil its mission. A supporter of the Oxford Movement, he witnessed its disintegration and collapse. A passionate critic of the Roman Catholic Church, he saw his two closest friends join it.

Religion was central to Gladstone's life. But its all-pervasiveness makes it easier either simply to assume its presence, or ignore it entirely. Most historians have concen-

[1] BL Add. MS 44827.

trated upon Gladstone the politician, and especially his years as
Prime Minister. This is not surprising. Yet it has led to a curious
neglect of the religious side of his life, which was to him primary
and which, he believed, gave meaning to his political
endeavour. While often stressing the religious foundation of his
life, historians have not attempted to define it, or relate it to his
political development.

    This neglect is due in part to John Morley's biography. His
*Life of William Ewart Gladstone*, published in three stout volumes
in 1903, remains the starting-point for any discussion of its
subject.[2] But in the introduction Morley warned his readers that
if they wanted 'the detailed history of Mr. Gladstone as
theologian and churchman', they would look in vain among his
pages. 'Nobody', he wrote, 'is more sensible than their writer of
the gap.'[3] And he excused himself on the ground that he lacked
the confidence and ardour of an adherent that was necessary if
the subject was to be treated with the understanding it deserved.

    In fact the omission was due as much to a deliberate
restriction placed on him by the Gladstone family as to the
conscious design of Morley himself. The family wished the more
intimate aspects of Gladstone's spiritual life to remain private
and they may have been unhappy at the prospect of a declared
agnostic writing about the religious life of so eminent a
churchman. Arthur Godley, later Lord Kilbracken, who had
been approached by the family as a possible biographer,
certainly felt the choice of Morley was a bad one for this reason.
It was 'very much like choosing a man who has been blind from
his birth, but a clever writer, to do the biography of Millais or
Burne Jones'.[4] Sir William Harcourt was blunter: 'You cannot
write about his religion because you don't believe it,' he told
Morley.[5]

    This supposed limitation has, however, been exaggerated,
and put in the form of Harcourt's remark it is patently absurd.
Like many Victorian agnostics Morley was not uninterested in

    [2] For Morley's biography see M. R. D. Foot, 'Morley's Gladstone: A Reappraisal',
*Bulletin of the John Rylands Library*, 51, Spring 1969, 368–80; and the discussion in A. O. J.
Cockshut, *Truth to Life, the art of biography in the 19th century* (1974), 175–92. For Morley
himself see D. A. Hamer, *John Morley, liberal intellectual in politics* (1968).
    [3] J. Morley, *The Life of William Ewart Gladstone* (1903), i. 3; hereafter cited as *Morley*.
    [4] *The Gladstone Diaries*, i (1968), Introduction, xxv.
    [5] G. M. Young, *Mr Gladstone* (1944), 4.

religious questions, nor devoid of what might be called a 'religious' sensibility. He had already written studies of Burke and Cromwell, so the interaction of politics and religion was not a theme foreign to him. Nor, in spite of his disclaimer, is the ecclesiastical side of Gladstone's life ignored in the biography. Religion was, he admitted in an early chapter, 'the biographic clue'.[6] Although concerned primarily with politics, for, as he declared on the second page, 'it was to his thoughts, his purposes, his ideals, his performance as a statesman . . . that Mr. Gladstone owes the lasting substance of his fame', Morley was willing to admit two hundred pages later that, 'all his activities were in his own mind one. This, we can hardly repeat too often, is the fundamental fact of Mr. Gladstone's history. Political life was only part of his religious life.'[7]

Religion was not, therefore, forgotten. Morley provided, for example, chapters dealing with Gladstone's first book on Church and State, the Tractarian catastrophe, and the Gorham case. But his narrative approach meant that the ecclesiastical side of Gladstone's life was compartmentalized and subordinate. While he repeated often that politics and religion were in Gladstone intertwined, they do not appear so, and for the first half of Gladstone's life this is rather distorting.

The importance of religious factors in moulding Gladstone's political vocation in the early 1830s, the ecclesiastical dimension of his Toryism, the centrality of his views of Church and State for his political philosophy, and the intensity of the intellectual crisis of the mid-1840s when this vision was abandoned, are all under-estimated. Ecclesiastical matters are seen as something essentially separate, episodes unconnected with the unfolding of Gladstone's political career as future Liberal Statesman. Thus while Morley acknowledged the significance of religion in providing the mainspring of Gladstone's personal life, the control it exercised, and the direction it gave to, his political development, especially in the 1830s and 1840s, tends to be obscured. This is a pity, for it seems from the concluding pages of the first volume that Morley was not, in fact, unaware of the crucial significance of Gladstone's ideas of Church and State,

---

[6] *Morley*, i. 52.
[7] *Morley*, ii. 200.

and the Oxford Movement, in his progress from Tory to
Liberal.[8]

An attempt to provide a more detailed account of Gladstone's
ecclesiastical development was made by D. C. Lathbury. In
1907 he published a short life of Gladstone in the *Leaders of the
Church* series edited by G. W. E. Russell. Three years later he
published the more important *Correspondence on Church and
Religion of William Ewart Gladstone* in two volumes.[9] The son of
Thomas Lathbury, the historian of the Non-Jurors, Lathbury
was a layman and an Anglo-Catholic Liberal.[10] Professionally
he was an ecclesiastical journalist and edited two High-Church
periodicals, *The Guardian* and the less well known, and short-
lived *Pilot*. He was a keen student of Anglo-Catholic history and
had a vast knowledge of ecclesiastical matters. He deserves
credit both for accurate transcription, and for a discriminating
sense of which letters were important and which were not. As a
source, therefore, his two volumes are invaluable but marred,
alas, by his decision to arrange his material topically instead of
chronologically. As so many topics overlap this is not merely
frustrating for the user, it is at times misleading. For example,
Gladstone's letter to Manning, 29 March 1837, is separated by
646 pages from another letter written on substantially the same
subject to the same correspondent just four days later.

The present study, like Morley's, does not attempt to provide
the detailed history of Gladstone as theologian and churchman.
To do so would be a colossal undertaking. The Gladstone papers
in the British Museum alone, the largest collection of any prime
minister, run to seven hundred and fifty volumes.

Rather, it focuses on the first fifty years of Gladstone's life and
on three interrelated themes: his becoming a High-Churchman;
the development of his ideas on Church and State; and his
relationship with the Oxford Movement. These years saw
Gladstone move from Toryism to Liberalism, a move which, it
will be argued, owed much to changes in his religious ideas and
attitudes in the 1840s and early 1850s. His acceptance of office

<hr>

[8] *Morley*, i. 631–4.
[9] D. C. Lathbury, *Mr Gladstone* (1907); *Correspondence on Church and Religion of William
Ewart Gladstone, selected and arranged by D. C. Lathbury*, 2v. (1910); hereafter cited as
*Lathbury*.
[10] For Lathbury himself, see the obituary in *The Guardian*, 16 June 1922, 450.

under Palmerston in 1859 has been taken as a suitable point at which to conclude. While not a decisive event in his political development, it was interpreted as marking a definite change in his party allegiance. By the late 1850s, also, the crisis of the Oxford Movement had come to an end and the terms of the religious debate had begun to alter.

On a more personal level it is the story of a friendship between three men: Gladstone, Henry Edward Manning, and James Hope (later Hope-Scott). Brought together in the 1830s by a deep religious commitment, they were to find that in the next decade circumstances and differing ecclesiastical convictions forced them apart. To write history in these personal terms is, perhaps, unfashionable. Nonetheless, the first half of the nineteenth century was a period of peculiarly intense friendships, passionate loyalties and fierce jealousies. To neglect these would be seriously to distort the history, especially the religious history, of the period.[11]

The study itself is based largely upon the six published volumes of Gladstone's *Diary* and upon letters and memoranda, still mostly unpublished. Besides the vast Gladstone deposit in the British Library, it draws upon the large and underused collection of family papers kept in the Clwyd Record Office at Hawarden; the correspondence of Gladstone, Manning, and Hope in the Hope-Scott collection in the National Library of Scotland, which includes a small though fascinating collection of Gladstone's letters to the ecclesiastical lawyer E. L. Badeley; the correspondence of Gladstone with Samuel and Robert Wilberforce; his letters to Pusey, Keble, and Newman; his letters to Edward Hawkins, Provost of Oriel; his letters to Lord John Manners, Lord Lincoln, and Richard Monckton Milnes; as well as a number of smaller collections and individual letters. It also makes use of the very important letters of Manning to Gladstone, which Manning's biographer Purcell thought had been destroyed, but which were discovered by the Abbé Alphonse Chapeau, who, in 1955, edited them as a thesis for the University of Paris.

[11] For the importance of friendship in the history of the Oxford Movement, see the classic account by R. W. Church, *The Oxford Movement. Twelve Years, 1833–1845* (1891), especially the comparison with Florence of *Quattrocento*, 141; and the eloquent evocation by D. Newsome, *The Parting of Friends* (1966).

The nature of the sources and Gladstone's involved prose style, as well as his tendency to draw fine distinctions, have meant a considerable amount of quotation. I hope that this has not become excessive. It seemed to me more sensible to quote at length in many instances than resort to contrived or misleading paraphrase.

In focusing on Gladstone's religious development and his friendships, and in organizing the material as I have done, I am conscious of assuming knowledge of the political and ecclesiastical background more than, perhaps, I should. The line between history and biography is not an easy one to draw. Like Morley, I would not be presumptuous enough to suppose that this difficulty has always been successfully overcome. Gladstone said of reconstructing the income-tax that he did not call the task Herculean, because Hercules could not have done it. I would, again with Morley, simply plead: 'It may be that Hercules himself would have succeeded little better.'[12]

Unlike Morley, however, I am fortunate in that many historians have in recent years written extensively about the religion and politics of Gladstone's time. I am more than happy to acknowledge my debt to them.

---

[12] *Morley*, i. 2.

# THE MAKING OF A HIGH CHURCH TORY:
## 1809–1838

# EVANGELICALISM AND CALLING: 1809–1832

Gladstone's early religious development presents two major problems: the nature of his evangelicalism and his choice of career. Why did the product of an evangelical home forsake the tradition of his family and become a High-Churchman? Did this development closely parallel that of other supporters of the Oxford Movement who came from evangelical backgrounds? Again, why as a young man destined by his father for a career in public life, did he decide to become a clergyman and then, subsequently, resolve to enter politics after all? Was this his own free choice or was it, as popularly held, a decision forced upon him unwillingly by an autocratic and overbearing father?

In old age Gladstone described his home environment as 'strictly Evangelical' and his early creed as 'that of the Evangelical School, whose bigotry I shared but whose fervour if it possessed me at all possessed me only by fits and starts'.[1] Like many memories, however, this description both of the religious culture into which he was born and of his own response to it, gives an over-simplified and somewhat misleading picture.

For although the Gladstone family was evangelical, this was due as much to their Scottish background, to a compound of Lowland earnestness and Highland episcopalianism, as it was to the permeation of 'vital religion' among the English upper classes at the end of the eighteenth century.

Gladstone's parents had married in 1800. His father, John, was a wealthy Liverpool merchant who originated from Leith, his mother, Anne Mackenzie Robertson, was the daughter of the Provost of Dingwall.[2]

John Gladstone had arrived in Liverpool some twenty years

---

[1] *Autobiographica*, 26 July 1894, 148–9. For Gladstone's later appraisal of evangelicalism see *Gleanings*, vii. 201–41.

[2] For the career of John Gladstone and the family background of W. E. Gladstone, based almost entirely on the family papers at Hawarden, see S. G. Checkland, *The Gladstones, A Family Biography, 1764–1851* (1971).

earlier. The son of Thomas Gladstones a Leith corn merchant, he had come south like many Scots before him in search of better prospects and after a few years as a corn trader had diversified and vastly extended his business interests moving into property, shipping and cotton, and acquiring sugar plantations in the West Indies. By the second decade of the nineteenth century he had amassed an enormous fortune and become one of Liverpool's leading merchants.

In leaving home he had shown himself a far bolder and more ambitious man than his father. Thomas Gladstones was content with his lot and not anxious to exploit his business possibilities further. Indeed he regarded money as a temptation and its accumulation as a positive hindrance to spiritual progress, a conviction rooted in his religious beliefs.

He was not a native of Leith, but had come from the small town of Biggar in the Lowlands where the Covenanting tradition still lingered. When he was ten years old the revivalistic outburst known as the 'Cambuslang Wark' had swept through the upper wards of Lanarkshire. Together these influences had bred a faith that was stern, dogmatic and puritan. He felt no sympathy for the moderate party then dominant in the Scottish Church, and as an elder in the North Leith Kirk he played his part in rooting out moral laxity and enforcing the strict Calvinistic discipline as generations had done before him. He lived ever conscious of the reality of death and the inevitability of divine judgement.

> I entreat you will not let the affairs of this life so occupy your attention as to shut out a serious concern for the more important interests of another life, [he urged John on his twenty-third birthday.] For we know neither the day nor the hour we may stand before the awful Tribunal.[3]

John Gladstone, however, quietly discarded the severer elements of this rigid faith. His temperament was different. He was less afraid of the corrupting possibilities of worldly success. He had little of his father's sensitive conscience, his inhibitions, or his sense of guilt. His own religious convictions were genuine enough but they were simple, practical and unreflective. They did not prevent him owning slaves on his Demerara plantations when the need for a profitable new source of investment

---

[3] Checkland, op. cit., 18.

required it, nor from attacking the abolitionist cause, however incompatible that may have seemed to his fellow evangelicals in the 'Clapham Sect'. He was also circumspect enough to ensure a return of 5 per cent on the money he spent building new evangelical churches in the Liverpool suburbs.

He regarded intellectual speculation in religious matters with suspicion:

> I have not looked into either the sermon or answer which you sent your mother [he wrote to the more theologically minded William.] I have no relish for such controversy on points of doctrine most of which have their origins in the notions of theologists, for I do not consider such discussions as edifying in their nature or necessary to salvation, whilst we have the Bible to resort to as our guide and instructor.[4]

And in a letter concerning a cousin he proffered his twenty-one year old son advice very different from that his father had given him forty years before.

> I believe him aimiable and well disposed, [he wrote of the youth,] but he seems so occupied with preparing himself for the next world that he is disposed to abandon the concerns of this, such a course, so taken, never fails to lead to the neglect of both its duties and obligations.[5]

As there was no Scottish Church in Liverpool he worshipped initially with other Scots in Benn's Garden Chapel. But this arrangement proved unsatisfactory and in 1792, the year of his first marriage, he was one of a syndicate of seven who helped establish a Scots Kirk in Oldham Street, with a Caledonian School opposite. When his first wife Jane Hall died childless six years later, his second marriage was solemnized in St. Peter's Parish Church and in 1804 he paid £203 for two seats in the newly-built St. Mark's Church. By then he seems to have ceased regularly attending presbyterian worship and counted himself a member of the Church of England.

Perhaps it was his new wife, anxious for a more congenial ministry, who persuaded him to make the change. Anne Mackenzie Gladstone remains a shadowy figure. She died at the age of fifty-three when William was twenty-five and he remembered her as 'a woman of warm piety but broken health'.[6] Her frailty and submissiveness contrasted with the commanding

---

[4] J. Gladstone to W. E. Gladstone, 4 Mar. 1831, Hawn. P. Cf. the remarks of Thomas Gladstones to his son above.

[5] J. Gladstone to W. E. Gladstone, 2 July 1831, Hawn. P.

[6] *Autobiographica*, 149.

personality of her husband. Perhaps that in itself is significant. How they came to meet is unclear though they may have been brought together by James Fraser, a local coal merchant of Highland episcopalian stock, who was later William's godfather.

Despite her stoutly episcopalian and Jacobite ancestry, her own religious convictions inclined to evangelicalism and she soon found a place within the mainstream of Liverpool evangelical church life. She was prominent in the SPCK, the Mariners' Church and the Ladies' Auxiliary Bible Society. She became a friend of William Wilberforce. She corresponded with Hannah More and a visit to that formidable evangelical matriarch was among William's earliest memories.[7] He also remembered a visit to Cambridge where, no doubt at his mother's bidding, his father consulted the renowned evangelical leader, Charles Simeon, about suitable incumbents for the two churches he had built.[8] In June 1817 when the prominent Scottish evangelical Thomas Chalmers visited Liverpool, the Gladstones acted as hosts.

William himself was inclined to doubt that his mother influenced his religious opinions.[9] But it was she who set the devotional tone in the Gladstone household and his earliest apprehension of religion must have been conditioned by the ordered pattern of evangelical piety, its family prayers, churchgoing, and strict sabbath observance which was part of the fabric of his home life.

In a letter of 1818 or 1819 his mother wrote that she believed William, then about ten years old, to have been 'truly converted to God'.[10] Whatever that implied, it meant at least that the young lad had absorbed fully and unselfconsciously the language and religious ethos surrounding him. How fully he had done so we can gauge from a verse taken from a long poem, typical of many scattered among his early papers, which he wrote for his favourite sister Anne, aged nearly thirteen, at Christmas 1822:

[7] *Autobiographica*, 15.
[8] *Autobiographica*, 14.
[9] *Autobiographica*, 150.
[10] G. W. E. Russell, *Mr Gladstone's religious development: a paper read in Christ Church, May 5, 1899*. 2nd ed. (1899), 7.

I see my Saviour languish on the tree
I see the big drops on his forehead now
Lord let me come—Come nearer unto Thee
And kiss thy wounds and bathe Thy bleeding brow.[11]

Ann was the eldest of the Gladstone children. There were six in all. William Ewart, named after his father's friend, was the fifth child and the fourth son. He was born on the 29 December 1809. His elder brothers Thomas, Robertson and John Neilson were separated by less than three years and so tended to form a natural group apart from their younger brother. As a result, William was a rather isolated little boy and in consequence grew closest to Anne and to his younger sister Helen Jane.

He became deeply fond of Anne and her early death in 1829 after long years of illness was a tragic blow. She became an idealized saintly figure in his imagination, an impossible standard of purity and zeal against which to measure himself. For years afterwards he solemnly recorded the anniversary of her death in his diary, and his frequent self-disparagement there gained much of its intensity from the contrast he felt between his supposed sinfulness and her undoubted perfection. 'O is it possible that such a saint can have held communion with such a devil?' he asked himself in 1831.[12]

She was also his godmother and perhaps this made her more anxious to act as religious guide and confidante, a duty she fulfilled with due earnestness. On the occasion of his confirmation, for example, she wrote recalling her own, attributing her ill-health to lack of dependence on God's grace then, and exhorting William to take seriously the years of youth, 'In time we must reap the fruit of the seed then sown, and I feel that I reap it now . . .'.[13] She did not scruple to reprove him if she felt he was likely to be led into error. Her moral code, while it did not forbid card games or drinking, would not permit a visit to the theatre without serious misgivings. On one occasion, for instance, she was extremely displeased by William's 'inconsistent' conduct in visiting the theatre with his brother Robertson and reminded him of their mutual agreement made some

---

[11] W. E. Gladstone to A. M. Gladstone, 24 Dec. 1822, Hawn. P.
[12] *Diary*, i, 17 Apr. 1831.
[13] A. M. Gladstone to W. E. Gladstone, 7 Feb. 1827, Hawn. P.

years before never to go anywhere where they could not seek
God's presence or undertake anything on which they could not
seek His blessing. Her warning was blunt: 'the end of these
things is Remorse, even if it please to God to give us that
Repentance which is unto Life'.[14] Not only did she guide his
conduct, she seems also to have influenced the development of
his theological opinions. Her own, while evangelical, were
somewhat eclectic. Although her parents read the moderate
evangelical magazine the *Christian Observer*, she became an avid
reader of the new and more aggressively Calvinist *Record* and
frequently sent it on to her brother when he was away from
home. Yet she had, William later recalled, 'an opinion that, the
standard divines of the English Church were of great value'. It
was this insight he later maintained, that started him on some
'by paths of opinion' between school and university which led to
his first divergence from the religious tradition of his youth.[15]

In 1815 the Gladstone family moved from Rodney Street to
Seaforth House some five miles down river from the centre of
Liverpool. William began his education there at the small parish
school attached to St. Thomas's Church which his father had
built. It was run by the incumbent, the Revd William Rawson,
whom Gladstone remembered as a man 'of high No Popery'
opinions.[16] In fact this description is rather misleading for
Rawson, recommended to John Gladstone by Simeon, seems to
have been a good example of a moderate evangelical: earnest,
hardworking, loyal to the Prayer Book, with a distaste for the
more extreme views beginning to circulate in evangelical circles
in the 1820s. Although Gladstone could not recollect being
influenced by him, he did sometimes write from university to ask
his views on controversial issues and clearly thought of him as a
man of sincere and balanced convictions.

At the age of eleven William was sent to Eton following in the
steps of his brothers Robertson and Thomas. John Gladstone
was acutely conscious of the limitations of his social background
and lack of education. He had therefore determined that his sons
should enjoy the opportunities denied him which his wealth

---

[14] A. M. Gladstone to W. E. Gladstone, 15 Aug. 1827, Hawn. P.
[15] *Autobiographica*, 140.
[16] *Autobiographica*, 20.

could now buy. Above all he nurtured the hope that they would eventually achieve distinction in public life, and the road to success in that sphere lay through the public schools and the universities. He had begun to realize that he could never now achieve the political influence he craved. Although of some importance in local politics, he never secured the cherished nomination for Liverpool itself and though he was an MP for some nine years, first for Lancaster, then Woodstock, and finally for Berwick where he was unseated for bribery in 1827, his parliamentary career was undistinguished and ended in humiliation. His hopes of achieving national political fame he transferred to his sons.

His desire that they should succeed outweighed any fears he might have had about the brutality of the public schools or their low reputation in evangelical circles for 'sound religion'. William Wilberforce, for example, deeply concerned for his sons' spiritual welfare, had discounted a public school education 'for its probable effects on eternal state'.[17] Mrs Gladstone, however, may have felt greater foreboding for she had heard of 'the very awful state of the Church at Eton'.[18] Perhaps it was in deference to her that the Gladstone boys were spared the horrors of the lower school.

In fact only William enjoyed his time there, no doubt because of the four sons he alone had the capacity to sustain his father's ambitions.[19] John Neilson had early taken an independent line and entered the Royal Navy. Robertson began at Eton in 1819 but was clearly unsuited to the school or to politics. After two years he was taken away and sent to Glasgow College where the curriculum and atmosphere was more suitable for an intending merchant. Tom, the eldest, went to Eton in 1817 but was desperately unhappy from the beginning. He found work difficult and his situation a trial. Depressed and lonely, he asked several times to leave and although in the end he stayed five years he never reached the sixth form.

As William overlapped with Tom in his first year the

[17] C. H. E. Smyth, *Simeon and Church Order, a study in the origins of the Evangelical Revival in Cambridge in the 18th century* (1940), 52.
[18] Checkland, op. cit., 130.
[19] His father realized this, see his remark in *Diary*, i. 10 Aug. 1826. 'You shall be my biographer William.'

transition from the quiet and ordered routine of Seaforth House was less painful, though the attitude to religion at school caused him considerable distress and bewilderment. For a sensitive boy from a devout home the cold formality of chapel, the carefree indifference of so many boys to religion and the easy going amorality of the schoolboy code came as a chilling shock. Not long after his arrival he wrote to his mother that he had never seen anything 'so really shameful as the whole system of going to Church'. It was impossible to derive the least good from it and he felt it was only 'an invention of the masters to cheat the fellows out of their time'.[20]

He later recalled that at Eton 'the actual teaching of Christianity was all but dead though happily none of its forms had been surrendered'.[21] There was certainly no religious instruction as such except the occasional study of the Greek New Testament, Tomline's *Elements of Theology*, and a sermon on Sunday mornings. These were seldom to his taste and letters home often contained complaints about the preacher's manner or message.[22]

Chapel was primarily a roll call and the services were often conducted merely mechanically. The nearest approximation to direct religious teaching was the custom called 'prose' when the upper school assembled between 2 and 3 p.m. on a Sunday afternoon and the Headmaster, the notorious Dr Keate, gave out notices and then read from a book such as Blair's *Sermons*, or a short passage from the classics with some moral content and then set the theme for the next week.[23]

Some effort was made, however, in relation to confirmation, for in June 1826 he wrote to his mother, 'I must do Eton the justice to say that the Masters take a good deal of pains in preparing fellows for confirmation.'[24] His own preparation eight months later seems to have been something of an exception, which may explain his remarks to A. C. Benson in old age pouring scorn on the perfunctory instruction he had received.[25]

[20] W. E. Gladstone to A. Gladstone, 29 Oct. 1822, Hawn. P.
[21] *Gleanings*, vii. 138.
[22] See e.g. the letter to his mother, 23 Nov. 1825, Hawn. P.
[23] A. C. Benson, *Fasti Etonenses* (1899), 297.
[24] W. E. Gladstone to A. Gladstone, 27 June 1826, Hawn. P.
[25] Benson, loc. cit., 500.

The confirmation in 1827 seems to have been arranged at short notice, for William was told only seven days in advance. Nonetheless, his tutor the Revd H. H. Knapp, a kindly, easy-going and scholarly man, did read the boys a few sermons relating to confirmation and suggested some biblical passages and the Catechism for study.

Such brevity, however, mattered little in William's case. His own piety was already well advanced: now seventeen, he had read the Bible regularly since childhood and to this staple diet he had begun to add various quite weighty works of theology as his diary, begun it seems three years earlier, clearly shows.

Shortly before confirmation he had begun regularly reading the Gospels on Sunday evenings with help from D'Oyly and Mant's *Notes*, and both before and after he systematically tackled the two volumes of Tomline's *Elements*. He finished this four months later and pronounced it 'as far as I can judge a very good and useful work'. Both these books, it is interesting to note, were representative of 'high and dry' theology and their authors renowned opponents of the evangelicals.[26] According to Gladstone's later recollections, he had been brought up to believe that D'Oyly and Mant's *Notes* were heretical.[27] This did not perturb him at the time, though in August he read Thomas Scott the evangelical commentator for comparison, so he was clearly conscious that they represented different standpoints.[28]

Gladstone was confirmed on 1 February by Bishop Pelham of Lincoln, who urged the Etonians 'to maintain the practice of piety, without luke warmness, and above all, without en-thusiasm'.[29] It was ironic, given the deep sense of unworthiness with which the young Gladstone approached this act of commitment, that he was confirmed by an archetypal example of a time-serving, place-seeking, nepotistic Hanoverian prelate.[30]

---

[26] G. P. Tomline, *Elements of Christian Theology*, 2v. (1799).

[27] *The Holy Bible with introductions etc. arranged by G. D'Oyly and R. Mant* (1817), see *Autobiographica*, 149.

[28] Thomas Scott's *Commentary on the Bible*, first issued in weekly parts between 1788 and 1792, was a vital evangelical work. J. H. Newman wrote in the *Apologia* that Scott was the influence 'to whom (humanly speaking) I almost owe my soul'.

[29] Benson, op. cit., 500. See also *Diary*, i, 1 Feb. 1827.

[30] R. A. Soloway, *Prelates and People, Ecclesiastical Social Thought in England 1783–1852* (1969), 84.

One distinctive feature of his school days, however, was his apparent unwillingness to communicate his religious feelings to those about him. How far this was due simply to adolescent embarrassment and how far it stemmed from a conscious or deliberate reluctance to parade his convictions is difficult to say. Whatever the cause, such reserve was unusual in an evangelical, and this failure to witness more openly to his faith may have provided an added reason for the feelings of self-depreciation which are a feature of his diary. Getting his thoughts down on paper was perhaps his main means of sharing them and besides the diary he kept a private notebook in which he confided melancholy verse and meditations on religious themes.[31]

Perhaps he feared that too open a display of evangelical sentiments would excite ridicule, including, perhaps, mockery of his social origins. At school and university Gladstone was keenly aware of the contrast between his mercantile and provincial background and the aristocratic and more cultured homes of his contemporaries. In the presence of noble blood he felt something akin to awe. No doubt part of his fascination for the brilliant Arthur Hallam derived from the poise and cultivation the younger boy possessed as a result of his upbringing among the Whig intelligentsia. It is interesting that although both boys enjoyed an intense, almost classic, public school friendship and swapped intimacies about politics, philosophy and literature, Gladstone could never remember them talking much about religion.[32]

Though he tended to keep his religious convictions to himself, in all other respects Gladstone surrounded himself with like-minded boys who were more likely to arouse hostility for being self-consciously highbrow than by being sanctimonious. This coterie comprised such boys as W. W. Farr, Frederic Rogers, Arthur Hallam, Francis Doyle, Charles Canning and the effervescent James Milnes Gaskell. Together they launched a successor to the *Etonian*, the *Eton Miscellany*, which Gladstone edited under the pseudonym Bartholemew Bouverie, and a sixth form debating Society called the Eton *Literati*.

---

[31] BL Add. MS 44801.
[32] *Autobiographica*, 30.

Gladstone later doubted whether he had strong political leanings while at Eton.[33] This is not borne out by his correspondence, which is full of political comment and a lively awareness of matters of the day. 'We are getting very deep into Politics; I am afraid too much so,' he wrote to his father in July 1826,[34] and two months later Hallam was writing to Farr how during the holidays he had received letters from Gladstone and others 'breathing politics at every pore'.[35]

This enthusiasm for politics came partly from following his father's political career and partly from the infectious excitement of the set in which he moved. Gaskell, for example, was obsessed with politics and organized private political debates on the Pitt–Fox period in defiance of the school authorities who regarded this as too recent for the susceptible minds of school boys.

Gaskell was a Whig from a Unitarian background. Later, while up at Oxford, Gladstone paid a visit to his family at Thornes House, near Wakefield. The occasion remained vivid in his memory for Mrs Gaskell made the remark that anyone united to Christ by faith and love was surely saved, whatever the faults of their opinions.[36] This observation, he recalled, shook his inherited evangelical assumptions and lay like a seed, destined long to remain in his mind until finally germinating.

His political convictions at this time were staunchly Canningite.[37] This was a reflexion of his upbringing. His father had initially supported the Whigs and radicals, but as well as changing his ecclesiastical allegiance, he had also changed his political sympathies. In the Liverpool election of 1812 he was instrumental in persuading George Canning to contest the seat and thereafter remained a prominent supporter of Canning and later of Huskisson. William himself developed an adolescent admiration for Canning that bordered on hero worship. After

---

[33] *Autobiographica*, 33.

[34] W. E. Gladstone to J. Gladstone, 7 July 1826, Hawn. P.

[35] 24 September 1826, M. Zamick, 'Unpublished Letters of Arthur Henry Hallam from Eton, now in the John Rylands Library', *Bulletin of the John Rylands Library*, xviii (1934), 221.

[36] *Autobiographica*, 149–50.

[37] *Autobiographica*, 30. See his letter to W. W. Farr, 15 Sept. 1827, ibid., 194–5.

Canning's death in August 1827, he published in the *Miscellany*, a poem he had written two years earlier as a tribute and followed it later with another seventy lines inspired by his visit to Canning's grave in Westminster Abbey. The strong Canningite flavour of his youthful Toryism also explains why he ardently supported Catholic emancipation when his supposed evangelical antipathy to Romanism might suggest otherwise.[38]

He left Eton at the end of the autumn term in 1827. 'But oh! If anything mortal is sweet, my Eton years, excepting anxieties at home have been so!'[39] he wrote in his diary nostalgically. His Eton years had certainly been formative. He had shown the beginnings of academic promise, though as much through hard work as natural brilliance. He had more than held his own among his peers and had established friendships that would endure for life. But above all he had gained there the educational and social grounding necessary for the future his father had marked out for him. He would not have to return to the business world of Liverpool. A clear route lay before him, to Oxford and the House of Commons beyond. Of the Gladstone sons he, at least, was set to fulfil his father's expectations.

Before going up to Oxford in the Michaelmas term 1828 he crammed with Dr J. M. Turner at Wilmslow in Cheshire. His stay was cut short, however, when Turner's wife fell ill and on 11 April he left to join his family in Edinburgh. But before he left, Turner gave him an introduction to an Edinburgh clergyman who was to have an important influence on the course his religious development would take at Oxford, which made this short period between school and university more significant than might have been expected.

This clergyman was the Revd Edward Craig, a young man of high Calvinist opinions, who was minister of St. James's Chapel, Broughton Place. Craig had come to Edinburgh in the early 1820s from St. Edmund Hall, the centre of Oxford evangelicalism, and once established had created something of a stir in Edinburgh ecclesiastical circles by a sweeping attack on episcopalian teaching, especially concerning the doctrine of baptismal

---

[38] See letters to W. W. Farr, 22 Nov. 1826, *Autobiographica*, 184–5, and to P. Handley, 23 July 1828, BL Add. MS 44352, f. 64.
[39] *Diary*, i, 2 Dec. 1827.

regeneration which he vehemently rejected.[40] He was also the author of the resolutions sent by the Edinburgh Bible Committee in 1825, protesting against the British and Foreign Bible Society's policy of including the Apocrypha in bibles to be sent to the continent, and with other 'anti-apocryphists', all from the extreme wing of evangelicalism, had set up a Corresponding Board severing all connection with the London Society.[41]

Gladstone visited Craig almost daily during his six week stay in Edinburgh and attended his chapel regularly, though not exclusively. He went, at least once, to Craig's extempore prayer meeting for communicants and spent his time reading some of Craig's published works.[42] When he left Edinburgh on the 6 June Craig gave him introductions to other evangelicals in Oxford including Dr J. A. Macbride, Principal of Magdalen Hall.

Whether Gladstone felt drawn to the extreme Calvinism of Craig is difficult to say. He later recalled how deeply shocked he had been when Craig cooly asked him, 'Is your father a Christian?'.[43] But he may not have been as repelled as subsequently he liked to think. Meeting Craig forced him to think more deeply about his own theological position. It introduced him, at an age when his reliance on his family's views was beginning to weaken and he was beginning to forge his own adult personality, to a type of evangelicalism unlike anything he had encountered before. Indeed until that time he was probably unaware of the tensions developing within the evangelical camp, perhaps even unaware of differences in emphasis and belief within evangelicalism at all.

---

[40] For an account of this see W. Walker, *Life of Rt. Rev. Alexander Jolly , D. D., Bishop of Moray* (1878), 106–108. Craig was taken to task for his 'novel' ideas by a fellow episcopalian the Revd. James Walker, later Bishop of Edinburgh, and a pamphlet war ensued. Craig was also an opponent of the Scottish liturgy and supported a fellow evangelical D. T. K. Drummond, Minister of St. Thomas's Episcopal Chapel who in 1842, under pressure from episcopalian authorities, resigned from the church and set up an independent chapel where the English Prayer Book of 1662 was used.

[41] Moderate evangelicals like Simeon and Henry Venn were philo-apocryphists. The anti-apocryphists comprised the extremist neo-pentecostal wing, men like R. Haldane and E. Irving, see A. Haldane, *Memoir of the Lives of Haldane, of Airthrey, and his Brother J. A. Haldane* (1852).

[42] *Diary*, i, 2 June 1828.

[43] *Autobiographica*, 144.

One concrete result of this encounter with Craig was his own
resignation from the Bible Society. He wrote to William Rawson
to inform him and received a reply regretting that he felt it
necessary to take such action since the Society had ceased to
circulate the Apocrypha and had altered its rules to prevent it
happening again.[44] On the question of baptismal regeneration,
however, Gladstone came to a conclusion totally opposed to
Craig's. Whether he had formed any precise convictions about
the matter before may be doubted. Not all evangelicals denied
the possibility of regeneration accompanying baptism, but they
denied that it must necessarily do so. They believed only
conscious faith in Christ could bring about the justification of
sinful man. Baptism was merely the rite of admission into the
visible church and was a badge or token rather than an actual
channel of grace.

Since the publication of Richard Mant's *Appeal to the Gospel* in
1812, however, and the ensuing controversy, denial of baptismal
regeneration was becoming a touchstone of evangelical orthodoxy. Gladstone must have come upon most of the arguments
for and against the doctrine through Craig's controversial
writings. On returning to Liverpool in June he re-read Craig's
*Respectful Remonstrance* and the reply to it by the episcopalian Dr
Walker. This stimulated him to undertake a thorough investigation of the question and he began assembling the opinions of
Anglican authors on the subject in order to reach a definite
conclusion.[45]

The next day he began an article in the *Quarterly Review* which
adduced patristic testimony in its favour and was particularly
struck by the inclusion of St. Augustine among the witnesses, for
Augustine was regarded in the evangelical tradition as the
soundest of the Early Fathers.[46] Throughout the next month he
diligently continued his researches, sharing his discoveries with
his sisters. In August he went to Cuddesdon to cram with the
Revd A. P. Saunders and it was there that his thinking
crystallized. In a delayed reply to a letter from Helen requesting
his judgement on the matter he announced his acceptance of the

[44] Rawson to Gladstone, 29 July 1828, BL Add. MS 44352, ff. 70–1.
[45] BL Add. MS 44719 ff. 126–86.
[46] *Quarterly Review*, xv (July 1816), 475–511. A review of two tracts by R. Mant and
three tracts in reply to them.

doctrine. The letter, studded with quotations from the Bible, the Fathers and Anglican divines, gave his considered verdict:

> Regeneration is a birth: the principle of life only is imparted therein: it is an admission into the covenant: continuance in its blessings being independent of it. The only time we have regeneration mentioned in the Bible is when it is expressly applied to the Bath of Baptism . . . I remember the time when I had a horror of anything that upheld the Doctrine of Baptismal Regeneration Fool that I was: every Sunday repeating a belief in one baptism for the remission of sins and yet neither knowing nor caring for its spiritual grace. Strange it may seem for one who is indeed among the poorest and the darkest of the 'unlearned and most able' to speak of conviction: nevertheless I do not see how the argument from the Apostles' preaching can be answered and how can I, dare I, refuse assent to a doctrine I cannot deny and a reason I cannot refute . . .[47]

But while this was a divergence from mainstream evangelical teaching, it made little immediate difference to his overall theological stance, though as he later realized, it 'opened the way for further changes'.[48]

Gladstone was up at Oxford from October 1828 until December 1831. His time there was of crucial importance for his subsequent mental development. Although in one sense an extension of Eton, for many of his friends were up at Christ Church with him, it was much more. For despite the outward success, crowned by triumph in the Union and a Double First in the Schools, these years were years of inner doubt and unsettlement.

The problem revolved around the question of identity and, linked with it, vocation. These years saw a prolonged debate with his family and within his own soul about his future career. At school he had been quite prepared, indeed eager, to fulfil his father's intentions for him: 'From the faint idea which I am enabled to form of my future profession, I should suppose (am I right?) that it was of consequence to me to begin the study of law as early as possible.' he had written to John Gladstone two months before his fifteenth birthday.[49] And when he left Eton he had inscribed on a number of envelopes 'The Rt. Hon. William Ewart Gladstone M.P.'[50] But between school and university his

[47] W. E. Gladstone to H. J. Gladstone, 24 Aug. 1828, Hawn. P. Helen's letter is dated 2 August 1828.
[48] *Autobiographica*, 150.
[49] W. E. Gladstone to J. Gladstone, 3 Nov. 1824, Hawn. P.
[50] P. M. Magnus, *Gladstone: a biography* (1954), 13.

mind changed. Perhaps a career in politics was not now his vocation; perhaps God required him, despite his father's wishes, to cast aside worldly fame and offer himself in a more obviously religious way. Should he become a priest? He appears to have raised the matter with his sisters and his mother. They were sympathetic, even enthusiastic, to this new inclination.[51]

When and why this change occurred is difficult to judge. The death of Canning may have produced a certain disenchantment with political life, a feeling that great possibilities had died with him. Certainly Gladstone found little to admire in Wellington. Undoubtedly the quickening of his religious feelings during the Edinburgh visit in the spring played its part. Perhaps it was then that the idea was born. The vigour with which he set about the matter of baptismal regeneration could well be explained by this.[52] The death of the beloved Anne a few months later would then have had the effect of further confirming him in this new path. Certainly once the idea had taken root it was not lightly cast aside. It remained an underlying source of tension and uncertainty throughout his Oxford career until finally, early in 1832, the matter was resolved.

His first year in Oxford was a period of deepening religious intensity. He made friends soon after arrival with a number of particularly devout young men of an extreme evangelical persuasion whose focus was St. Ebbe's Church. The curate there was the Revd Henry Bulteel whose high Calvinism was later to cause notoriety in the University, and led eventually to episcopal censure and Bulteel's secession from the Church of England for the Brethren.[53] Gladstone seems to have made contact with this group through Henry Moncrieff whose brother James he had met in Edinburgh in the spring. Moncrieff[54] was at New College and was a nephew of John Bird Sumner, the evangelical Bishop of Chester. Others in the group were Thomas Tancred, Alfred Hanbury of St. Mary Hall, Charles Childers

[51] Checkland, op. cit., 246.

[52] BL Add. MS 44719, f. 235. 'Every man, it appears to me, whose mind has been in any way accustomed to contemplate the prospect of labouring as a Minister in the Vinyard of Christ, must feel the immense importance of using every means which may conduce to settle his opinions on the question of Baptismal Regeneration.'

[53] For Bulteel see W. R. Ward, *Victorian Oxford* (1965), 72–5.

[54] Moncrieff became a Church of Scotland minister, disrupting in 1843.

who later, like Hanbury, took orders, and an Irishman, Owen Blayney Cole. Benjamin Harrison, later a member of Newman's circle and the man chiefly responsible for introducing Gladstone to the Tracts, was also connected with them.

It was their practice to hold prayer meetings and Bible study in their rooms and in his first term Gladstone became, at least an occasional attender of these.[55] It was at one such meeting that he met R. W. Sibthorp, then an evangelical clergyman but better known later as an unstable convert and reconvert to Rome.[56] Through Hanbury and Moncrieff, Gladstone was also introduced to a Mr Charrière, an elusive figure, who seems to have attended Bulteel's Church and whose daughter was, two years later, to become the first recipient of Bulteel's new found gift of spiritual healing.

As with Edward Craig, it is difficult to assess how deeply Gladstone's relationship with this group materially altered his religious convictions. Looking back he described this small evangelical group as 'for the most part sharply Calvinistic which partly held and partly repelled me'.[57] No doubt their fervour provided a congenial contrast to the rather stagnant religious atmosphere of Oxford. The Tractarian storm still lay in the future.

> You may smile [Gladstone used to say long after,] when told that when I was at Oxford, Dr. Hampden was regarded as a model of orthodoxy, that Dr. Newman was eyed with suspicion as a low churchman, and Dr. Pusey as leaning to rationalism.[58]

Apart from the evangelicals around John Hill at St. Edmund Hall with whom Gladstone seems to have had no contact, the evangelical group centred on St. Ebbe's, and the Noetics in the Oriel Common Room, the prevailing tone of Oxford religion was 'high and dry'. Moreover the college services and the behaviour of many undergraduates was as painful to Gladstone as the situation he had encountered at Eton. He assiduously attended chapel, the University Sermon and the fortnightly communion, scrutinizing the number present. But he was conscious of being in a pitifully small minority. As he wrote in

[55] *Diary*, i, 5 Dec. 1828; 16 Nov. 1829.
[56] See J. Fowler, *Richard Waldo Sibthorp: a biography* (1880), 45–6.
[57] *Autobiographica*, 141. See also *Gleanings*, vii. 211–12.
[58] Quoted in *Morley*, i. 57.

March 1829, 'The state of religion in Oxford is the most painful spectacle it ever fell to my lot to behold'.[59]

His mood became darker during these years. The contrast between God and sinful humanity became sharper, the choice between religious obedience and the snares of the world more urgent. His own feelings of sinfulness became more pronounced and because of this his standards became more stringent and the vice of those around him a great burden.[60] He became openly critical of his fellow students and gained a reputation in some quarters for priggishness.[61] But how far his *theological* convictions (as opposed to his religious *feelings*) underwent substantial change is less clear.

He later maintained that he had continued to hold moderate evangelical opinions throughout this period.[62] This is probably true, but even as a young man he was never satisfied until he had investigated a question thoroughly and reached his own conclusion. He had accepted baptismal regeneration even though it fitted uneasily into the evangelical schemae. Similarly his notebooks at this time show him wrestling with issues like predestination and justification by faith, prompted no doubt by discussions with these young men.[63] But it is clear from these jottings that he was searching for solutions to these questions that were theologically satisfying and not merely acceptable to those he mixed with.

Any evaluation of his religious feelings is complicated by his use of language. From his family circle and from his evangelical associates he had learned the vocabulary of a distinctive religious tradition. To what inner reality this language corresponded is harder to gauge.[64] He tackled theological questions in

[59] *Lathbury*, i. 2; see also *Checkland*, op. cit., 219.
[60] See *Diary*, i, 29 Dec. 1828; 29 Dec. 1829; 24 Dec. 1830. These summing-ups are particularly harsh.
[61] See the incident in *Diary*, i, 24 Mar. 1830 and Checkland, op. cit., 245–6.
[62] *Autobiographica*, 141.
[63] See especially BL Add. MS 44801, ff. 31, 50.
[64] For example BL Add. MS 44801, f. 69, June 1830. 'Tell me not of any cause of salvation save the free mercy of God in the precious blood of Christ: of any instrument, save the faith that clings to his cross: of any test save the meek and abiding glories of a Christian life—of purity and self-denial—of energy and zeal—of love and peace. Deem it not in vain I say, nor dishonour the mighty scheme by forgetting, that from the pierced side of Jesus together with the blood to atone, flowed the water to purify.'

the same systematic manner and with the same relentless energy he tackled everything else. But as when evaluating the effect on him of his vast reading, it is difficult to know how far his thinking on paper correlated with his actual experience. Did his soul really apprehend the particular doctrines of which he wrote, or was he impelled principally by a thirst for knowledge and theological coherence? This question cannot be answered but it has interesting implications. In terms of his inner religious experience was Gladstone ever really an evangelical of the classic type? Did he ever feel what as a professed evangelical he was meant to feel?

There is certainly evidence to suggest that Gladstone was wary of committing himself too deeply to this evangelical group. He wrote to Craig in December 1829 asking whether it was proper to attend the extempore prayer meetings in college rooms and about the differences between Sibthorp and Bulteel on the matter of predestination and election.[65] He also wrote to Rawson to solicit his views on Bulteel, for he had become convinced that Bulteel's theological position was founded on a partial view of scripture. Rawson seems to have known little about him, but his reply is an illuminating comment on the new forces infecting evangelicalism from a man reared in the evangelical tradition of Simeon and the Venns. There were, he wrote, 'many men in the present day, good men, glorifying God, whose notions appear extremely crude and who deviating from "the good old way", wander "in endless mazes lost".'[66]

Although initially impressed by Bulteel, Gladstone's enthusiasm for him lessened; he could not follow Bulteel in his Calvinistic predestinarianism nor in his view that the atonement was of benefit only for the elect. Such high Calvinism startled him. He heard the controversial University Sermon Bulteel preached on 6 February 1831 and felt moved afterwards to write to him about it. He was saddened, however, when as a consequence of open-air preaching the Bishop of Oxford withdrew Bulteel's licence.[67] But when shortly afterwards Bulteel became involved with Irvingism, Gladstone wrote to

---

[65] For Craig's reply see BL Add. MS 44352, ff. 141–2, 15 Dec. 1829.
[66] Rawson to Gladstone, 1 Mar. 1831, BL Add. MS 44352, f. 183.
[67] *Diary*, i, 14 Aug. 1831; W. E. Gladstone to J. Gladstone, 19 Aug. 1831, Hawn. P.

Helen that spiritual healing and speaking with tongues were a delusion, an example of the morbid temper of the age.[68]

This preoccupation with religion provoked mixed feelings among Gladstone's more secular friends. In the Michaelmas term of his second year for instance, Gaskell wrote derisively to his parents,

I much regret that Gladstone has mixed himself up, as he has done, with the St. Mary Hall and Oriel set, who are really, for the most part, only fit, as Robinson said, to live with maiden aunts and keep tame rabbits.[69]

It was also a source of growing disquiet to his brother Tom, then a trainee barrister in London. About a year before Gaskell's letter, near the end of his brother's first term, Tom had visited William in Oxford and discussed with him at great length his new choice of career. At William's wish he agreed to broach the subject with their father and seven days later reported back by letter. His reply was to the point and somewhat cool. He assured William that their father was not angry with him for failing to raise the matter earlier and had no intention either of thwarting his wishes or of constraining his choice of career. He had, however, made it clear that no hasty decisions were to be made. So long and so anxiously had their father looked forward to William entering the law with the object of using it as a spring board to public life that he wished him to take ample time to weigh the matter before coming to a decision. And he added that he had himself expressed some doubts as to William's capability as yet to decide on this course of action.[70]

Though John Gladstone was largely unperturbed by William's fervent religiosity, Tom found it increasingly difficult to accept with such patient good humour. Of all the Gladstone children he remained closest to the basically conventional religion of his father. His younger brother's seeming obsession with religious matters was both distressing and irritating to him. William was aware of this and in an effort to increase brotherly understanding proposed that they should be more open with each other and discuss unreservedly all matters of importance

[68] W. E. Gladstone to H. J. Gladstone, 23 Oct. 1831, Hawn. P.

[69] C. M. Gaskell (ed.), *An Eton Boy. Being the Letters of James Milnes Gaskell from Eton and Oxford 1820–1830* (1939), 170–1.

[70] T. Gladstone to W. E. Gladstone, 3 Dec. 1828, Hawn. P.

that concerned them, particularly religious matters, so that the 'painful differences of sentiment' between them might be diminished.[71] Tom would have none of it: 'Let us abide by the charitable principle of allowing each other his own unchallenged sentiments,' he replied. ' *Yours* are imbibed evidently very much more strongly than *mine*.' In future, rather than being more open with his brother, he declared he would abstain entirely from any discussion of religious matters at all.[72]

This principle remained unbroken for fifteen months until the summer of 1830 when the issue of William's choice of career was raised again, this time in a more definite way. Throughout this time William's mind had remained strongly inclined to the Church and in August he decided the matter could be left open no longer. He resolved to write to his father directly and ask permission to prepare for holy orders after graduation.

The year 1830 had been one of particular emotional stress and disappointment. He felt dissatisfied with himself, disgruntled by his own slackness and his lack of progress in religion. He had entered for the Ireland Scholarship with considerable hope of success, only to have it dashed. Shortly afterwards he had been beaten up in his rooms by a group of undergraduates who, as he put it, were 'living in sin and had rejected Christ their Saviour'. This had prompted a phase of even greater introspection.[73]

He was also spending increasingly more time with a pious young man of evangelical inclinations called Joseph Anstice.[74] In July they studied together under Saunders at Cuddesdon where long periods of hard work alternated with equally long discussions on religious matters.

It was while here, on 4 August, that William wrote to his father about his future career. He was in a highly suggestible and rather overwrought frame of mind. Discussion with Anstice had turned to the question of purity of motive. William had been stirred. Nine days later the two young men walked into Oxford together and were caught up in the pandemonium of the

---

[71] W. E. Gladstone to T. Gladstone, 20 May 1829, Hawn. P.

[72] T. Gladstone to W. E. Gladstone, 22 May 1829, Hawn. P.

[73] *Diary*, i, 24 Mar. 1830, 25 Apr. 1830.

[74] Joseph Anstice (1808–36); later Professor of Classical Literature, King's College, London.

County election campaign. The whole sight plunged William into gloom: 'On Monday when I was in Oxford and saw the people parading with flags and bands of music my first impulse was to laugh, my second to cry: and I thought how strangely men had missed the purpose of their being.'[75] Next day he agonized alone. With souls sinking daily into death how futile academic studies seemed; how irrelevant, how self-indulgent. The following day he struggled to put his thoughts on paper.

It was an extraordinary letter, tortuous and verbose, its language florid and its sentiments extreme. The world was in the grip of evil and despair. Opposed to the apostasy of man stood the love of God. No obligation was more absolute than making this fact plain. No vocation offered greater scope for doing this than that of a priest. 'None which can compete with the grandeur of its end or of its means—the end, the glory of God, and the means, the restoration of man to that image of his Maker which is now throughout the world so lamentably defaced.'[76]

His father's reply, one sixth the length of his own, was sympathetic but recommended further patience. If, after graduation, William still continued to think in the same way he would not oppose him, but the matter could not be decided until then. Gently he suggested that William's own view of the situation was too high-flown and that it was unrealistic to suppose that the priesthood offered the peculiar possibilities William asserted.

William replied immediately, thankful for the advice and pleased to have caused no offence. His mood had in any case altered. He felt quieter and with his pent up emotions released had begun to feel that, after all, he should accept the guidance of others, at least for the time being.[77]

The matter now became one of family debate. Even Tom decided to break his principle of not communicating on religious subjects. He informed William that while he had written nothing in an unbecoming manner his father was none the less disappointed and felt William was forcing a decision unnecessarily early. He went on to give some brotherly advice. The

---

[75] *Diary*, i, 8 Aug. 1830, describing the scene on 2 August 1830.
[76] The letter and his father's reply is printed in *Morley*, i. 635–41.
[77] W. E. Gladstone to J. Gladstone, 12 Aug. 1830, Hawn. P.

'extravagance of religious effervescence' which William's letter displayed repelled him. 'For God's sake, my dear William', he counselled, 'look at human nature through a fairer glass—do not believe that it is so utterly worthless as you describe it.'[78]

William, highly charged once more, could not resist this opportunity to rush into the lists of religious controversy. He sent Tom a long letter outlining his beliefs in an endeavour to put Tom's mind at rest about his supposed feelings about the utter worthlessness of human nature. Alas, if anything, it simply confirmed Tom's worst fears![79]

Throughout the summer and into the autumn letters continued to fly. Robertson and John Neilson were brought in and their opinions sought.[80] But by the end of the year forces were to emerge that would significantly alter the terms of the debate and in the New Year of 1831 a different note was being heard. 'I cannot tell you how I rejoice at your having determined upon the Law,' Tom wrote to William.[81] And almost a year later on 7 January 1832 William began a letter to his father that was to settle the matter once and for all.[82]

This letter, quite as long though less dramatic than the previous one, made it clear that his mind had completely changed. It was not that his estimate of mankind's situation had altered. If anything he was more gloomy. But what had altered was his analysis of the situation and his former belief that the best way in which he should grapple with it was as an ordained minister of the Church. He now believed that the sin and misery of the world was the result of a chronic malaise within the social and moral order. The civilized world was approaching crisis. The foundations of society, its primary obligation to God and the obligations of man to man, were being undermined, sapped by a new and alien philosophy spreading gradually and silently;

[78] T. Gladstone to W. E. Gladstone, 13 Aug. 1830, Hawn. P.
[79] W. E. Gladstone to T. Gladstone, 15 Aug. 1830; T. Gladstone to W. E. Gladstone, 23 Aug. 1830; W. E. Gladstone to T. Gladstone, 1 Sept. 1830; T. Gladstone to W. E. Gladstone, 11 Sept. 1830, Hawn. P.
[80] W. E. Gladstone to R. Gladstone, 14 Aug. 1830, 6 Sept. 1830; W. E. Gladstone to J. N. Gladstone, 29 Aug. 1830, 30 Dec. 1830, *Lathbury*, ii. 223–8. The letter of 29 Aug. 1830 is to J. N. Gladstone and not to his father as Lathbury suggests.
[81] T. Gladstone to W. E. Gladstone, 24 Jan. 1831, Hawn. P.
[82] *Autobiographica*, Appendix 2, 220–9.

a philosophy which exalted self-will and undermined hierarchy and obedience to lawful authority.

In this situation when the designs of evil against mankind were on such a general and comprehensive scale there were perhaps special possibilities for those following a career neither limited to particular technical functions nor confined in too specific a way. A career in public life afforded tremendous opportunities of serving God and meeting the challenge of the age, provided it was accompanied by religious zeal, consistency and single-mindedness.

It was only here that William faltered. These qualities were, he felt, the very reverse of his own character and conduct. But he was prepared to leave it to the will of Providence. If he proved unfitted for the task, or if his vocation was motivated only by a craving ambition it would become clear and he would then seek out a humble and safer walk of life. All this, he felt, fitted in exactly with his father's wishes as far as he understood them. He would study the law and when the time or circumstances allowed it he would enter some sphere of public life.

The Reform Bill crisis was the occasion for this surprising change. The atmosphere engendered in 1830 and 1831 had a galvanic effect upon him. In Gladstone's mind the issue took on almost apocalyptic significance. Here, indeed, was that alien philosophy which was dissolving away the old order: democracy. The impact of the crisis was dramatic. With remarkable suddeness he embraced a doctrinaire high Toryism markedly different from his previous convictions and from those of his family.

Despite his intense preoccupation with religion at Oxford his interest in politics had not waned. He had formed an essay club called, immodestly, by his own initials which, like the one at Eton, acted as a forum for political and intellectual debate. In February 1830 he had given his first speech in the Union and three months later was made secretary. On 11 November, the autumn after his first letter to his father, he introduced a motion of no confidence in the Duke of Wellington's administration. It was carried by a single vote and at the same meeting he was elected president. His skill in debate was now apparent and he had risen rapidly to a position of importance in the political life of the university. It gave him considerable though not unalloyed pleasure: 'This has been my Debating Society year: now I fancy done with. Politics are fascinating to me, perhaps too fascinating,'[83] he wrote in his diary at the end of that year.

But his greatest debating triumph still lay in the future. At the end of March the first Reform Bill reached a crucial phase when it received its second reading by only one vote. Gladstone threw himself into frenzied campaign against it. With his tutor Charles Wordsworth, a staunch high Tory, he formed the Oxford Anti-Reform League, stuck up placards around the town, and organized a petition which was signed by some four-fifths of the graduates and bachelors resident in the university. 'Gladstone is quite furious in the cause,' Charles Wordsworth wrote to his brother Christopher.[84]

On 17 May, in a debate which lasted three days, 'a debate such as was never known in the Society before',[85] he spoke for three-quarters of an hour on the amendment that the Reform Bill threatened to change not only the form of government but would also ultimately break up the very foundations of the social order. It was carried by ninety-four votes to thirty-eight. But what was remembered was Gladstone's speech. It had enormous impact. Sir Francis Doyle looking back described it as the oratorical event of his time at Oxford.[86]

It was a passionate indictment of the philosophy behind 'this Jacobin bill', a plea for the true statesman:

to look to the *principles* established by God for the well being of nations and with those principles to live or die, instead of endeavouring to govern his course by phantoms which are themselves perpetually shifting—the frail and fleeting shadows of human waywardness.[87]

There was no room for compromise or a pragmatic acceptance of change. Stability and good government lay only through loyalty to the Constitution that embodied and developed these principles, the Constitution which was 'the object under Heaven and the things of Heaven, of our deepest reverence and as surrounded with a halo of accumulated glory which is essen-

---

[83] *Diary*, i, 29 Dec. 1830.
[84] 28 Apr. 1831, C. Wordsworth, *Annals of My Early Life, 1806–46* (1891), 85.
[85] W. E. Gladstone to R. Gladstone, 20 May 1831, Hawn. P.
[86] F. Doyle, *Reminiscences and opinions of Sir Francis Hastings Doyle 1813–85* (1886), 114. Speech notes are in BL Add. MS 44721, ff. 23–34. This account of its content differs from that in Checkland, op. cit., 249–50.
[87] BL Add. MS 44721, f. 34.

tially fadeless'.[88] In the University, where the prevailing political tone was 'Church and King', such baroque sentiments had great appeal. Gladstone's father was less enthusiastic, though young Helen Jane was totally captivated. 'In spite of your reforming predelictions Mamma, you could not fail to admire William's noble, nervous, glorious speech, one of the very few in which the Arm of All Strength is named, one apart from the apostate crowd,' she wrote to her mother.[89] Another young man deeply impressed by Gladstone's performance was his friend Lord Lincoln,[90] son of the ultra-Tory Duke of Newcastle.

It was from this speech that Gladstone's political career derived. Unless its intensity and extremism are understood, his change of mind, the forsaking of a clerical career for a life in politics, is incomprehensible. Only in the light of his violent opposition to the Reform Bill can the sentiments expressed in the letter to his father in January 1832 be appreciated.

When he had first conceived the idea of ordination he had seen the influence it afforded purely in pastoral terms, in bringing individual souls to Christ. The events of his last eighteen months at the university which reached their climax in his speech at the Union, convinced him that this alone was insufficient. It was not merely individual souls that must be brought to the foot of the Cross, it was the whole political and social order that had lost its bearings and stood in urgent need of redemption. The philosophy implicit in the Reform Bill symbolized this for him. The letter to his father was the working out of the implications of this for his own life. In an effort to serve God and the Church the young Gladstone made a contract with the World.

His final months in Oxford were spent in intense preparation

[88] Ibid.

[89] For John Gladstone's attitude to the Reform Bill Crisis see Checkland, op. cit., 250. He wrote to his son that although he enjoyed reading his speech, he felt William had gone astray 'when you connect religion with political controversy, and which I think would, on this occasion have been left out for the reasoning founded upon it, and the conclusions you draw from it, do appear to me, even if they were called for, much over strained'. J. Gladstone to W. E. Gladstone, 12 July 1831, Hawn. P. For Helen's remarks see H. J. Gladstone to A. Gladstone, dated simply Friday 1831, Hawn. P.

[90] Henry Pelham Fiennes Pelham Clinton, 1811–64; M. P. Nottinghamshire; Peelite; 5th Duke of Newcastle 1851.

for his final examination. Classics was first, in November, and maths followed a month later. He was placed in the First class in both, as Peel had been twenty-three years earlier. In the mood of 'thrilling happiness' he made his farewells, wrote to his mother and to friends, had tea and left Oxford on the coach for London.[91]

It had been decided that like many young men down from the university Gladstone should round off his education with a continental tour. Consequently, accompanied by his brother John Neilson, he left England in February 1832 for Italy, travelling through Belgium and France and returning via Germany. These six months were important to him for two reasons. Firstly they enabled him to see for himself the Roman Catholic Church and the part it played in the life of its people. Secondly it was during this time that he received the offer from the Duke of Newcastle to stand as MP in the coming election at Newark.

Seeing the practical workings of the Catholic Church at first hand was important in William's own religious development. His first impressions were unfavourable. He witnessed mass for the first time in the Cathedral at Brussels and pronounced it 'an unmeaning and sorrowful ceremony'.[92] In Paris he was appalled by the lack of any regard for the Sabbath. He inspected the graves in the Père la Chaise, but was painfully disappointed to find not one epitaph on the graves that expressed the sentiments of 'sound Christianity'.[93]

On the other hand he enjoyed his first visit to the Vaudois. These Alpine Protestants, the descendants of the medieval Waldenses had always figured highly in evangelical literature as the bearers of authentic Christianity during the dark period of Papal domination. Gladstone's interest in them had been long-standing. He had first read about them while at Eton. 'They alone have kept the faith pure and undefiled from the age of the Apostles,' he had written to his brother John in 1826,[94] and the fruit of his researches had been a poem, 'The Song of the Vaudois Women', which was included in the *Miscellany*. He

[91] *Diary*, i, 14 Dec. 1831.
[92] *Diary*, i, 5 Feb. 1832.
[93] *Diary*, i, 11 and 15 Feb. 1832.
[94] W. E. Gladstone to J. N. Gladstone, 29 Jan. 1826, *Lathbury*, ii. 222.

confessed that he 'would rather see them than anything else on the Continent', and his two day visit in the company of a Waldensian pastor, M. Bonjour, delighted him.[95]

He arrived in Rome on the last day of March and spent Holy Week there attending the main ceremonies in St. Peter's and the Sistine Chapel. The whole experience deeply affected him. Despite his antipathy to Romanism the pain of Christian disunity pressed upon him for the first time.[96] He felt the awe and grandeur of the Catholic system coupled with a sense of unease.

Shortly afterwards he went on to Naples. Here he fell in with a young Polish count called Orlowsky, a liberal-minded Catholic whose ignorance of the English Church appalled Gladstone. They spent much time together discussing the differences between their two churches and this set Gladstone about examining the Prayer Book in much greater detail than he had ever done before. On 13 May he wrote in his journal:

To coming into Catholic countries, and to some few books, I owe glimpses which now seem to be afforded me of the nature of a Church, and of our duties as members of it, which involve an idea very much higher and more important than I had previously had any conception of.[97]

Much later he looked back to this as a moment of great illumination. Having previously taken his religious teaching directly from the Bible, now the figure of the Church rose before him as a teacher too. He realized how incompletely he had absorbed the doctrine and discipline of the Prayer Book, how much continuity the Church of England had with its Catholic past.

It presented to me Christianity under an aspect in which I had not yet known it: its ministry of symbols, its channels of grace, its unending line of teachers joining from the head.[98]

Seven weeks later he arrived in Milan to find waiting for him a letter from Lord Lincoln inviting him to accept his father's nomination in the election at Newark. This 'stunning and overpowering proposal' left him 'in a flutter of confusion'. He wrote home for his father's advice.[99] The family were unani-

---

[95] *Diary*, i, 3 Mar. 1832. Cf. his later recollections, *Autobiographica*, 142.
[96] *Diary*, i, 6 and 7 Mar. 1832.
[97] *Diary*, i, 13 May 1832; see also 8 May 1832.
[98] .26 July 1894; *Autobiographica*, 143.
[99] *Diary*, i, 6–8 July 1832.

mous. At Geneva, on 15 July, he wrote to accept the Duke's invitation and began the return journey home.

Far sooner than he could have anticipated the call to political life had come. The lingering doubts about his choice of career that had dogged him in the early stages of his tour had disappeared. Buttressed by his father's approval he now had the opportunity to put into practice the commitment made seven months before. The idea of serving God in the tranquility of a parish had been abandoned. Politics was no longer the object of adolescent fascination or an arena for displaying oratorical prowess. It was to be one of the battle fields of the Cross. Before him lay the opportunity of becoming one of God's providential instruments in the divine regeneration of society. It was with this extraordinary sense of mission that the young Gladstone embarked upon his parliamentary career.

# 2

# POLITICS, THEOLOGY, AND FRIENDS:
## 1833–1838

On 7 February 1833 Gladstone took his seat in the newly reformed House of Commons. Eight years later, in 1841, when the long tottering Whig ministry finally fell, he became a member of Peel's second administration. The years between form a distinct period both in his political and his religious life.

Politically these years saw him move steadily to the forefront of parliamentary life. In 1835 he first experienced political office. Three years later he published *The State in its relations with the Church*, a fourth and extended edition of which appeared in 1841.[1] By the end of the decade he had achieved sufficient renown to be dubbed by Macaulay in a famous phrase, 'the rising hope of those stern unbending Tories'.

In the religious sphere these years saw him move further from his early evangelicalism to a High Church position, which underlay his first book and which was expressed more fully in his second, more theological work: *Church Principles considered in their results*, published in 1840.

This period also saw the beginning of an intense friendship with two young men, Henry Manning and James Hope which, cemented by shared ideals and aspirations, was of central importance to him until its dramatic rupture in 1851.

Gladstone's early Toryism has been too readily dismissed with Macaulay's ultra-Tory stereotype, as if the young Gladstone was merely a black reactionary and a cypher of the Ultras.[2] Of course evidence can be marshalled to support such a

---

[1] For a discussion of this book and its significance for Gladstone's political development see chapter 3 below.

[2] For the politics of the 1830s and 1840s see especially N. Gash, *Reaction and Reconstruction in English politics, 1832–1852* (1964); *Sir Robert Peel, the life of Sir Robert Peel after 1830* (1972); and R. M. Stewart, *The politics of protection, Lord Derby and the protectionist party, 1841–1852* (1971). For Church and State see G. I. T. Machin, *Politics and the Churches in Great Britain 1832 to 1868* (1977).

view. His voting pattern in the 1830s, for instance, does suggest a Canute-like mentality. His second major speech delivered on 8 July 1833, six days before Keble mounted the pulpit of St. Mary's to declare 'National Apostasy', was no less searing in its attack on the 'desecration' involved in the suppression of the Irish bishoprics.[3] He supported the Irish Coercion Bill and Fleetwood's attempt to strengthen the laws relating to Sabbath observance. He opposed the Maynooth grant, the abolition of flogging in the forces (while voting to retain the award of commissions on the basis of purchase and patronage), the abolition of church rate, the removal of Jewish disabilities, the introduction of Roman Catholic prison chaplains and the admission of dissenters to the universities. Moreover, he owed his seat to the patronage of a man in most respects the archetypal ultra-Tory, who, in the 1829 election had served eviction notices on forty of his tenants who had dared to vote Whig, justifying his action with the notorious remark that 'he had the right to do as he liked with his own'.[4]

But Gladstone's conservatism was never simply the unthinking desire to preserve the *status quo* or the stolid maintenance of privilege. Nor was it a matter of political faction. Although he was the Duke of Newcastle's nominee, Gladstone seems never to have consciously acted as part of an organized Ultra pressure group. Though friendly with Sir Robert Inglis, Peel's trouncer in the 1829 Oxford election and the leading Protestant constitutionalist, there is nothing to suggest that Gladstone was influenced by him or that he saw any conflict between such cordiality and his growing devotion to Peel. Similarly there was a clear difference between Gladstone's position and that of the Irish Protestant Ascendancy wing of the Tory party. While sharing their belief that Ireland was organically linked to England and that the Churches of England and Ireland stood or fell together, Gladstone never envisaged revoking Catholic Emancipation or of solving Irish problems by brute force.

In fact Gladstone's Toryism was highly individual. His political opinions, he told a friend on his return from the Continent in 1832, were 'of a cast, I believe, rather melancholy and severe, than violent or ultra in the ordinary sense of these words'.[5] What was distinctive was the religious fervour that underpinned it. Having entered politics convinced that nothing less than a divine regeneration of society could counteract the rising tide of secularism and false thinking threatening the social order, Gladstone had cast the Tory party in the role of the God-given agent for such a regeneration. Only under Tory leadership, he believed, could government be re-established on a sounder footing and the Church of England helped to reassume its rightful role as matrix of the nation.

This approach to politics, so different from that of his father, undoubtedly owed as much to temperament as to intellectual conviction. With the Tories reduced to a rump and ranged against them a conglomeration of Whigs, radicals and Irish, all committed in Gladstone's eyes, to a war of attrition against the Established Church and a further stripping of the religious character of the State, it was easy to invest the Tory party with a providential destiny. Gladstone always needed to feel that he was acting to great purpose. He loved causes. Perhaps this approach to politics was even a psychological necessity for him. Having abandoned the idea of entering the Church, he needed to see politics in this exalted way in order that, almost as a compensation, his new career could satisfy, as the priesthood would have done, his original religious longings.

What then was his early political creed? In old age he looked back to this period with misgiving. His education had made him glorify in an extravagant manner the moral character of the State and the religious mission of the Conservative party. Burke, whom he read constantly during his undergraduate years, had misled him. One thing stood out above all: he had never learned to appreciate the importance of liberty as a political principle or the necessity of individual freedom for a right understanding of authority. 'Where lay the root of this folly?' he asked. 'It lay here. Early education, civil and religious, had never taught me, and Oxford had tended to hide from me, the great fact that liberty is a great and precious gift of God and that human excellence cannot grow up in a nation without it.'[6] Liberty

[5] Gladstone to Handley, 9 Aug. 1832, BL Add. MS 44352, f. 244.
[6] *Autobiographica*, 12 July 1892, 37.

certainly played no part in the young Gladstone's political thinking. Indeed it was because the Reform Bill appeared to be based on the premise that government derived its authority from the majority will that Gladstone saw in it the work of 'Anti-Christ' and attacked it as a threat to the foundations of the social order. 'Human will,' he said in his famous speech in the Union,

has nothing whatever to do with the foundation of government—it can neither establish nor overthrow its legitimacy—divine will alone is its ground—and as to human opinion, it is only valuable and deserving of regard in exact proportion as it is calculated from the virtue and ability of those who hold it, to embody and develop those eternal laws which alone are the source of authority and which alone purpose to us the objects of true and legitimate obedience.[7]

Freedom was not something intrinsically good. In the abstract it was not even a legitimate object for human beings either to desire or pursue. He made this clear in an essay, *On the Principle of Government*, written soon after the speech.[8] 'Restraint and freedom from restraint', he wrote, 'stand upon an equal footing in a moral point of view, and both are good or evil according to their results, and according to their results alone.' Moreover:

No restraint is *necessarily* an evil except what prevents men from following this rule of right conduct. And restraint which gives men a tendency to follow it, is just as much a *good* as the opposite kind of restraint is an evil. Contrariwise no freedom is necessarily a good except that which consists in the removal of restraint upon *right* conduct. And freedom which consists in restraint upon evil conduct being removed, is a positive evil *as much* an evil as the opposite freedom is a good.[9]

However convoluted the prose, the meaning is clear. Gladstone felt liberty was good only when it resulted in a man choosing what authority demanded. Since the very act of choosing allowed for the possibility of wrong choice, Gladstone wished to limit liberty as far as possible. In framing a constitution, he wrote, the right principle was 'not to give as much political liberty to the subjects as can be considered compatible with the maintenance of public order, but as little. A minimum of representation and not a maximum is I think the first object to be desired.'[10]

[7] BL Add. MS 44721, f. 24.
[8] Ibid., ff. 1–17.
[9] Ibid., f. 6.
[10] Ibid., f. 16.

There is little here that can square with the emphasis on freedom, the majority will and utility that formed the core of nineteenth-century political liberalism. It was an unashamedly authoritarian structure where subordination was considered natural and to be enforced where necessary by positive coercion. Even Gladstone, however, while upholding the right of the sovereign power to exercise coercion for the purpose of doing away with 'ridiculous and intolerable absurdities or mischiefs', was sufficiently realistic to admit that such action should only be taken under pressure of necessity: 'this principle is one which requires infinite caution in its application: society is bound by its own laws: the supreme power is no more entitled than the meanest subject to transgress them'.[11]

Moral progress was, in Gladstone's view, as much the concern of government as administration and the maintenance of public order. 'Restrict the sphere of politics to earth, and it becomes a secondary science,' he wrote shortly after his election for Newark reflecting on the prospect ahead.[12] This was the mistake of Locke and especially the Utilitarian thinkers Bentham and Mill. They had removed the ethical dimension from the scope of government and substituted a defective view of the State and a degraded system of personal morality.

The utilitarian principle calls for correction at the very outset. It should not be the greatest happiness of the greatest number but of the greatest virtue. Happiness is the right and reward not of existence alone but of existence combined with and governed by virtue.[13]

Ethics could never be divorced from politics. To do so was to violate the very nature of political society. The two were complementary, ethics dealing with the government of individual man, politics with the government of collective man. One grew out of the other, politics taking over where ethics finished.[14]

And for Gladstone moral progress was, of course, synonymous with submission to the will of God. Political society was a natural institution, bound by fundamental laws fixed by the

---

[11] Memorandum on the Irish Church Property Bill, 28 June 1834, BL Add. MS 44723, f. 107.
[12] 27 Nov. 1832; *Memoranda*, 19.
[13] BL Add. MS 44725, f. 290, 21 Oct. 1835.
[14] Ibid., f. 140.

mandate of divine justice. Social obligation was therefore no mere matter of expediency. The relation of the members to the body was to be determined by a natural and ordained relation, like that of the members of a family to a father, 'and not as one originating in the choice and therefore shaped by the fancy of those who are comprehended in it'.[15] Thus the view that the will either of the individual or of the majority was a rightful arbiter in matters of government should be denounced. The notion of *Vox populi* was an absurdity. As he wrote in 1835:

The *Vox populi* should be the servant of the *mens populi*, the *mens populi* of the *Vox Dei*, the *Vox Dei* is the servant of the *Mens Dei*.[16]

The paternity of these ideas is not difficult to trace given Gladstone's education. The major influence was undoubtedly Aristotle whose *Rhetoric, Ethics* and *Politics* formed the staple of the Oxford Classical School. Gladstone did not read Plato's *Republic* until 1832 after he had left Oxford. While at Oxford he also read with great intensity three authors who themselves had been greatly influenced by Aristotle: Hooker, Bishop Butler, and Burke.[17] The influence of Butler and Aristotle was lifelong and in later years he placed them with Augustine and Dante, 'my four doctors', as the teachers to whom he owed most.[18]

Gladstone drew from Aristotle a particular view of politics encompassing the whole of man, the refusal to divorce politics from ethics, the supremacy of truth as an objective structure, and a vision of the unity of the world with its own inner moral harmony. In a short memorandum written towards the end of 1835 he surveyed prevalent theories of government.[19] These, he felt, numbered six: the divine right of kings, the notion of contract as found in Hooker and Burke, the same notion as developed by Rousseau in his *Contrat Social*, the theory of delegation, the theory of expediency which he associated with

---

[15] Ibid., f. 174.

[16] Ibid., f. 211.

[17] He read Hooker intensely from 12 July to early October, 1829. His interest in Bishop Butler culminated in his edition of Butler's *Works* 2v. (1896) and his *Studies Subsidiary to Bishop Butler* (1896). This edition was planned as early as the 1830s; see BL Add. MS 44725, ff. 236–40. When Hallam left Eton, he gave him 'a superb Burke'; *Morley*, i. 42. He read Burke during the Reform Bill Crisis. For the importance of Aristotle and Butler, see letters to son Willy, *Lathbury*, ii, 1 Aug. and 18 Oct. 1860, 163–4.

[18] *Morley*, i. 207.

[19] BL Add. MS 44725, ff. 190–216.

Paley, and finally, what he regarded as the truest view, government as a natural, and therefore divine, obligation, 'which we believe under pagan modification was the principle as contained in the Politics of Aristotle: as they are distinctly owned in the Commentaries of Blackstone.'[20]

Gladstone's social vision was similarly hierarchical and paternalist. At the top was the monarchy, an hereditary institution bound by the law of nature, exercising its power analogously to that of a father over his children.[21] Gladstone also upheld the principle of an hereditary aristocracy, for a strong aristocracy meant the dispersal of power. When his friend Denison asked him in 1833 for an outline for a speech against a motion in the Oxford Union condemning the principle as an evil, Gladstone willingly complied.[22] Hereditary rule and primogeniture, he argued, were both endorsed by biblical authority. Since everyone agreed in the principle of inheritance in relation to property, it was not unreasonable to believe in the transmission of honour and power. Despite abuses among the aristocracy, such as 'a tendency to profligency', they fulfilled a positive role as a third force between monarch and people, a force whose power would be rendered nugatory if they were either elected by the people or appointed by the monarch. Intellectual capacity was not the only requisite for the due exercise of political power: an interesting view coming from a young man with a Double First.

The loftiness of sentiment and honour, which is certainly the *besetting virtue* of an aristocracy *per se* . . . is well worthy of being admitted into that compound to which . . . we are to commit the work of legislation.[23]

Gladstone's ideas on aristocracy and their role in the political order demonstrate more than anything the deep rooted need to idealize which characterized his early politics. He was acutely conscious of aristocratic status: 'People call Lord Lincoln my friend and he acts as such but it is well for me to remind myself of the difference of rank between us,'[24] he wrote of his patron's son. After his election for Newark he described the thoughts that

[20] Ibid. f. 190.
[21] Ibid. f. 196.
[22] BL Add. MS 44722, ff. 194–201, 11 Apr. 1833.
[23] Ibid., f. 196.
[24] 26 Dec. 1834; *Memoranda*, 40.

came to him as he rode through Sherwood Forest to the Duke's seat at Clumber. The oak trees, some with branches bare and blackened, others green and youthful, suggested to him the image of the English aristocracy: wealth, authority, ease, the proud and exclusive spirit generated by the sense of high birth, even their more dissolute tendencies. As a body the aristocracy had an influence both penetrating and pernicious. Why?, he asked himself rhetorically:

Because they were men. It does not follow, that they are to be rooted out. Birth, wealth, station, are as well as talent and virtue among the natural elements of power, and we must not war with nature's laws.[25]

Burke could have written much the same and there is also an echo here of the wistfulness of Coleridge's *Lay Sermons* addressed to the aristocracy, lamenting that they had not done all they could for the nation.[26] From the son of a Liverpool merchant such sentiments seem strangely quaint, but despite his background Gladstone was quite adamant that 'unequality is essential to a good state of society', and that the notion of human equality was nothing better than 'a monster'.[27]

However, the idea that stood at the nub of his political thinking, and certainly that nearest to his heart, was the unitary nature of Church and State. To maintain this was, he believed, one's chief political duty and the true politician would seek ways of developing and applying this principle in defiance of the extraordinary forces working against it.

The full implications of this were developed in his first book, but many of the ideas expressed there were among his political convictions from the beginning. They developed partly from the ancient tradition of the Anglican political theology stemming from Hooker, which had never been entirely eclipsed by eighteenth century theories of alliance, and partly in response of his own needs.

It is under the high and noble aspect of a church sanctifying a state, that we ought to contemplate the alliance between them, [he confided in a notebook early in the 1830s.] The functions of a government, unless the true doctrine of the necessity of a national religion be overthrown, become highly spiritual, if only it be sensible of its true character. It is charged in our country with the

[25] 28 Nov. 1832; *Memoranda*, 23.
[26] I owe this comparison to Dr David Nicholls.
[27] BL Add. MS 44722, f. 195, 11 Apr. 1833.

solemn duties of spreading its religion along with its civil establishments and on a scale of adequate liberality.[28]

As religious and secular concerns were inseparable in the life of the body politic, so also they should be inseparable in the life of the individual politician. This was not of course a distinctively high Tory view. It was probably best exemplified in this period by two evangelicals, Wilberforce and Shaftesbury, and perhaps formed part of Gladstone's evangelical legacy. Such a view obviously met a very real personal need for without it the religious foundation of his political vocation would have disappeared. That he was conscious of this can be seen from a comment from one of his note books:

Consider the effect of the anti-establishment principle in a Christian view of the profession of a politician: it removes, I say, the one great anti-septic element from it. What Christian of a sincere heart will accept powers capable in the ordinary course of things, of use *for* Christianity, but to which he shall be forbidden to apply them?[29]

It is important to realize, in view of subsequent events, that Gladstone applied this view of Church and State with its full rigour to Ireland. Of all the problems facing parliament, 'Ireland is the darkest spot of all,' he wrote to his brother Tom in 1833.[30] His first speech attacking the Irish Temporalities Bill has already been noted. But denunciation of sacrilege was probably too recondite an argument for the maintenance of a church that served the needs of less than one tenth of the population. He told his father that his speech had been heard with kindness and indulgence but confessed, 'it is after all uphill work to address an assembly so much estranged in feeling from oneself'.[31]

Gladstone never denied that there were reasons of expediency for upholding the Irish establishment. He was quite convinced, for example, that the Irish Catholic clergy were politically seditious and that popery as practised in Ireland was irredeemably corrupt, 'a faith so steeped in the worst of human passions that its disease is virulent and pestilential,' he wrote to Monckton Milnes, who had counselled moderation and even suggested the possibility of State support for Catholicism as a

[28] BL Add. MS 44815, A. f. 13.
[29] BL Add. MS 44821, D. f. 21, December 1834 or early 1835.
[30] W. E. Gladstone to T. Gladstone, 4 Jan. 1833, Hawn. P.
[31] W. E. Gladstone to J. Gladstone, 9 July 1833, Hawn. P.

means of expiating the Irish problem.[32] Before such a menace the Irish Protestant Church was a bulwark and defence, and its clergy were a rallying point for peace and order.

'The Union is necessary to the Empire—the Protestants to the Union—the Church to the Protestants,' he wrote in an article for the *Dublin University Magazine* in 1834.[33] But expediency was not enough. The real reason for supporting the Irish establishment was that England and Ireland were organically linked.

Are we one nation or are we not? If not, the union is a shadow, and cannot subsist. If we are can one nation have opposite churches? The church is one. Therefore the Church of England is part of the United Church of England and Ireland. In this the Catholics are a majority in their particular part, a minority in the whole.[34]

Higher considerations were indeed necessary and by the mid-1830s as he refined and deepened his thinking, he had begun to evolve a rationale for the Established Church that went beyond the usual arguments based on history and the Bible. The national establishment of religion was not a matter of expediency nor simply part of the national homage to God as evangelicals tended to aver; it was part of the intrinsic nature of the State as such.[35] The State was a moral entity capable of distinguishing between truth and falsity. A religious establishment was therefore more than the means of christianizing the nation, it was the articulation of the nation's religious conscience. As he wrote to his father in 1835:

I hold the belief, that the state is bound to teach *truth*; not indeed that it need exclude from its favour every shade of opinion except one, but that it is bound to observe the substantial unity of that which it teaches, as matter of duty in the first instance and of expediency in the second.[36]

What should be clear from this survey of Gladstone's early political thinking is that it was a purely theoretical construction, developed in response to his own needs, mainly through a dialogue with political philosophers of the past. It could not,

[32] Gladstone to T. Monckton Milnes, 3 Nov. 1835, Houghton MSS, Box 9, f. 134.
[33] BL Add. MS 44681, f. 23, May 1834; apparently unpublished.
[34] BL Add. MS 44723, f. 114, 28 June 1834.
[35] See the interesting account of his conversation with Lord Ashley after his speech in support of Church rates, 17 Mar. 1837, *Lathbury*, ii. 344–7.
[36] W. E. Gladstone to J. Gladstone, 11 Mar. 1835, Hawn. P; cf. his speech on Church rates, 15 Mar. 1837, *Hansard*, 3 series, XXXVII, 489–502, and his letter to Manning, 5 Apr. 1835, *Lathbury*, i. 23–38.

therefore, easily be translated into a programme of practical action. Indeed, it was difficult to express in parliamentary or party terms at all. Many Tories would have respected its strong religious tone or its stress on the hierarchical ordering of society, but Gladstone's Toryism was too lofty, too philosophical to be readily understood by the bulk of Tory MPs in the House of Commons.

Moreover, Gladstone saw his political creed as much more than a party matter. He was convinced that mere Toryism would be unable to meet the dangers of the contemporary situation. He wrote to his friend T. D. Acland, another young High-Churchman, who hoped to enter the Commons:

With delight indeed would I see you in Parliament, and a hundred more men, who, sound in their politics (as the term is commonly understood) yet brought something more than such politics to the task of rescuing, rectifying and securing the institutions of the country.[37]

But he was only too aware how few of his colleagues thought in these terms, and a year later when trying to persuade Acland to stand for Bath, he was forced to admit how anxious this made him. While sure that parliamentary Toryism agreed in all material points with Acland's own convictions, 'on those Church questions, which are now the cardinal and paramount criteria of political principle, a large portion of them [i.e. Tory MPs] may be inclined (unhappily I think) to yield more than you would'.[38]

The difference between Gladstone and his party leadership in religious matters and the tensions this produced for him can be illustrated by his attitude to the West Indian education problem that occurred during Peel's short-lived first ministry in 1835. Peel gave Gladstone a junior position at the Treasury and then, after the election, made him Under Secretary at the Colonial Office, thus recognizing his undoubted talent as well as placating the Duke of Newcastle and the Ultras by offering his candidate (together with his son) minor office.

Within a couple of months it was proposed to alter the educational system of the West Indies by supplanting the

---

[37] A. H. D. Acland (ed.), *Memoir and Letters of Sir Thomas Dyke Acland* (1902), 76.
[38] Gladstone to Acland, 10 Dec. 1835, Bodleian Library, Oxford, MS Eng. lett. d. 89, f. 3.

distinctively Anglican religious education by a system based on
more comprehensive principles. This horrified Gladstone. On
the 27 February he saw the 'harrowing details' of the scheme.[39]
A few days later he was in conversation with his chief, Lord
Aberdeen, on the matter and contemplating resignation.[40]

The scheme envisaged by the government involved giving
financial support to different denominations. To Gladstone this
was dangerously latitudinarian; the government would be
tacitly admitting that there was no important distinction
between different churches in matters of faith. Gladstone saw
this as a surrender of the true principle upon which the
Establishment was based and a relaxation of the Establishment
principle so important in its possible results that the matter
ought to be weighed with very great caution.[41] The 'great law of
the unity of national faith' had already been violated by the
endowment of the Roman Catholic seminary at Maynooth and
by the recognition accorded to the Roman Catholic establishment in Canada. No further violation could be contemplated
without struggle.

In fact the matter was never pressed, for a few weeks later the
government fell and the Whigs returned to power. None the less
it was a warning, both of the sensitivity of Gladstone's
conscience and of the attitude to the Established Church current
in government circles. After the onslaught launched by the
Whigs, Gladstone had expected a Conservative ministry to leap
immediately to the Church's defence. But while supporting the
idea of an Anglican Establishment it was clear that Peel and his
colleagues were not prepared to enforce exclusive Anglican
claims in all spheres. Had Gladstone thought more, he might
have sensed that the Tory party would, in the end, prove
inadequate to the distinctively religious mission he had assigned
it.

For Gladstone's theological development the 1830s were a
crucial decade. By the early 1840s his mind had he felt, when
looking back, attained a certain fixity. He had moved from the
evangelicalism in which he had been bred to a position which he

[39] *Diary*, ii. 27 Feb. 1835.
[40] *Morley*, i. 125.
[41] BL Add. MS 44724, f. 10, 21 Mar. 1835.

regarded as loyally Anglican yet authentically Catholic,[42] and in this position he was to remain for the rest of his life.

What transformed Gladstone's theological outlook was a new understanding of the doctrine of the Church. 'It happened once to me, on the top of a coach between London and Eton,' Gladstone wrote, 'to hear a conversation in which the interlocutors were a "converted" private soldier and an unconverted comrade, of the foot and life guards respectively. There came a turn in it at which the first named of the two put the question, "Come now, what is the Church of England?" To which the other replied, "It is a d————d large building with an organ in it." I think this expressed the ideas of my childhood.'[43] By the mid 1830s however, he had come to accept the Church as a divine institution with a magisterium based upon her apostolic pedigree.

His emotional conversion to this view, during his visit to Italy in 1832, has already been described. The deep and lasting impression this made can be verified from his diary, for six years later when he entered St. Peter's again he immediately recalled his earlier visit and that awe-inspiring conception of the unity of the Church it had given him. 'That idea has been upon the whole, I believe, the ruling one of my life during the period which has elapsed since,' he wrote. 'It does not lose its force.'[44]

But it would be wrong to isolate unduly this experience. The visit to Italy only set his mind in motion; its implications took several years to be worked out. Nor was it entirely unprepared. In his last year at Oxford his tutor had been Charles Wordsworth, a vigorous High-Churchman. His sudden conversion to high Toryism during the Reform Bill crisis may also have had implications for his religious outlook of which he was only dimly aware. A higher conception of the State could have made him more open to the attractions of a more definite conception of the Church. Similarly, by accepting the doctrine of baptismal regeneration he had opened the door to a firmer ecclesiology, for if a sacrament of the Church defines one's status as a Christian, rather than grace mediated outside the Church through private

[42] 17 Dec. 1893; *Autobiographica*, 158.
[43] *Autobiographica*, 149.
[44] *Diary*, ii, 8 Oct. 1838.

reading or prayer, then a more definite doctrine of the Church becomes not only possible but logical.

His investigation of this matter had also introduced him to the writings of a wide range of theologians, making him more aware of his own heritage. Again, although he later felt that Hooker's exposition of Anglican claims came to him as a mere abstraction,[45] it is difficult to believe that his intense study of that judicious divine a year later, had no repercussions for his religious outlook when it was obviously formative for his political thinking.

In general, the evolution of his theological opinions owed little to the direct influence of others. He embraced a more Catholic conception of Anglicanism independently of the Oxford Movement, though later he felt it may have had an indirect influence. Owing to the Tractarians, Catholic ideas were, so to speak, 'in the air' affecting his thinking without him appreciating it, in the same way as he later believed, the ancients like Seneca and Aurelius were unconsciously indebted to Christianity although they would have denied it.[46]

He wrote in old age that he had not seen the Tracts.[47] Here his memory played him false, for his college friend Benjamin Harrison had latterly come under the influence of Newman and sent him some of the earlier ones as soon as they were published.[48] But he was probably right in assigning them little significance in actually forming his views, they merely confirmed and reinforced what he had already come to accept. It is a great pity that Gladstone's letters to Harrison have not survived,[49] for from Harrison's side of the correspondence it is possible to see the young Gladstone moving gradually towards a more High Church position.

'I send you two Oxford tracts,' Harrison wrote to Gladstone

---

[45] *Autobiographica*, 150. It seems that Gladstone introduced B. Harrison to Hooker, see Harrison to Gladstone, 23 Dec. 1830, BL Add. MS 44204, f. 4.

[46] 17 Dec. 1893, *Autobiographica*, 158; and 26 July 1894, ibid., 146 for the impact on his thinking of Dante and Augustine, both of whom he read systematically in the late 1830s. The influence of Dante is partially explored by Owen Chadwick in 'Young Gladstone and Italy', *Journal of Ecclesiastical History*, xxx, (Apr. 1979), 243–59.

[47] *Autobiographica*, 158.

[48] Benjamin Harrison (1808–87), domestic chaplain to Archbishop Howley 1843–8, Canon of Canterbury and Archdeacon of Maidstone 1845–87.

[49] Harrison's papers were burnt by his widow on his death.

in November 1833, enclosing the first of the series, 'to shew you how exactly you have arrived at the line which they drew respecting the Apostolical succession and Episcopacy as related to each other.'[50] And nearly a year later he wrote, 'Your remarks about the irresistible force of the argument for an apostolic succession give me much pleasure.'[51]

But theological opinions in this period were in a very fluid state and historians assign labels only at their peril. Gladstone's churchmanship was always very individual and his movement towards Anglo-Catholicism, if indeed that label adequately represents his mature theological position, was no simple progression. At the same time as he was writing to Benjamin Harrison about the necessity of episcopacy or the uncatholic views of Dr Arnold, he was corresponding with his mother or his aunts in as fervent evangelical prose as he had ever written in boyhood.[52]

In fact Gladstone did not so much react against the tradition in which he had been brought up as assimilate to it Catholic doctrine regarding the Church and the sacraments. He would have said, as Pusey did to his cousin Shaftesbury, that he wished not so much to oppose evangelicalism as 'to supply its defects'.[53] Or perhaps it would be more accurate to say that both as evangelical and High-Churchman his theology was always, as regards the fundamental doctrines of grace and salvation, essentially Augustinian.[54] Gladstone did not need to surrender much of the evangelical tradition because so many of its tenets were part of the common stock of an older religious tradition to which he was always committed.

Gladstone believed that traditional Anglicanism was embodied in the Book of Common Prayer and the Articles of Religion, and that these could be interpreted in a sense entirely consonant with the teaching of the undivided Church. His main criticism of the evangelicals was that their doctrine often fell

[50] Harrison to Gladstone, 10 Nov. 1833, BL Add. MS 44204, f. 12.

[51] Harrison to Gladstone, 27 Oct. 1834, ibid., f. 52.

[52] See Gladstone to Aunt Johanna Robertson, 18 June 1834, Hawn. P.

[53] MS copy of letter from E. B. Pusey to Earl of Shaftesbury, 17 May 1852, quoted in D. W. F. Forrester, 'The Intellectual Development of E. B. Pusey 1800–1850', (1967), 204. Unpublished Oxford D.Phil. thesis.

[54] Autobiographica, 152.

below the standards set by these authorities and this was due, he believed, to evangelicals adopting high Calvinist views.

However near he came to accepting these views himself while at Oxford, he had consciously abandoned them before entering parliament. While in Venice in 1832, for example, he heard a sermon from a young Irish clergyman and noted in his diary that the views expressed were more decidedly Calvinistic 'than are strictly warranted by the tenets of the Church whose orders he bears'.[55] Four months later in an interview with the Duke of Newcastle, he complained of the harm done by Low Churchmen preaching Calvinist doctrine and his remarks showed that he was aware of men of the older High Church school like Hugh James Rose and the new *British Magazine*, and looked on them with approval.[56]

Where then did Gladstone differ from the evangelicals in this formative period? If we take as normative evangelicalism the moderate Calvinism of Simeon and the *Christian Observer* school, rather than the high Calvinism of Bultecl, or the pentecostal enthusiasms of Edward Irving, then Gladstone's position was not radically different on many issues. In fact the only central evangelical tenet that Gladstone actually rejected was the doctrine of assurance, and this he did for reasons as much philosophical as theological. He believed, following Butler, that probability was the guide to life and he applied this principle, like Ockham's razor, to both the evangelical claims of personal assurance and to Roman Catholic claims of infallibility.[57]

But in this he was tilting not at most evangelicals, but at that small number who claimed no one possessed a justifying faith 'unless he can pronounce absolutely of himself that his soul is at that moment in a state of salvation, pure in the sight of God as washed in the blood of the Redeemer'.[58] It is curious how unaware Gladstone was of the strength of moderate evangelical opinion in the 1830s.[59] His memoranda on theological matters

[55] *Diary*, i, 24 June 1832.

[56] 9 and 10 Oct. 1832; *Memoranda*, 27–8.

[57] See his memorandum, 'Considerations of Christian Experience', 17 Apr. 1835, BL Add. MS 44724, f. 54. For his opinion of Irving see the account of his visit to Irving's chapel, W. E. Gladstone to J. Gladstone, 28 and 30 Jan. 1833, Hawn, P. The second letter describes what he witnessed as 'delusion' and 'little short of madness'.

[58] BL Add. MS44724, f. 59.

[59] See David Newsome, *The Parting of Friends* (1966), 8.

during this period show him anxious to refute opinions that he evidently regarded as mainstream evangelical opinion when, in fact, they were the views of the extremist wing. It is difficult to account for this except in terms of his own experience. Having become engrossed in church defence where High-Churchmen were taking the initiative, he seems to have ceased moving in those circles where evangelical opinion of a moderate kind continued despite the excesses and indiscipline of the few.

How Gladstone's understanding of Anglican theology developed during these years can best be illustrated by his reactions to three books, each representing a different theological tradition, which he read during the 1830s: Joseph Milner's *History of the Christian Church*, Alexander Knox's *Remains*, and William Palmer's *Treatise on the Church of Christ*.

Milner's *History of the Christian Church*, published in the 1790s, was written from a definite evangelical viewpoint.[60] It was an attempt, as Milner put it in his introduction, to present a history of *real* and not merely *nominal* Christianity. Gladstone read and noted it in August and September 1836.[61]

He took Milner to task on three points: firstly for speaking of effusions of the Spirit without defining his terms (Gladstone was probably thinking of the dangers so adequately demonstrated at Edward Irving's chapel); secondly, for Milner's discussion of episcopacy. Gladstone was unhappy to find that he regarded church order merely as a matter of form, just as one might compare one form of government with another in the secular world. Thus his attitude was one of expediency,

Whereas the real question to be discussed, [Gladstone wrote] undoubtedly is this: whether there is not a special gift communicated by Christ to his ministry—whether that gift was not appointed to be transmitted from man to man . . . and whether such transmission was not further ordained to take place through the authority of an order of single individuals whom we term Bishops.

Thirdly, he took Milner to task for his tendency to separate the gift of grace from the visible sign in the sacraments. Gladstone felt that such a separation was impossible for it was the visible sign that secured the inward spiritual grace. The

---

[60] See J. D. Walsh, 'Joseph Milner's Evangelical Church History', *Journal of Ecclesiastical History*, x (1959), 176–7.
[61] BL Add. MS 44726, f. 136, 1 Sept. 1836.

evangelical revival, he wrote a year later, 'took grace out of the casket'. Like the sixteenth-century Reformers who went too far in reaction to the abuses of Rome, some evangelicals had tended to see grace 'in some inward unattested act of communion between God and the soul', thus overlooking the appointed means by which grace was conveyed.[62]

Because Alexander Knox, the recently deceased Irish lay theologian, anticipated some of the distinctive emphases of the Oxford Movement, Gladstone's attitude to him is particularly interesting.[63] The Tractarians themselves were, on the whole, suspicious of him. Keble, for example, although admiring Knox's *Treatise on the Eucharist*, felt his attitude to Methodists far too indulgent and felt his theology in general too eclectic for his taste.[64]

Gladstone read Knox's *Remains* in March 1835 and was much impressed.[65] Having been raised outside the High Church tradition he was probably better able to appreciate Knox's strictures of its arid legalism. Knox had been a friend and admirer of John Wesley and his theology was something of a synthesis of Caroline High-Churchmanship and evangelical warmth. 'He has in the first place vindicated . . . one may almost hope for ever, against the outrages of the scoffer and the saturnine contempt of formalism, the great and essential doctrine of an inward and vital religion,' wrote Gladstone.

He was also impressed by Knox's emphasis on the ideal of complete holiness, of the necessity of 'going on to perfection' which was where Knox's affinity with Wesley was at its strongest. He also felt that Knox had shown convincingly the dangers of mysticism, that the undivided contemplation of the Divine Essence 'is not appointed to constitute the habitual state or furnish the constant sustenance of our souls. Such contemplation is final, its triumph and reward'. And Gladstone was particularly impressed by Knox's teaching of baptismal regeneration. He has, he wrote:

    [62] BL Add. MS 44727, f. 192. In a discussion of the doctrine of justification by faith alone, 1 Oct. 1837.
    [63] See Y. Brilioth, *The Anglican Revival, Studies in the Oxford Movement* (1925), Chapter 2.
    [64] See Keble to Sir John Coleridge, 23 Oct. 1839, Bodleian Library, MS Eng. lett. d. 134.
    [65] Notes in BL Add. MS 44724, ff. 73–6, 24 Mar. 1835.

unfolded with great ability the beautiful results of that Catholic doctrine which ascribes a spiritual efficacy to the Sacrament of Baptism . . . so that while none can suspect him as others have been and perhaps justly suspected, as using the doctrine of baptismal regeneration in order to supersede the notion of subsequent spiritual agency, he has with great ability vindicated the truth that Christ desires in his Kingdom not only naturalised but also native subjects.

But although Gladstone found much to admire in Knox's work he also found blemishes, and nothing highlights more clearly Gladstone's own interesting combination of Catholic ecclesiology with evangelical soteriology than his criticisms of Knox's position. On the one hand Gladstone took Knox to task for taking a 'high' view of the sacraments but a 'low' view of the Church:

His religion is very much individualised. It seems to recognise no brotherhood. It does not receive the aids of sympathy. It does not appear to have any constant reference to laws, privileges, obligations, common to all. It has a large intercourse with the Almighty, but the communication is with his own mind alone, it has not witnesses nor partners.

This criticism shows clearly how advanced Gladstone's views had become for in fact Knox did hold the doctrine of the visible Church and saw its catholicity resting in the possession of an unbroken episcopate, in the liturgy, and in the appeal to the Christian antiquity. His idea of the Church was that of a *via media*, but was far more catholic than most eighteenth century theologians, even those who would be described as High-Churchmen.

But if he was defective in a Catholic direction, he was also defective in his understanding of justification and the atonement. Knox seems to have held a moral theory of the atonement and Gladstone felt he was not firm enough on the expiatory nature of Christ's crucifixion. It was not enough to say, as Knox did, that we must trust in our Redeemer for salvation, without a clear perception of the vicarious character of his suffering. Only this view could produce, Gladstone believed, the sense of sin necessary for the healing of a stricken will.

Knox's most serious error in Gladstone's eyes, however, was his denial of the forensic view of justification. Although Knox upheld that faith unites us in Christ and makes us depend on him alone as the source and cause of our salvation, Gladstone felt that Knox had deprived faith of its special office by denying that it procured for us, instrumentally, an extrinsic or imputed righteousness. It was not sufficient to see Jesus as the cause of our salvation by his impartation of himself to us and our assimilation to him, unless one was prepared to accept the 'link by which we connect his work with its individual application to ourselves, a forensic justification'. There was no need, Gladstone asserted, for Christians necessarily to have a distinct intellectual apprehension of justification as the natural precondition of their filial status, but he was quite convinced that the forensic view of justification was the doctrine of scripture and the teaching of the Church of England in its articles and homilies.

Gladstone was prepared to admit, however, that Knox's denial of this doctrine did not have the destructive consequences evident in other theologians, and that it was dangerous to be too preoccupied with its precise formulation. Two years later in a long memorandum[66] he went further, arguing that Knox had probably been led to deny the doctrine because he was repelled by the harsh and revolting manner in which it had often been expressed. There was, he believed, 'an idolatry of this doctrine against which we must protest'.[67] This he illustrated by pointing out that Melanchthon had condemned Wycliffe's views, while Milner had found even St. Augustine unsound. The essence of a Church did not depend, Gladstone felt, on a correct interpretation of this doctrine,[68] though many of the current misunderstandings were due to one-sided teaching in evangelical circles and the 'wretched degeneracy of sanctification teaching in this country until recently'.[69]

Gladstone read Palmer's *Treatise on the Church of Christ* at the suggestion of his friend James Hope shortly after its publication and took it abroad with him in 1838. Probably no single work of contemporary theology influenced him as much and at the end of his life he described it as 'the most powerful and least assailable defence of the position of the Anglican Church from the sixteenth century, especially from the reign of Henry the Eighth onwards'.[70]

[66] BL Add. MS 44727, ff. 178–92, 1 Oct. 1837.
[67] Ibid., f. 186.
[68] One of the reasons for his hostility to Lutheranism at the time of the Jerusalem bishopric, see below, p. 172.
[69] BL Add. MS 44724, f. 76.
[70] *Later Gleanings* (1898). 294.

William Palmer of Worcester College, represented the conservative strand of Oxford High-Churchmanship in the 1830s.
Gladstone had already read his study of the sources of the prayer
book, *Origines Liturgicae*, published in 1832. The *Treatise* was a
full-scale attempt at an Anglican systematic theology.

Palmer was Irish, which may account for his virulent attitude
to Roman Catholicism, and had been influenced by Knox,
Knox's friend Bishop Jebb, and Dr George Miller under whom
he studied at Trinity College, Dublin. He had a strong sense of
the Church as a divine institution, the necessity of episcopacy
and the dangers of private judgement in religious matter,
together with a horror of dissent. Although he accepted the
Reformation as necessary for ridding the Church of abuses, he
believed the Church of England was essentially continuous with
the pre-Reformation Church and therefore regarded Roman
Catholics in both England and Ireland as schismatics.[71]

Gladstone found Palmer's book 'remarkable'. Looking back
he wrote: 'It took hold upon me: and gave me at once the clear,
definite and strong conception of the Church which through all
the storm and strain of a most critical period has proved for me
entirely adequate to every emergency and saved me from all
vacillation.[72] Newman, he believed, had passed from evangeli-
canism to Romanism without ever coming to a true conception
of the historic Church, the conception 'on which Palmer's great
book is founded'.[73]

His enthusiasm, however, did not override his critical judgement.[74] He found Palmer's extreme rigour in regard to non-
episcopal communions distasteful, preferring to trust in the
biblical maxim, 'By their fruits ye shall know them.' Nor did he
feel Palmer was correct in maintaining that there could not be
two separated communions in the same place both upholding
the essence of the Church. He was also unable to accept Palmer's
insistence that members of the Church were never, under any
circumstances, to join in the worship of separatists, and he felt it

[71] W. Palmer, *Treatise on the Church of Christ* (1838), i, 458, 'I repeat, as a fact which
ought never to be forgotten, that WE DID NOT GO OUT FROM THEM, but, as the
apostle says THEY WENT OUT FROM US . . .'
[72] *Autobiographica*, 152. See also H. C. G. Matthew, 'Gladstone, Vaticanism and the
Question of the East' in D. Baker, ed., *Studies in Church History* (1978), xv. 421.
[73] *Autobiographica*, 157.
[74] For his comments see BL Add. MS 44728, ff. 136-40, 19 Aug. 1838.

both wrong and imprudent to maintain that the magistrate should enforce the decrees of the Church by temporal penalties.

More interestingly, he felt that Palmer talked too often about the teaching of scripture and tradition without drawing a distinction between the respective senses in which each can be said to teach, thereby, perhaps unconsciously, compromising the authoritative supremacy of scripture. In fact Palmer did uphold the supremacy of scripture in matters of faith and accepted tradition only to corroborate scripture when it was distorted or unclear. He did, however, believe that universal primitive tradition was infallibly true. Gladstone, following Butler, rejected this, though he liked Palmer's stress, particularly in the second volume, on the role of the testimony of the Church and his view that faith could not be founded solely upon the individual examination of scripture.

Gladstone later believed that his study of Palmer completed for him what the inspection of the Prayer Book at Naples had begun. It gave order and system to his conception of Anglicanism as well as historical depth.[75] It also shows that while fed by many streams, his churchmanship was particularly indebted for its understanding of the Church, the ministry and the sacraments to the older, more conservative, High Church tradition. Before he had become deeply involved in the Oxford Movement his theological position was becoming set. He had reached a position that was, he believed, Catholic yet in agreement with Anglican formularies. This was the standard by which in the next decade he was to judge the non-Juring sentiments of Keble and the more openly pro-Roman theology of Keble's disciples.

This position Gladstone expressed most systematically in *Church Principles considered in their results*. Published in 1840, it was written as a companion volume to his book on Church and State to make more intelligible the theological position that underlay it. But much of it was a reworking of material written at various times during the previous decade, and so it provides both a convenient summary of his theological position as well as giving some insight into his hopes for the future.

As a theological work, however, it had little impact. The press ignored it and though it was noticed by a few religious journals,

[75] 26 July 1894, *Autobiographica*, 146.

only the *Cambridge Univeristy Magazine* reviewed it favourably. As Morley remarked, 'it was still born'.[76]

Gladstone was sorely disappointed, for although disclaiming originality he felt his position in parliament, where church problems were of pressing concern, gave him an understanding of the religious difficulties of the time denied those living in more secluded situations and that a defence of the Established Church by a political lay man might arouse more interest than a similar treatise emanating from a country vicarage.

The title itself helps locate it within a particular tradition. A return to 'Church principles' was the clarion call of the conservative wing of High-Churchmanship and an appendix to the book contained extracts to support the argument drawn from representatives of that school like Bishops Heber, Jebb, Mant, Philpotts, and Van Mildert.

But Gladstone was quite aware of recent stirrings among High-Churchmen and held out the greatest hopes for their success, although he recognized that any such revival would display 'much of hesitation, of defect, and of incongruity, while upon its road to the amelioration it desires'.[77] Church principles, however, were not something peculiar to 'certain pious and learned individuals in the University of Oxford',[78] and part of his aim was to make that clear.

While not minimizing the Church's current difficulties, the self-confidence of the book reflected the growing optimism evident in Anglican circles as the Whig ministry weakened. He wrote in his concluding observations: 'I close at length this review of the religious position of the Church of England, full of the most cheerful anticipations of her destiny and without the remotest fear, either of schism among her children or of any permanent oppression from the State, whatever may befall the State itself.'[79]

The book itself was divided into two parts. The first discussed in three chapters the main doctrines which Gladstone believed were of special value in present circumstances: the doctrine of a

[76] *Morley*, i. 181. See also the letter of Gladstone to Lord Lyttelton, 9 Dec. 1840, *Lathbury*, ii. 49.
[77] W. E. Gladstone, *Church Principles considered in their results* (1840), 320.
[78] Ibid., 17.
[79] Ibid., 528.

visible Church with its own inherent authority; the doctrine of grace in the sacraments; and the doctrine of apostolic succession.[80] A fourth element, the notion of Catholic consent in contrast to the protestant principle of private judgement, he had already discussed in his previous book, and his exposition concluded with a chapter scrutinizing the specific claim of the Church of England to be the catholic church of the land.

The second part, a chapter of over two hundred pages, dealt with the implication of these doctrines for the contemporary situation and took the form of a detailed refutation of three common objections: that Church principles tended to Romanism; that they placed the Church in a false and uncharitable position as regards other Protestants, and that their general acceptance was divisive.

Gladstone's aim was to refurbish old truths. As he wrote in the opening section, 'To explore an old way, not to survey a new one, is the work of him who would be a reformer in religion'.[81] Yet he was aware that the chief threat to Christianity now came from Utilitarian philosophy and the liberal theology emanating from Germany that exalted private judgement, took a subjective view of truth, and regarded submission to dogma as superstition. Like Newman in Tract 73, therefore, Gladstone was concerned first to meet the rationalist attack on revealed religion for he realized that unless the objective nature of belief in dogma was established at the outset, his subsequent argument would be in vain.

His second chapter was therefore devoted to a refutation of the attempt to reduce Christian doctrine to the measure of human understanding. Christianity did not, he declared, oppose the understanding but transcended it.[82] Rationalism over-emphasized the intellectual faculty; it applied the Gospel only to the mind without taking into account that the mind, like the rest of human nature, was fallen. Catholic Christianity, on the other hand, stood for the total redemption of man, soul and body and the sacramental principle meant that the natural entry of grace came not through the understanding but the

[80] Ibid., 28.
[81] Ibid., 25.
[82] Ibid., 36–7.

affections, and was, therefore, anterior to the understanding. Teaching and instruction were partial and inadequate as instruments of salvation. Grace was mediated through rites and institutions, channels which were distinct, mystical and the outward representation of an inward living power.[83]

In one other respect Gladstone also showed his awareness of new currents of thought breaking surface. Four years before Newman's *Essay on the Development of Christian Doctrine*, Gladstone devoted several pages to what he called 'the theory of progression in religion'.[84]

He recognized that even those committed to the fundamental immutability of Christian truth had to concede that in every age there had been particular modifications in belief and practice. No religious system possessed 'subjective immobility'.[85]

But his own conclusions on this matter were conservative. While it was possible *a priori* that the Church develops while retaining her essential principles, in the way that 'an oak unfolds the life which it has carried seminally within it from the acorn',[86] there was no evidence that this had actually occurred, at least not sufficient to assert it as a recognizable principle. The matter was, he believed, extremely complex. In any given age the Church was progressing in some respects and regressing in others, a point he illustrated with reference to the thirteenth century, a supposedly dark period in the Church yet one that had produced Dante.[87] He preferred himself, not the organic image of acorn and oak, but the more 'static' image of a ship at anchor, 'The ship retains her anchorage yet drifts within a certain range, subject to the wind and tide.'[88]

Gladstone's arguments for the doctrines of the Church, the ministry and the sacraments displayed no striking originality but they were expressed with a freshness that contrasted happily with the dry and legalistic formalism into which much early nineteenth-century High Church theology had degenerated. He defended the idea of a visible Church from Roman errors on

    [83] Ibid., 83–4.
    [84] Ibid., 7. See D. Nicholls, 'Gladstone and the Anglican critics of Newman', in J. Bastable, ed., *Newman and Gladstone: Centennial Essays* (Dublin, 1978).
    [85] *Church Principles*, 13; 6.
    [86] Ibid., 9.
    [87] Ibid., 10–11.
    [88] Ibid., 8.

the one hand and protestant neglect on the other, while also attacking the Erastian attempt to derive ecclesiastical authority, and not merely the Church's civil rights and temporal jurisdiction from the State.

His whole chapter displayed a vivid sense of the Church as a divine institution and he quoted extensively from the Pauline epistles and the *Acts of the Apostles* to show that the idea of the Church as the Body of Christ was no vague metaphor and that the Church was entrusted with the lofty aim of mediating Christ's total redemption to the world and transforming it.[89]

He was concerned to analyze why this conception had been lost and to stress the advantages that would result from reviving it. Similarly, when treating the sacraments, he was anxious not only to state biblical and patristic testimony but also to enter into dialogue with the contemporary trends that had led to 'the modern and diluted notion of Sacraments'.[90] Again, his survey of the evidence for the doctrine of apostolic succession was supplemented by a discussion of its moral uses and advantages. Gladstone was well aware of the Englishman's natural anti-clericialism, and so was particularly impressed with the conception of the Church found in the Epistles of St. Ignatius, especially his view of the laity, 'And thus it is a mistake to suppose that the effect of Catholic principles is, unduly to elevate the clergy with relation to the people—it is much rather, to raise the position of both.'[91]

Throughout the book Gladstone's motive was to assert these doctrines in order to safeguard and enhance the truth that Christianity was a religion of grace and that within the economy of salvation the Church was the appointed means of grace. As he wrote, developing the image he had first used when writing on justification, grace was a 'gem'.

This gem, destined for an earthly use requires a casket—this casket a keeper. the casket is found in the Holy Sacraments; the keeper in their appointed, hereditary and perpetual guardians.[92]

In the second half of the book, aimed at meeting objections to Church principles, Gladstone displayed an awareness of the

[89] Ibid., 96–7; 107–8.
[90] Ibid., 166.
[91] Ibid., 269.
[92] Ibid., 278.

current situation and a surprisingly eirenic spirit. Thus while invoking the primitive Church as a standard by which to judge Roman innovations he recognized that the Roman Catholic Church shared many of the doctrines he was asserting and that she possessed the essentials of a church and a valid apostolic commission. Indeed Rome had more to commend her than many churches which had separated from Rome, where zealous reformation of abuses had terminated in denial of the faith.[93] Although the dark side to the Roman Church was evident from the abuses in Italy, a more intellectual and positive kind of catholicism was reviving in Germany associated with such men as Möhler and Görres.[94]

Gladstone was also anxious not to unchurch dissenters though he could not countenance any relaxation of the formularies of the Church of England even though some felt these placed the Church in a false and uncharitable relation to other Protestants. The zeal of many dissenters made him humble but doctrine was to be judged ultimately not by its moral results but by its truth. Many Protestants, he believed, would not wish to be considered members of the Church if it was defined in a Catholic sense, for they believed the Church was invisible. There need be no dispute between such people and the upholders of Church principles, for no one denied their communities were churches in the sense they defined them. For a Catholic, the best and purest form of the church could only be one that possessed the apostolic succession. But Gladstone felt it was impossible either to assert or deny that a non-heretical church that lacked the apostolic succession was a true church or not. The doctrine of apostolic succession was not, he believed, necessary for salvation, and quoted in support of this view the seventeenth century divines Bramhall and Laud. Nor did he believe that an upholder of Church principles need deny the efficacy of dissenting sacraments. 'When the fact of holiness is established, the inference of grace is certain.'[95]

Finally he defended Church principles from the charge that

[93] Ibid., 332.
[94] Ibid., 350-60.
[95] Ibid., 415, 420-1.

they introduced division within Anglican ranks. That their reaffirmation would produce schism he considered baseless. If anything their reaffirmation had brought more people into the Church than it had driven out. In recent years their reassertion had been completely beneficial for the internal welfare of the Church:

And in practice it is wonderful how, within the last few years, the more general and rapidly growing comprehension of Church principles has actually produced these results; approximation of opinion, deep consciousness and agreement in faith, strong sense of brotherhood, and general concurrence in the pursuit of the great purposes of the Church and of religion.[96]

He also included within this discussion a survey of Anglican theology since 1688, which gives an interesting perspective on his understanding of English Church history. After 1688 the tone of Church principles had, he believed, been 'grievously lowered and relaxed'.[97] The eighteenth century had witnessed a great decay in theological learning: 'Butler indeed and some others are bright lights upon the waste,' he wrote after quoting from latitudinarians like Hoadly and Paley.[98]

But with the evangelical revival a happier era had begun and Gladstone saw this revival as a herald of the movement for Church principles in his own day.

The evangelicals had aroused men from their slumbers by preaching again the vital doctrines that bore directly on personal salvation: the fall, the atonement, justification by faith, and sanctification by the Holy Spirit. If they did not appreciate fully the doctrine of a visible church this was because, Gladstone believed, they saw such lofty claims 'frequently associated with personal luke-warmness in religion, and with gross administrative abuse.'[99]

It was inevitable that their reaction was one-sided and had resulted in 'Strange and unauthorized admixtures'[100] like Wesley's notion of perfection and assurance and the high Calvinism of Toplady and Berridge. But the answer to this one-

96 Ibid., 441.
97 Ibid., 442.
98 Ibid., 460.
99 Ibid., 467.
100 Ibid., 468.

sidedness was the current movement for Church principles which both supplemented the work of the evangelicals and corrected their eccentricities. Gladstone wrote:

Does it seem a startling assertion that the doctrines of Catholic consent, of grace in the Sacraments, of succession in the ministry, of visibility in the Church, are the natural and effective complement, and the best guarantee of those doctrines of personal religion, for the lively and general exhibition of which we owe so much to the Romaines, the Newtons, the Scotts, the Cecils, and those who preceded and followed them?[101]

For over a century theology had been haunted, he believed, by three false oppositions. The first, between faith and obedience, had been overcome. The second, between grace and the sacraments, and the third, between the scriptures and the Church, ought at last be resolved:

The last twenty years, and in particular the last ten, have witnessed a resolute and determined inculcation of church principles, by men whose sympathies, with respect to the earlier doctrinal struggle of the preceding generation, were far more with the promoters than with the opponents of that movement.[102]

Church principles, therefore, were nothing less than the authentic doctrine of the English Church consonant with the spirit of primitive Christianity. Their acceptance enabled the Church of England to stand as a reformed Catholic Church, an authentic *via media* between the Roman, the Protestant bodies, and the Churches of the East. 'The Church of England,' he wrote, 'appears to be placed in the very centre of all the conflicting forms of Christianity.'[103] It had before it, therefore, a providential mission in helping to bring about the visible unity of all Christian peoples. And on this lofty and optimistic note he brought the volume to a close.

The change in Gladstone's theological position had implications for his involvement in church affairs and his attitude to ecclesiastical matters in parliament. In at least two instances during the late 1830s his new found High Church beliefs prompted particular action. The first related to the Church Pastoral-Aid Society and showed Gladstone identifying, con-

---

[101] Ibid., 470–1.
[102] Ibid., 473.
[103] Ibid., 507.

sciously, himself with other High-Churchmen for the first time in a public way.

The CPAS was set up in February 1836 under the chairmanship of the prominent evangelical Ashley, later Lord Shaftesbury, in an attempt to meet the pastoral needs of urban areas, and Gladstone was invited to become one of the Vice-Presidents.[104]

It soon became apparent, however, that there was serious disagreement over matters of policy, particularly the proposed use of lay assistants in pastoral visiting. High-churchmen wanted such lay agency limited to candidates for holy orders, under the direction of the incumbent, but the majority of the committee, who were evangelicals, were unwilling to abandon or limit lay help in any way.

Gladstone apparently accepted the invitation to join without studying the constitution in much depth. When its implications were pointed out to him by two High Church friends, Robert Williams and A. H. D. Acland, his anxiety grew. It seemed to him indefensible that lay agents should be examined and authorized not by bishops, or even parochial clergy, but by a body of laymen who had been neither examined nor authorized themselves.

He was reluctant, however, to go as far as Acland who now saw the whole thing merely as an evangelical ploy and who felt its work should be restricted to raising funds to be put at the unrestricted disposal of the bishops.[105] There was, he believed, enough common ground within the society, given its sincere attachment to the Church and the common obligation to defend its formularies. The time was not ripe to prompt controversy, especially when evangelicals seemed to be coming to a better appreciation of Church principles. But as the situation developed he became increasingly aware that compromise was impossible.

After a committee meeting in early February 1837 he wrote in his diary: 'A good spirit but a blank in the place where church

---

[104] E. J. Speck, *Church Pastoral-Aid Society: Sketch of its Origin and Progress* (1881).
[105] A. H. D. Acland to Gladstone, 3 Dec. 1836, BL Add. MS 44092, f. 8.

principle should be, on many hands.[106] A week later he spoke in favour of an amendment to the constitution, restricting assistance only to clerics.[107] The amendment was lost and the High Church element eventually withdrew. In July they met together to form their own society, the Additional Curates Society, under the supervision of stalwart High-Churchmen like Joshua Watson and Benjamin Harrison senior. To this society, formed in strict conformity with existing ecclesiastical discipline, Gladstone subscribed, and continued for much of his life to play an active role.[108]

Another instance of his growing commitment to the High Church cause was his interest in the Church's role in education. In his book on Church and State he had voiced concern about the annual state grant which, from 1833 onwards, had been divided equally between the National Society, a Church body, and the dissenting British and Foreign School Society. While anxious not to dismiss this arrangement out of hand, he pointed out that because of it public funds were being used to support schools not associated with the Established Church, thus infringing the Church of England's exclusive right to the control of education.[109]

In April 1838, at Bishop Blomfield's invitation, Gladstone joined the National Society's Council. This had become increasingly open to High Church influence in the 1830s and Gladstone was one of several young High-Churchmen, including his friend Henry Manning and S. F. Wood, who acted as a kind of 'ginger group' to uphold the Church's rights in this sphere and resist the State's pretensions. For it was becoming clear by the late 1830s that the government, far from allowing the Church greater rights in education intended to intervene more actively.

Early in 1838 they put forward a series of proposals to forestall State action in the training of teachers in an effort to goad the National Society into action and force the Church to take seriously her right to educate the English people. Each diocese was to have a diocesan board of education, a seminary and a central college. There were to be 'middle schools' to which

---

[106] *Diary*, ii, 9 Feb. 1837.
[107] Ibid., 16 Feb. 1837.
[108] Ibid., 31 Jan. 1838, 3 Feb. 1838. See *Centenary of the Additional Curates Society* (1937).
[109] See his comments in *The State in its Relations with the Church* (1838), 249–50.

promising pupils from the parochial schools would be sent, a religious syllabus was drawn up strictly in accordance with Anglican teaching and proposals made for a system of inspection. It was only the intensification of the conflict between the Society and the government due to the setting up of a committee of council to control education that put paid to their proposals.[110]

Gladstone in fact carried his struggle into the House of Commons itself. As a member of a select committee in 1838 he voted against the suggestion that a board of education should be established under the control of parliament. The following year this committee was set up with Dr Kay as its secretary (a clear indication in itself that the government had abandoned its role as paymaster and intended to be its own agent in education). Tory pressure had already forced Russell to abandon the plan to establish State Normal Schools. On 20 June, Stanley moved an amendment to the government resolution increasing the grant to £30 000 incorporating a request to the Queen to rescind the order in council constituting the committee of council. Gladstone, in a speech the *Standard* described as perhaps the best he had yet delivered, supported him.[111] He took the opportunity of lashing the government's proposals, arguing that they amounted to a recognition of all forms of religion by the State and therefore enunciated a new and unconstitutional principle. While its first result would be to supply the people with education, its ultimate consequence would be the destruction of the principles of national religion on which the State was founded. The government escaped defeat by only five votes and Gladstone, by his uncompromising stand, showed that he was now one of the leaders of the Church party within the Commons.

The other major development that took place in the 1830s was the growth of Gladstone's friendship with Henry Edward Manning and James Robert Hope. He had not been intimate with either of them at Oxford. Manning had come up to Balliol a year before him, while Hope came up to Christ Church from Eton the year after, as a fastidious young man of seventeen. He

[110] Newsome, op. cit., 219–22.
[111] Notes for the speech, BL Add. MS 44649, ff. 275–7.

and Manning, however, shared the same private tutor, Charles Wordsworth, for some six weeks during the long vacation of 1830.[112]

At that time Manning seemed set fair for a political career. He commanded a certain awe as an all-rounder and had made something of a name for himself in the Union where Gladstone was to succeed him as President. But the crash of the family banking firm, Manning and Anderdon, ended these ambitions and on leaving Oxford he spent a chastening fifteen months as a clerk in the Colonial Office. During this time, however, he was decisively influenced by the evangelical sister of his friend Robert Bevan, and underwent a conversion experience which led him to return to Oxford to study for holy orders. He was a changed man. He was ordained shortly before Christmas 1832 and went to serve as curate to John Sargent, Rector of Lavington and Graffham in Sussex, whom he succeeded on Sargent's death in May 1833.

Three months later he wrote to Gladstone for the first time, but a regular correspondence did not begin until April 1835 when a minor problem at SPCK brought them together. From then onwards their friendship deepened into one of the most important friendships of Gladstone's life until it was shattered by Manning's conversion to Roman Catholicism in 1851. 'No one was so intimate with him as I was in his Anglican days,' Gladstone assured Edmund Purcell, Manning's biographer, in the summer of 1897. 'We were in close and constant communication.'[113]

This was no polite exaggeration. Between 1835 and 1851 nearly four hundred letters passed between them: letters which

---

[112] For Manning see Newsome, op. cit., especially 146–50, 200–10; E. S. Purcell, *Cardinal Manning*, 2v. (1898); J. Oldcastle, *Memorials of Cardinal Manning* (1892); S. Leslie, *Henry Edward Manning: His Life and Labours* (1921); and A. Chapeau, 'Manning the Anglican' in J. Fitzsimons (ed.), *Manning: Anglican and Catholic* (1951). Fr. Chapeau has edited the letters of Manning to Gladstone which were previously thought to have been destroyed but which Chapeau discovered during the Second World War at the House of the Oblates of St. Charles, Bayswater. See A. Chapeau, 'The letters of Manning to Gladstone, 1837–1851', unpublished thesis, Paris (1955). Purcell's biography is, of course, notorious and was heavily criticized for its bias when it appeared. Gladstone wrote to Purcell: 'You have so pierced Manning's innermost interior that it really seems if little more remains for disclosure in the last day when the books are opened.' 14 Jan. 1896, *Lathbury*, ii. 341.

[113] Purcell, op. cit., Preface viii.

contained their own deep feelings on matters of mutual concern. Critiques of parliamentary bills, disdain at the Church's opponents in parliament, anxiety at the work of the Ecclesiastical Commissioners, the problems of the Universities, the progress of Church Principles, the situation in Oxford: all these and much else were examined and discussed. 'The correspondence', wrote Sir Shane Leslie dryly, 'was of Rome and Canterbury, of Church and State, of Church without State, of State without Church—and world without end.'[114]

For Gladstone the correspondence was the outpouring of his innermost and heartfelt convictions. In Manning he discovered a friend committed, like himself, unreservedly to the cause of the Established Church in a period of trial. 'Politics would become an utter blank to me', he wrote to him in 1835, 'were I to make the discovery that we were mistaken in maintaining their association with religion.'[115]

Manning understood such sentiments. Perhaps the attraction each had for the other derived partly from the fact that each was what the other had originally wished to be. But both men were also responding to the religious pressures of the age.

Like Gladstone, Manning had begun to move away from evangelicalism. In his early clerical days he was a decided Low Churchman: 'His *fides* was always *fiducia*', Gladstone recalled in old age.[116] But his position changed as he pondered the question of his own priestly authority. What authority had he for entering the homes of his parishioners and instructing or admonishing them? By 1835 when he preached the Visitation Sermon at Chichester he was stressing both the importance of continuity and the necessity of the apostolic succession. The next year he wrote a reply to Wiseman's lectures on the difference between the Catholic Church and Protestantism, which he published in the *British Critic* under the signature of 'A Catholic Priest'.

By the late 1830s, therefore, both Manning and Gladstone had arrived at a similar theological position and a firm commitment to the cause of the Church. Their thinking crystallized in their published works which to some extent

---

[114] *Leslie*, op. cit., 52.
[115] 5 Apr. 1835, *Lathbury*, i. 23.
[116] Gladstone to A. W. Hutton, 21 Apr. 1892, BL Add. MS 44215, f. 256.

complemented one another. In 1838, when Gladstone published his *State in its relations with the Church*, Manning published a sermon with a lengthy appendix under the title *The Rule of Faith* which repudiated the notion that Scripture needed no interpreter and stressed the role of tradition, thus bringing upon him the wrath of the evangelicals. And in 1842, two years after the publication of *Church Principles*, he published his first full-length book, *The Unity of the Church*, a theological and historical exposition not unlike Palmer's which was, according to Manning, inspired by Gladstone and dedicated to him.

The other friendship of crucial importance for Gladstone in the 1830s was his friendship with James Hope.[117] Indeed in the late 1830s and early 1840s their friendship was peculiarly intense. Hope had more influence over him, he later believed, than any other person at any period of his life except, perhaps, Hallam.[118] The comparison with Hallam is significant. Like Hallam, Hope was aristocratic, slightly younger than Gladstone, and naturally refined. He was strikingly handsome, rather delicate but with a strain of severity.

His background was Scottish and military, his father, Sir Alexander Hope, being the Governor of the Chelsea Hospital. His mother hoped he would become a clergyman but he inclined to the law. At the age of nineteen, however, he spent some weeks caring for the family's aged nurse and this quickened his religious feelings. After his election as a Fellow of Merton in 1833, at the young age of twenty, he became increasingly preoccupied with religion and went through a period of profound spiritual unease during which he contemplated taking orders.

It was shortly after this that his friendship with Gladstone really began. They had been acquaintances at Eton and Christ Church, but in the summer of 1835 Gladstone was invited to dine at the Hopes. The following spring he called on Hope in his rooms in Chelsea Hospital.[119] The occasion remained vivid in his mind, though it went unrecorded in his diary.[120] Hope, surrounded with folios and books, opened the conversation on

117 For Hope, see R. Ornsby, *Memoir of James Robert Hope-Scott* (1884), 2v.
118 See *Autobiographica*, 151, G. W. E. Russell, op. cit., 14 and Ornsby, op. cit., ii. 274.
119 Gladstone to Miss Hope Scott, 13 Sept. 1873, Ornsby, op. cit., ii. 274.
120 Perhaps it was 24 February 1836, at the time of the controversy over Hampden.

the controversies then raging in Oxford and declared gravely that, in his opinion, 'the Oxford authors were right'.[121] Gladstone later declared how he had felt himself 'under the reception of a profound and powerful religious impulse'.[122] His relationship with Manning was, perhaps, a relationship of intellect and will. Manning was proud, self-possessed, stern. Hope was more complex, more enigmatic. 'He possessed', Gladstone later wrote, 'that most rare gift, the power of fascination, and he fascinated me'.[123]

In July he wrote Hope a letter and the following February they began corresponding regularly. They soon found themselves being drawn together by their common religious concerns, initially their interest in a missionary society for Upper Canada and then in the difficult question of the relations of Church and State. Hope had by now resolved his spiritual dilemmas. Increasingly influenced by Tractarianism he had decided to dedicate himself to the Church in the realm of ecclesiastical law, and to serve her at the parliamentary bar with much the same attitude and fervour as Gladstone in the House of Commons.

Thus as the 1830s came to an end Gladstone stood poised and expectant. His religious position was now fixed. In the House of Commons he had achieved renown. He had developed a political philosophy which, with the sands of Whiggery running out, could form the basis of a new political creed for Toryism. The Church seemed set once more to regain her lost privileges and to gather into her communion her separated children. He had moreover, found two men with whom he could unite in a common creed and in a common purpose. Gladstone: Manning: Hope. As that formidable prelate Henry Philpotts, Bishop of Exeter, declared, these were the three men to whom the country had chiefly to look in the coming time: 'Manning in the Church, Gladstone in the State, and Mr. Hope in the Law.'[124]

---

[121] Ornsby, op. cit., i. 106.
[122] Ibid.
[123] Gladstone to R. Ornsby, 15 Oct. 1883, *Lathbury*, ii. 322.
[124] Ornsby, op. cit., ii. 74.

# CHURCH AND STATE: 1838–1859

3

# THE IDEAL DEFINED: 1838

*The State in its relations with the Church* was the manifesto of Gladstone's early Toryism. It was as much a political vision, an ideal, as it was a contribution to the contemporary debate about the relationship of Church and State. It summed up the movement of his mind since entering politics and was the starting point for his subsequent advance.

The book was published in December 1838.[1] Gladstone had begun it the previous July and completed the first draft in under three weeks. James Hope then read it, made some valuable suggestions including the title, and saw it through the press while Gladstone left for his second visit to Italy.

It dealt with questions that had long preoccupied him. As early as 1832, shortly before he received the invitation to contest Newark, he had written to his father from Verona that what was most needed at the present time was a discussion of 'the *principles* which bind society together, direct the mutual conduct of governor and governed and determine their relations'. These were, he believed, very rarely made the subject of serious enquiry and he expressed the desire to turn his reading to these matters and to study both the historical and legal aspects and the works of authors who had investigated the subject in a more philosophical way.[2]

The immediate stimulus to write, however, came in the spring of 1838 when the prominent Scottish and presbyterian theologian, Thomas Chalmers, lectured on the establishment and extension of National Churches before an audience of

---

[1] For other discussions of the book see A. R. Vidler, *The Orb and the Cross* (1945); B. M. G. Reardon's brief survey in *From Coleridge to Gore* (1971), 488–92; and for this and other matters see the seminal introduction to volume iii of Gladstone's *Diary* by H. C. G. Matthew, especially pp. xxv–xxxviii.

[2] 25 June 1832, *Lathbury*, ii. 228.

London society.[3] Gladstone, who as an undergraduate had broken bounds to hear Chalmers preach in a local baptist chapel, was one of his most assiduous hearers. But not all he heard was to his liking: 'Such a jumble of Church, un-Church and anti-Church principles as that excellent and eloquent man Dr Chalmers has given us in his recent lectures, no human being ever heard', he wrote to Manning describing the scene.[4]

Despite Chalmers's eloquent vindication of the establishment principle, his attack on the Voluntaryists and his views on the spiritual independence of the Church, Gladstone could not but lament the grave deficiency in theological outlook of a man who, as he put it: 'flogged, the apostolical succession grievously, seven bishops sitting below him: London, Winchester, Chester, Oxford, Llandaff, Gloucester, Exeter and the Duke of Cambridge incessantly bobbing assent'.[5]

Gladstone's own work, however, created quite as much notoriety when it appeared. It quickly ran to three editions. 'Gladstone's book is making a sensation,' Newman wrote to Mrs Mozley early in January.[6] Archbishop Howley of Canterbury and Bishop Blomfield of London both expressed their approval. Chevalier Bunsen, the Prussian diplomat and ecclesiastical enthusiast, sat up all night to read it. 'It appears to me', he wrote to his friend Thomas Arnold, 'the most important and dignified work which has appeared on that side of the question since Burke's considerations.'[7] A copy was immediately dispatched to Frederick William of Prussia, who had it translated into German by the theologian Tholuck. *The Times* was more ambivalent in its response. Leaders described the book as bold, trenchant and profound, but early in the New Year the tone changed and it attacked Gladstone's 'popish biases' which

[3] T. Chalmers, *Lectures on the Establishment and Extension of National Churches* (1838). For Gladstone's attitude to these lectures see *Autobiographica*, 42–3. Chalmers attacked the Voluntary principle declaring that there could be no 'free trade in Christianity', Chalmers, op. cit., 6. He argued, however, that any form of Protestantism could be established, the State making its choice for territorial, economic and fiscal reasons. He specifically rejected the doctrine of the apostolic succession as an assertion of exclusiveness, op. cit., 72.
[4] 14 May 1838, quoted in *Morley*, i. 171.
[5] Ibid.
[6] A. Mozley (ed.), *Letters and Correspondence of John Henry Newman* (1891), ii. 248.
[7] F. Bunsen, *A Memoir of Baron Bunsen* (1868), i. 493.

showed he was, after all, 'contaminated with those new fangled Oxford bigotries'.[8]

Gladstone's purpose in writing was to vindicate the idea of a National Church established by law, to show that despite recent events the Church of England was the only possible church to be so established, and to commend this to the Tory party in the hope that it would provide them with a coherent set of principles on which to base their future ecclesiastical policy.

The repeal of the Test and Corporations Act, Catholic Emancipation and the Reform Act had altered forever the basis on which the Establishment rested. Whigs and Utilitarians even questioned the right of the State to interfere in ethical or religious matters at all. Government, Gladstone told Samuel Wilberforce, was:

progressively and rapidly abdicating all in its province that is most worthy all that recognised the moral being, the personal duties and responsibilities of nations: descending out of the very highest region of excellence into the character of a machine not losing indeed as yet its power any more than other machines.[9]

More was needed, therefore, than a refurbishing of outworn arguments. A satisfying intellectual justification of the concept of an Established Church had to be found. 'Our inquiry', he wrote at the beginning of his study, 'is into the grounds and reasons for the alliance not its terms.'[10]

In fact the discussion ranged over a number of separate but interrelated topics: the relationship of Church and State itself; the effect of Establishment on the tone of personal religion; the Royal Supremacy; liberty of conscience and toleration; and a survey of the present constitutional and administrative practice in England and abroad.

The main burden of the argument, however, was in the second chapter where Gladstone attempted to ground the connection of Church and State in natural law. Central to his thinking was the notion he had discovered in Hooker of the moral personality of the State. The State for Gladstone was not merely a social or economic entity, an aggregation of individuals, it was a moral agent possessing a conscience, capable

[8] *The Times*, 19 and 21 Dec. 1838, 4 and 21 Jan. 1839.
[9] Gladstone to Wilberforce, 25 Apr. 1838, BL Add. MS 44343, f. 16.
[10] *The State in its relations with the Church* (1838), 5.

of discriminating between truth and falsehood in religious matters.

Churchmanship could not, therefore, be divorced from statesmanship. Just as an individual was endowed with a conscience accountable to God, so also the individuals comprising the governing body of the State could not remain indifferent in moral or religious matters but were bound by their collective conscience to profess a religion and seek to promote it.[11]

Because the establishment of a particular Church was on the basis that it embodied the truth, there could in Gladstone's view, be only one Established Church in a nation. The State should seek to promote the purest form of religion, which Gladstone argued, invoking the idea of probability, was 'the Catholic Church of Christ'.[12] The Bible, the sacraments, the historic creeds and primitive tradition, clergy validly ordained and standing in the apostolic succession, were witnesses to the catholicity of a Church. In England, therefore, the State was bound to establish and maintain the Church of England, because it bore all these characteristics while other denominations: Quakerism, Independency, Presbyterianism for example, were deficient in one or more.[13]

This, in bald outline, was the theory. Several other points, however, need to be noted. Firstly, Gladstone specifically rejected Hooker's ideal of the congruency of Church and State. The English nation was not one society which bore two different names but rather two societies, one ecclesiastical, one civil, co-extensive with one another. He had criticized Chalmers for omitting from his discussion of the matter any notion of 'the divine constitution of the visible Church'.[14] For Gladstone the Church was an independent institution and although the State needed an alliance with the Church to realize its full moral character, to the Church itself any such alliance was of secondary importance:

Her foundations are on holy hills. Her Charter is legibly divine. She, if she should be excluded from the precinct of government, may still fulfil all her

[11] Ibid., 21, 31, 106.
[12] Ibid., 26.
[13] Ibid., 66.
[14] Ibid., 21.

functions, and carry them out to perfection. Her condition would be anything rather than pitiable, should she once more occupy the position which she held before the reign of Constantine. But the State, in rejecting her, would actively violate its most solemn duty and would, if the theory of the connection be sound, entail upon itself a curse.[15]

Establishment, therefore, in no way compromised the Church's spiritual integrity. The alliance of Church and State was an alliance of equal and independent bodies, and if the Church's sovereignty was compromised it had the right, indeed the obligation, to dissolve its connection with the State and renounce its civil privileges, deplorable though, Gladstone believed, such a contingency would be.[16]

In ideal circumstances Church and State would function in harmony, while each retained independence in its own sphere. Gladstone described this relationship in the form of a metaphor. The Church was, he wrote, 'independent without exercising the right of separate action, independent as two watches are independent while indicating the same hour and going at the same rate; or as two men are independent who become companions on a journey reserving their right to part when the roads which they have to follow shall diverge'.[17]

Secondly, Gladstone refused to press his view of the union of Church and State to its logical conclusion with regard to other religious bodies and so there was, as part of his theory, an uneasy and rather grudging acceptance of the idea of toleration, justified mainly on pragmatic grounds.

He did not hesitate to declare that the theory of toleration had become associated with consequences pernicious and ultimately hostile to the true principles on which the Establishment rested. Unrestricted liberty of conscience, the principle implicit in protestantism, led inexorably to the stripping from government of its higher ends and duties. Political liberalism had the same corroding effects and had gone hand in hand with religious liberalism.[18] But although the situation England had entered in 1829 with Catholic Emancipation would logically lead to a

[15] Ibid., 4.
[16] Ibid., 121.
[17] Ibid., 120.
[18] Ibid., 231.

situation where all Churches would have either equal regard from the State or none at all, Gladstone did not envisage a reversal to previous constitutional arrangements, still less discrimination or persecution. The State was incompetent to exercise constant and minute supervision over the religious opinions of its inhabitants, and to punish people for religious error would mean it assuming a function that belonged wholly to the Church. Moreover, to coerce an individual was to break down 'the natural freedom which God had given to man'.[19] But toleration need not be a euphemism for indifference and his plea was that the existing situation, although not the best or most natural basis for the Establishment, was nevertheless an intelligible one and should be defended from any further invasion.

Gladstone's argument was not, therefore, without difficulties and inconsistencies which marred its inner intellectual coherence.

Although he had attempted to write from a political rather than a theological point of view he had not succeeded. While his argument for a national religious Establishment as the ethical dimension of an organic State was powerful and the invocation of natural law to justify it was impressive, his justification for the State adopting a specific type of Christianity was less convincing. It relied entirely on the supposed superiority of a particular view of what constituted the Catholic Church. Underpinning his argument, therefore, were definite and unargued theological presuppositions which to other Christians would seem arbitrary. He was not unaware of this, for shortly after the book's publication he wrote to James Hope: 'It is quite evident that the real connexion of my subject with the belief in the visibility of the Church and the doctrine of Catholic consent upon the interpretation of disputed Scripture will render it more difficult as well as more important for the principles of my book to make way.'[20] No doubt it was for this reason that he decided to expound his theological premises at greater length in *Church Principles* two years later.

Another area where the argument was unsatisfactory was the

[19] Ibid., 75.
[20] Gladstone to Hope, 11 Jan. 1839, BL Add. MS 44214, f. 62.

question of the relationship between the individual and the State. Gladstone had argued for the Establishment on the ground that the individual politician needed to sanctify his task by the agency of religion. But what of the man holding public office who was not a Churchman?

Writing three years earlier he had asserted that 'the Roman Catholics and Dissenters, who sit in Parliament, leave their dissention at the door'.[21] Although Parliament was a mixed body, made up of members of different denominations it was not a purely secular body. Those who were not Anglicans, he told Manning, had the right to sit but 'have no right to act there for their own religious communions'.[22] This presumption that dissenting MPs would not press the claims of their own denomination but meekly acquiesce in decisions favourable to the State Church was extraordinary in the parliamentary situation of the 1830s, in the virulence of the next decade it looked like wilful blindness.

Similarly Gladstone's attempt to reconcile liberty of conscience with the authority of the Church merely led him into an impasse. On the one hand he could not countenance coercion in religious matters, yet he castigated the notion that men of different creeds were equally well fitted to discharge civil office as fundamentally false, and that the development of religious toleration since 1688 had inevitably undermined the Establishment principle.[23]

The discussion of toleration was undoubtedly the weakest part of the book and one with which his opponents made great play. The Benthamite *Westminster Review* for example satirized what it regarded as the obvious implications of his theory: 'The ideas of State conscience and collective religion are not so clear to us as the Inquisition, the rack and the *auto da fé*.'[24] Since Gladstone never envisaged persecution this was rather harsh, but he had laid himself open to the charge and his acceptance of toleration, relying as it did on Utilitarian arguments and

---

[21] 23 May 1834, BL Add. MS 44681, f. 23.
[22] 23 Apr. 1837, *Lathbury*, i. 39.
[23] *The State in its relations with the Church* (1838), 217.
[24] *Westminster Review*, xxxvi (Oct. 1841), 308.

therefore on a philosophical tradition he despised, was at odds with his whole argument for a Confessional State.[25]

His only defence was that he never intended his theory to be pushed to its limits. As he wrote in the preface to the extended fourth edition: 'What political or relative doctrine is there which does not become an absurdity when pushed to extremes?'[26] In an age that lent towards an extreme and authoritarian form of Confessional State it was necessary to emphasize the rights of the individual conscience. But the present age was one that was inclined to secularize the State and ultimately curtail civil liberty by eliminating its religious guarantees. In this situation, therefore, the primary duty was to plead 'for those great ethical laws under which we are socially constituted, and which economical speculations and material interests have threatened altogether to subvert'. To declaim against intolerance was only a secondary duty. However true, this admission seems rather lame given the claims Gladstone was making.

There was then, a complete failure to grapple seriously or constructively with the problem of dissent. Gladstone criticized dissenters for their supposed exclusiveness, their lack of concern for the general religious welfare of the community and the fact that their position was contrary to the interests of the State Church.[27]

What is clear is that he was totally, and inexcusably, unaware of the growing strength of nonconformity and this considerably weakened the credibility of his argument. He later admitted as much in his *Chapter of Autobiography*. He had, he wrote in 1868, remained blind to the realities of the situation in the 1830s, and he admitted how astonished he had been by the increase of dissent shown by the 1851 Religious Census.[28]

---

[25] In many respects this position and others in the book is somewhat similar to the 'thesis-hypothesis' theory of continental Liberal Catholicism. Although there is no evidence to suggest that Gladstone derived his ideas from this source it is interesting to notice that he did meet and correspond with Rio and Montalembert, two of the leading French Liberal Catholics, and that in the fourth edition of his book he made specific reference to Lammenais. See W. G. Roe, *Lammenais and England* (1966), 111, M. C. Bowe, *François Rio, Sa place dans le renouveau Catholique en Europe, 1797–1874* (Paris, 1938), and Louis Allen, 'Gladstone et Montalembert', *Revue de Littérature Comparée*, xxx. 39–43 (Jan. 1956).

[26] *The State in its relations with the Church*, 4 ed. (1841), vii, viii.

[27] *The State in its relations with the Church* (1838), 92–3, 186–7.

[28] 'Chapter of Autobiography', *Gleanings*, vii. 144.

But the theoretical difficulties inherent in his theory lay at an even more fundamental level. He had jettisoned Hooker's identification of Church and State and argued that both were separate, independent and sovereign bodies. But unlike Paley, Warburton and other proponents of a 'two society' theory, Gladstone had rejected any alliance based on expediency or utility, and argued not only that it was of primary benefit to the State rather than the Church, but that the justification for the alliance lay not in the notion of contract but in natural law.

Yet all along Gladstone so stressed the spiritual independence of the Church that it is difficult to see in what sense, if any, the Church could be regarded as necessarily bound to the State. How could the bond between Church and State be part of the law of nature, and therefore by definition immutable, if the Church could whenever its authority was compromised by the State 'resign her privileges and act in her free capacity'?[29] Had Gladstone in fact formulated a coherent theory of a Christian commonwealth, or was it simply a desperate attempt to hold Church and State together when the split between them was already beyond theoretical repair?

Throughout the book there was an unresolved tension between an inclination on the one hand to emphasize the autonomy and authority of the Church, and on the other an equally strong inclination to emphasize the religious demands of the State.

Between these two conflicting inclinations, one feels, stood Gladstone, the priest turned politician, concerned that if the link between Church and State was dissolved his *raison d'être* as a Christian politician would be withdrawn. 'And I know not', he had written to Manning in 1837, 'how any man of conscience could become a politician, when that walk of life had become the only one in which a man may not avail himself of the opportunities placed within his hands for promoting the glory of God.'[30]

In a real sense, the particular view of Church and State Gladstone espoused was peculiarly fitted to meet his own needs and it is surely not too fanciful to see the book as a personal

[29] *The State in its relations with the Church* (1838), 120. cf. 116–17.
[30] Gladstone to Manning, 2 Apr. 1837, *Lathbury*, i. 31–2.

apologia written to convince himself and to suggest that any unresolved impulses stemmed from the tensions inherent in his own political vocation. The reviewer in the *Christian Observer* seems to have sensed this. The author's inconsistencies, he wrote, flowed:

from his attempt to combine with certain great principles, partly political and partly religious, which as a professed Protestant he appears anxious to recognise, and as a practical Statesman he is obliged, under existing circumstances, to apply.[31]

John Keble in his review had a similar perception when he ascribed the book's shortcomings to the fact that the author's 'wish' had been too clearly 'father of his thoughts'.[32] Keble's sensitive and intelligent review in the *British Critic* was undoubtedly the most impressive, but it was Macaulay's robust demolition in the *Edinburgh* that aroused the most interest and achieved lasting fame. As Gladstone himself admitted later in his *Chapter of Autobiography*, when interest in his book had faded, it lived 'only in the vigorous and brilliant, though not (in my opinion) entirely faithful picture drawn by the accomplished hand of Lord Macaulay'.[33]

Macaulay's religion was typically Whiggish: undogmatic, tolerant, erastian. What connection government could have with theological truth escaped him. 'Mr. Gladstone's whole theory', he wrote, 'rests on this great fundamental proposition that the propagation of religious truth is one of the principle ends of government as government. If Mr. Gladstone had not proved this proposition his system vanishes at once.'[34]

He made great play with the fact that Gladstone failed to distinguish between primary and secondary forms of human association so that the burden to seek religious truth lay equally on the State and, for example, canal companies.[35] He ruthlessly exposed the difficulties in Gladstone's treatment of toleration: 'But why stop here? Why not roast dissenters at slow fires?'[36] Exasperated at so bizarre a manifestation of an antiquated

---

[31] *Christian Observer*, May 1839, 288.
[32] *British Critic*, XXVI (Oct. 1839), 386.
[33] 'Chapter of Autobiography', *Gleanings*, vii. 104.
[34] *Edinburgh Review*, lxix (Apr. 1839), 235.
[35] Ibid., 239–41. Gladstone rectified this in the fourth edition.
[36] Ibid., 248.

mentality he fell back on ridicule. 'It is the measure of what a man can do to be left behind by the world. It is the strenuous effort of a very vigorous mind to keep as far in the rear of the general progress as possible.'[37] In fact, the review though witty was superficial. The rhetoric concealed the fact that Macaulay managed throughout to evade the real question, for, as Leslie Stephen later pointed out in his discussion of Macaulay's review: 'If, in fact, Government had as little to do as a Canal Company with religious opinion, we should have long ago learnt the great lesson of toleration. But that is just the very crux. Can we draw the line between the spiritual and the secular?'[38]

Keble on the other hand showed a shrewd awareness of the difficulty, though his point of view was as extreme in the opposite direction. He was one of those whom Gladstone probably had in mind when he wrote of churchmen 'growing cool in their approbation of the connection'[39] between Church and State, and the review highlighted the difference between Gladstone and the more radical Tractarians on this issue. Keble found much to admire. Here was 'no village theoriser, no cloistered alarmist, but a public man and a man of the world'.[40] He particularly liked Gladstone's discussion of the role of private judgement[41] and the stress on the permanency of the Church's doctrines and institutions.

But overall he was critical. He remained unconvinced that Gladstone had discovered an immutable basis for the Establishment in natural law. The arguments relied too heavily on secular considerations, on the social value and purposes of an Established Church, on expediency, and on measuring things

---

[37] Ibid., 256.

[38] L. Stephen, *Hours in a Library*, 3 series (1879), 300.

[39] *The State in its relations with the Church* (1838), 2.

[40] *British Critic*, XXVI (Oct. 1839), 356. Keble had wanted Newman to review it. See Keble to Newman, 31 Mar. 1839, Keble MSS, Keble College. 'It seems to me that a good field for saying something useful in the British Critic is afforded by Gladstone's book; have you engaged it for the Critic, if not, I hope you will take it yourself. It is excellently well meant but wants a little reconciling with Froude's views.'

[41] The right of the individual to read and interpret scripture for himself. This doctrine Gladstone traced to the Reformation. He attempted to show that in Anglicanism religious authority was based not on private judgement but Catholic consent as expressed in the Vincentian canon: *quod semper, quod ubique, quod ab omnibus*. For his full discussion see *The State in its relations with the Church*, Chapter 5, 'The Reformation, as connected with the use and abuse of private judgement'.

'by their visible results'. Gladstone had not escaped 'a certain utilitarian tone', and 'unconscious tinge, we will not say of Erastianism, but of State as distinct from Church policy'. If establishment was God's will for his Church, Keble argued, then it must be accepted even if the consequences in human terms seemed harmful. On the other hand if establishment was contrary to God's will, Christians could not acquiesce in it whatever benefits might result. When revealed rules and principles were at stake worldly prudence and political calculation mattered little. Churchmen should be prepared to stand 'in heroic imitation of the saints such as Athanasius who stood against the world and prevailed'.[42]

Gladstone had, he felt, ignored the scriptural arguments, especially Isaiah's analogy of the nursing fathers and nursing mothers, beloved of earlier Anglican apologetics, which provided a firmer basis than philosophy for the discussion of Church and State.[43] Gladstone's view of their relations seemed defective from an ecclesiastical point of view. Words like alliance, union or marriage were scarcely adequate, Keble believed, to describe the real relationship between Church and State. The word 'incorporation' seemed to him far more appropriate if it was understood in the traditional sense of 'the admission of any particular State, as of any particular individual, into the bosom of the Holy Universal Church reserving the Superiority, according to the idea of a corporation to the body adopting, for the benefit of the member adopted'.[44]

Above all Gladstone had, Keble believed, shied away from the appalling realities of the contemporary situation. He had professed to vindicate not only the abstract principle of establishment but also the particular form in which it appeared in England at that time. Here Gladstone the politician had been led 'to survey with too favourable an eye the alliance as it exists'.[45] His position in parliament blinded him to the terrible sin of the State in rejecting the Church. He did not fully appreciate how far the civil power had gone in usurping ecclesiastical authority. While he had acknowledged the gravity

---

[42] *British Critic*, XXVI (Oct. 1839), 358, 369–70.
[43] Isaiah 49:22–3.
[44] *British Critic*, XXVI (Oct. 1839), 359.
[45] Ibid., 367.

and danger in the State's recent actions towards the Church, Keble believed the situation was now beyond recall. 'He will go on in hope, believing against hope, after others at a greater distance have seen clearly that the time for hope is over.' It was better for the country to be ruined than for the Church to apostasize. There were enough 'secular' inducements for the State to maintain the Establishment, but this could mean the Church finding herself in an intolerable position. There was nothing more to be dreaded than that the Church, for fear of losing popularity or courting hostility, should in any way forgo her sacred principles for the sake of retaining her connection with the State.[46]

Here was the authentic voice of the new High Churchmanship. For the more extreme Oxford men only the spiritual integrity of the Church mattered. Fearful though they were of 'national apostasy', they were more concerned that the Church should be free than that the nation should be Christian. Though some, like Keble, still hankered after the Laudian dream, the younger men following Hurrell Froude, felt the old basis for the Establishment had been irrevocably destroyed and the Church must have liberty to fulfil its mission and direct its own destiny.

Such a view was impossible for Gladstone. As Keble rightly surmised, it cut at the root of his political vocation. He was in politics to serve the Church. He was not merely a party politician but a man in politics, using his position, as he put it, 'instrumentally for its ulterior purposes'. Moreover he genuinely believed in the religious view of the State he had put forward. Unlike Keble, he believed the State did have an unquestionable right to interfere in ecclesiastical matters as regards the Church's temporalities. Nor was there anything necessarily wrong, at least in theory, with the legislative powers the State wielded in relation to the Church. He was even prepared to acknowledge, again to Keble's dismay, that the State possessed the sole authority in matters of outward ecclesiastical discipline.[47]

But he was not entirely blind to the problems that gave rise to Keble's anxiety. As he had written to Manning three years earlier:

---

[46] Ibid.
[47] *The State in its relations with the Church* (1838), 30, 116, 131.

I think with you that if in contemplating the state and destinies of the Church, we set out from what we might call her sectarian interests, it is impossible to avoid lamenting her connection with the State, which in greatly enlarging the extent must also materially diminish the purity of her communion . . . I find far more considerations than one a more countervailing weight of reason and utility which induces me to banish this thought of discontent almost as soon as it has been tangibly entertained.[48]

Another Establishment theorist read Gladstone's book. When Thomas Arnold received it he welcomed it as 'a good protest against that wretched doctrine of Warburton's that the State has only to look after body and goods'.[49] But he was unable to endorse all he read. 'I like the substance of about half of it; the rest of course appears to me erroneous,' he wrote to the Revd F. C. Blackstone.[50] It is not difficult to guess which half the author of the *Oxford Malignants* took exception to. Arnold had carried Coleridge's ideas of a national Church further and in attempting to formulate his own idea of a Christian Commonwealth virtually eliminated the Church as a distinct society altogether.[51] As he had written, in the postscript to his *Principles of Church Reform*: 'religious society is only civil society fully enlightened: the State in its highest perfection becomes the Church'.[52] For him the Establishment was not something already existing, to be defended, but rather something to be realized in the future. He criticized Gladstone's theory because it made the promotion and propagation of 'religious truth' rather than 'man's highest perfection' the object of the State. 'Religious truth' could only be conceived as a set of dogmatic propositions to be found in a particular creed, Church or sect, and was therefore socially divisive. Doctrines like the apostolic succession, reliance on tradition or the concept of a priesthood were, Arnold maintained, superstitious and irrelevant and the Church should aim to be as comprehensive as possible.[53]

---

[48] Gladstone to Manning, 5 Apr. 1835, *Lathbury*, i. 23.

[49] A. P. Stanley, *The life and correspondence of Thomas Arnold* (1845), ii. 150.

[50] Ibid.

[51] T. Arnold, *Principles of Church Reform* (1833), ed. M. J. Jackson and J. Rogan (1962).

[52] Ibid., 163. Arnold's criticism of Gladstone is contained in an appendix to his inaugural lecture as Regius Professor of Modern History at Oxford, 'Introductory Lectures on Modern History (1842)', 49–50.

[53] For Gladstone's attitude to this, see his own remarks on Arnold's *Principles of Church Reform*, BL Add. MS 44803, f. 7, 30 Jan. 1833.

But perhaps the most interesting reaction to the book in view of Gladstone's subsequent development was that of his political master Peel. On receiving it we are told he quickly perused it and threw it down declaring 'that young man will ruin his fine political career if he persists in writing trash like this'.[54]

One of Gladstone's conscious aims in writing the book was to provide a coherent set of principles in church matters for his party when the Whig ministry at last fell. On 4 March 1838 he recorded in his diary a conversation he had had with his father.

I spoke to Mr. G. after dinner on the point I opened to Mahon at B[ridgewater] H[ouse]—viz. a definite principle on religious matters in the event of any C[onservative] Government being formed.

But neither the leader of his party nor the bulk of its parliamentary supporters were much interested in his principles. When it appeared in print J. B. Mozley, one of Newman's disciples, wrote to his sister:

Have you seen Gladstone's book? . . . It is a very noble book, I believe, and has damaged, if not destroyed, his prospects with the Conservative party. People are saying now 'poor fellow' and so on. Hope of Merton told Newman this, and what he had heard in town and also said persons out of the political world could not understand the sacrifice Gladstone had made.[55]

This was clearly an exaggeration. There were of course Tories like Sir Robert Inglis whose attitude to the Establishment was broadly similar to Gladstone's and who would press its claims with as much fervour. There were also no doubt an even greater number who felt, perhaps rather hazily, that it was the Tory party's duty to buttress the Church in its difficulties and to restore it to its rightful position. Many clergy outside parliament certainly felt so. Men like Hook of Leeds, the Wordsworth brothers, Palmer of Worcester, George Denison, members of the old High Church school, untouched by the radicalism of the younger Tractarians. Edward Churton, the rector of Crayke, was a typical example and in his *Letters of a Reformed Catholic* printed anonymously in 1838 he hailed Gladstone's work as 'a

---

[54] T. W. Reid, *The life, letters and friendships of Richard Monckton Milnes, first Lord Houghton* (1890), i. 316. One suspects that the account has been slightly 'improved'. Sir James Graham told Lord Teignmouth that Gladstone had sent him a copy, 'but confessed he could not understand it and that Sir R. Peel had regretted it having been written'. Lord Teignmouth, *Reminiscences of many years* (1878), ii. 226.

[55] A. Mozley (ed.), *Letters of J. B. Mozley, D.D.* (1885), 87.

sign of better days at hand', a voice of sense among 'the empty outcries of a spurious Toryism'.[56]

But Mozley's remarks, though exaggerated, pointed to the disturbing truth. The leadership of the Conservative party, however anxious to preserve the Church of England, were not interested in theoretical justifications of the Establishment. Their approach was empirical. They simply wanted to keep the existing state of affairs going as best they could and were prepared to accept the ambiguity of an Established Church in an increasingly pluralist society rather than seek a coherent intellectual legitimation for it. Catholic emancipation had already forced Peel into compromise, and his aim now was to consolidate the party around the defendable, rather than, as Gladstone seemed to do, defend a barricade that had already been breached. Indeed Gladstone, despite his intense political idealism, appears to have sensed this. In his diary for 23 July 1838 there is a revealing record of a conversation he had with Philip Pusey, Dr Pusey's brother, to whom he had given the manuscript. 'I told him for himself only,' Gladstone wrote, 'that I thought my own Church and State principles were within one stage of becoming hopeless as regards success in this generation.'

Yet he never regretted publishing the book and at the end of his life refused to place it among his recorded errors. The reason he gave is significant. When he had entered public life, he wrote in 1896, the prevailing creed of public men had been erastian. To get rid of this debasing system I even then felt an unconquerable desire, and one of the chief satisfactions of my political life has been to witness its progressive decay, which has now, I trust, nearly reached the stage of the last gasp. Now I make bold to say that my book on Church and State was the first manifestation from a political quarter of what was eventually to be a revolution in political opinion. It was anti-Erastian from beginning to end.[57]

[56] E. Churton, *Letters of a Reformed Catholic* (1838), vii. See also the reaction of S. F. Wood: 'Gladstone's book has given a standing place whereon to form a Church party in the House of Commons', S. F. Wood to Manning, 8 Feb. 1839, in Purcell, op. cit., 150.
[57] *Autobiographica*, 253.

# 4

# THE IDEAL DEMOLISHED: 1841–1845

Peel's government was to be the testing ground for Gladstone's theory. In June 1841 the Whigs finally fell and the Tories were returned with a majority of nearly eighty seats. Now, after almost a decade, it seemed as if the country had once more a government committed to the defence of the Established Church.

Despite the fears of some of his admirers, Gladstone's book did no perceivable damage to his parliamentary reputation. He was included in the small inner group that met with Peel throughout the summer to discuss policy and tactics, and it was clear that he would be given office of some kind.

His own ambition was to become Chief Secretary for Ireland. But on 31 August Peel offered him the Vice Presidency of the Board of Trade under Lord Ripon, a post that did not carry a cabinet seat, and which Gladstone accepted reluctantly, protesting his unfittedness. Although a position 'of great labour and responsibility', it was, he told Manning, 'as far removed as possible from nearly the whole of the subjects to which my mind has been habitually turned'.[1]

That was probably Peel's intention. Rather than place the young man where his religious views might cause embarrassment he sent him to a department where his undoubted aptitude for hard work could be profitably harnessed and his mind focused on political realities through the daily routine of administration. Facts and figures were to be the antidote to constitutional theorizing.

But mundane though his new duties seemed, the ecclesiastical bias of Gladstone's politics remained paramount and his vision of the Tory party's mission undimmed. His response to criticism of his book had not been to retract his opinions nor modify the argument, but rather to publish, in April 1841, a revised and

---

[1] Gladstone to Manning, 2 Sept. 1841, BL Add. MS 44247, f. 91.

expanded edition. On the very eve of its publication he showed his political stance had in no way softened by proposing the rejection of Divett's bill to remove the restrictions barring Jews from corporate office. The State was Christian, he argued, and therefore being Jewish was a disqualification for legislative office. Such a move would make it impossible to deny Jews the right to sit in parliament, would destroy the distinctive Christian basis of the Constitution and subvert the whole superstructure of national religion.[2]

A month later, in May, when the collapse of Melbourne's government seemed imminent, he had sat down and confided in a notebook his thoughts on the political situation.[3] 'All my reflections', he wrote, 'have brought me more and more to the conclusion that if the principle of National Religion (a principle, which is my bond to Parliamentary life) is to be upheld, or saved from utter overthrow, it must be by the united action of the Conservative party: not necessarily of every member of it, nor only of its members, but yet of the party as a whole and moving under its leaders.'

Yet the very nature of this conclusion prompted a sense of foreboding. What if the Conservative party did not live up to its high calling? What if it abandoned altogether 'the recognition of the Church, I mean of the Church as *the* Church—which recognition still remains almost unimpaired in Ireland still more near to absolute in England?'

Should this happen Gladstone would, he felt, have no other option than 'to accept the conditions of the age', 'to leave a way which is hopelessly barred' and to abandon parliamentary life altogether. The Church's interests could only be served by a party, not simply by the action of individual MPs: 'The principle of party has long predominated in this country: it now has a sway almost unlimited.' Whatever others might say, 'the time said to be that for resorting to individual action in Parliament is rather the time for abandoning Parliamentary action altogether'.[4]

He returned to the same theme some two months later. The

---

[2] *Hansard*, 3 series, LVII, 754, 31 Mar. 1841.
[3] 9 May 1841, BL Add. MS 44819, f. 57; *Diary*, iii. 105–6.
[4] Ibid.

union of Church and State is not, he wrote, 'a law of a primary kind, but a consummatory result of the development of Christianity in a people'. It was when the people had become members of the Church and had 'drunk of her spirit' that 'the State will harmoniously ally itself with her'. Therefore, he concluded, if the union between Church and State was endangered by the decline of Catholic principles among the people, the task of a committed churchman was not to attempt to reunite the two in the parliamentary arena, for a merely parliamentary evangelization was doomed to failure. Rather, he should assist in the reconversion of individuals to Catholic truth through the Church, for when this was done Church and State would reunite themselves. And he added: 'it may be difficult to determine the point of declension at which institutions in themselves wholesome must be surrendered: but there is such a point: retrospectively the fact, the practical issue will in most cases approximatively at least decide it'.[5]

How near at hand that point of declension was, Gladstone could not then have foreseen. Yet a mere three years later the 'practical issue' was to arise that convinced him it had indeed come. For in 1844, in an effort to meet some of the Irish grievances, Peel determined to increase and make permanent the annual grant to the Roman Catholic seminary at Maynooth, a grant Gladstone had attacked in his book as inconsistent with the Establishment principle.

On this issue Gladstone's theory was to founder. By now a member of the cabinet, he resigned from the government in January 1845. But he did so not to oppose Peel's policy but in order to make up his mind on the issue as an individual MP unconstrained by cabinet loyalties, and when the bill received its second reading, instead of voting against it as expected, he spoke and voted for it.

This quixotic behaviour scandalized some and baffled even more. But its oddness highlights the peculiar importance the issue had for him. It was to prove a landmark in his political development, one that in retrospect assumed symbolic significance. In old age he looked back on it as the crisis that broke his fetters: 'All my fetters were at once thrown off,' he wrote. 'In

[5] 24 June 1841, BL Add. MS 44729, f. 108; *Diary*, iii, 119.

short after Maynooth I had no great or serious mental change to make.'[6]

This, perhaps, gave a false finality to what was really a long and painful process of political, personal, intellectual and ecclesiastical readjustment. Nor was it entirely unprepared. But Gladstone was certainly right in assigning its decisive significance. Without this cathartic experience, a 'nightmare' as he described it,[7] his subsequent development would have been impossible. Only when the crucial importance of Maynooth in his intellectual development is appreciated does the course of his career become intelligible.

Between 1841 and 1845, therefore, Gladstone reluctantly abandoned the theory of his book as impossible, given the political circumstances of the time. Blinkered by his deep religious convictions and his abstract view of government, he had assumed that the Tory revival heralded a return to the ancient polity in Church and State. Actual experience of Peel's government, however, especially after 1843 when he became a member of the cabinet, convinced him that he had profoundly misjudged the situation. 'It was', he wrote in old age, 'only under the second government of Sir Robert Peel that I learned how impotent and barren was the conservative office for the Church.'[8]

Maynooth represented the turning point in this painful education, the conclusive demonstration of the glaring gap between theory and practice, political ideas and parliamentary reality. But what led up to it and what other factors contributed to the collapse of his ideal? These are worth examining in some detail.

It could be argued that the very nature of Gladstone's early political position made its eventual abandonment almost inevitable. He had confessed to François Rio, the French liberal Catholic, while writing the book that 'the straight lines of abstract speculation do not fit into the tortuous course of modern politics'.[9] He was right. The book was not a political

---

[6] *Autobiographica*, 51.
[7] *Diary*, iii, 25 Apr. 1845.
[8] *Morley*, i. 182.
[9] Gladstone to Rio, 28 July 1838: Bowe, op. cit., 156.

programme in any meaningful sense at all. It recommended no specific course of action, it was simply a vindication of the *status quo*. It demanded that the State undertake a more consistent attitude to the Established Church. Yet instead of suggesting ways of accomplishing this, it simply surveyed the current situation and pointed to the inconsistencies in the State's practice. As a theory it contained ambiguities, unargued premisses and unresolved tensions. As an attempt to provide the leadership of the party with a political ideology it was manifestly a failure.

Essentially, of course, it was the political theorizing of a young man, not yet thirty, who from the security of a proprietory borough, approached the world with a yearning for lofty principles, temperamentally disposed to great causes, a church-man fearless for his faith in an age of increasing secularism, a Tory for whom party was a means to an end. 'Reflection shows me', he had written in his diary in August 1840, 'that a political position is mainly valuable as instrumental for the good of the Church; and under this rule every question becomes one of detail only.'[10]

If to Macaulay he was the rising hope of those stern and unbending Tories, to others he was an enigma. *Fraser's Magazine*, for example, surveying Peel's ministry after its fall recalled the 'mysterious interest and intellectual individuality' with which the young Gladstone had invested himself at the outset of his career. His solemn earnestness, his sense of duty, 'the high and chastening spirit of religious obligation in all his speeches' had marked him out from most party politicians. But its conclusion was that he had assumed 'a moral position too elevated, too remote from the arena of conflict', and that he could not be looked upon 'to be one of the future guiding minds of the State'.[11]

Gladstone's position was, therefore, inherently vulnerable, and despite the outward self-assurance and the optimism that characterized his books he seems to have been aware of this. However hopeful, he recognized the possibility of failure. Indeed there was one area, that of the colonies, where the difficulties of maintaining his principles consistently had already

---

[10] *Diary*, iii, 16 Aug. 1840.
[11] *Frasers' Magazine*, xxxiv (Dec. 1846), 647–85. The article was by G. H. Francis.

become apparent to him. It was, he wrote later, colonial subjects that made 'a first breach in my Toryism'.[12]

The part that colonial affairs played in shaping Gladstone's political development should not be overlooked.[13] During his first years in politics they had been a major interest. He was, after all, the son of a plantation owner and his first experience of office, short though it was, had been as Colonial Under-Secretary. In the late 1830s, with that and experience of several select committees on colonial matters behind him, he had come to be regarded as the Conservative spokesman on the colonies.

But his real interest was as much the colonial Church as it was the colonies themselves, for it was in the colonies that the Establishment principle had been compromised most severely.

During Peel's first ministry he had almost resigned over the government's plan for West Indian education. In 1840 another sensitive issue arose, the Canadian clergy reserves. These reserves were land in Upper Canada that had been set apart by an act of 1791 for the maintenance and support of 'a protestant clergy'.[14] The precise meaning of 'protestant' in this context had not, however, been defined, and disputes arose as to whether it meant an Anglican monopoly or included non-Anglican protestant bodies like the presbyterians.

In June 1840 a bill came before the House of Commons from the Canadian parliament that aimed to settle the matter by selling the reserve lands and dividing the revenue among all the protestant bodies in a proportion determined by their estimated numbers. Although the terms were quite favourable to the Church of England the bill did, of course, undermine still further its exclusive claims and for this reason it might be expected that Gladstone would oppose it. But in fact he did not do so. He voted for the bill, the first occasion that he had ever voted on a different side to Sir Robert Inglis.

He was not unaware of the strong feeling among some churchmen, especially the episcopate, on this issue. But he felt it was impossible for the British Government to coerce the colonies in such a matter. 'We cannot mould colonial destinies against

---

[12] *Autobiographica*, 43.
[13] See Susan H. Farnsworth, 'Gladstone's policy toward the colonies, 1833–55', (1977), unpublished B. Litt. thesis, Bodleian Library, Oxford.
[14] W. P. Morrell, *British colonial policy in the age of Peel and Gladstone* (1930), 21.

colonial will,' he informed the Bishop of Nova Scotia.[15] The political changes wrought by the Reform Act, the diversity of religious beliefs in the colonies and the lack of agreement, even among Tories, on the real nature of a religious establishment, all made it difficult to enforce the will of the home government on its colonial subjects.

His actual speech in the Commons on the 15 June was an extremely interesting one for it highlighted plainly the tensions that underlay his position. If the colony was determined to have this bill then British notions were not to be forced upon it, he agreed. But he protested against being called upon in a parliament where British principles were acted upon, to abandon those principles and to be required to adopt the principles of a colony because they would not adopt the principles of the mother country. And, as if to justify himself against inconsistency, he declared that he did not regard this bill as in any way affecting the abstract principle of religious establishment but saw it merely as a way of dealing with a difficulty that had arisen under the 1791 Act.[16]

But however he liked to regard it, the settlement of the clergy reserves was yet another example of actual circumstances at odds with his theory. Though he had given the measure only reluctant support and justified it to himself and others on the ground that it involved no matter of principle, it was in a real sense a compromise as the more consistent stand of Sir Robert Inglis on the issue showed. Justice and prudence required that he act in the way he did. The only comfort left to him was to lament the fact that he had been forced to do so.

But though it was becoming increasingly difficult to impose 'national religion' in its full rigour on the colonies, the cause was not necessarily hopeless at home. Not, at least, if the Conservative party could be won over in sufficient numbers to a better appreciation of its religious mission. This could be done in two ways: conversion and infiltration. Gladstone was well aware of the limitations of the former. Though he had no desire to alienate needlessly men like Inglis and other rearguard defenders of the Protestant Constitution he realized that he could not hope for

[15] 9 June 1840; *Memoranda*, 121.
[16] *Hansard*, 3 series, liv, 1198; notes for speech in BL Add. MS 44650, f. 21.

much from them. Despite some common ground their understanding of the Church was too Protestant, their conception of
the Establishment was too Erastian and their solutions to many
issues too extreme for Gladstone's liking.

Nor could he expect to convert the existing Tory leadership.
'If I have differences from my leader, they are as I am convinced
not political but religious' he wrote in 1841.[17] Despite a high
personal regard for Peel, Gladstone realized that age and
education had already determined his religious attitudes.
Though a devout man Peel was, he later recalled, 'wholly anti-
church and unclerical, and largely undogmatic'.[18] The same
might have been said for Aberdeen and other leading Tories.

In fact Gladstone was so sensitive about the religious
differences between him and Peel that he was rather anxious to
defend himself from any charge of disloyalty. He was appalled
by the 'unjust, unwise, uncharitable'[19] attack on Peel's address
at the opening of the Tamworth Reading Room in the
Tractarian *British Critic* and felt it necessary to write to Peel
pointing out that the article 'excited the strongest sentiments of
dissatisfaction and displeasure among those who might upon
general grounds have been most expected to concur with its
views'.[20] Although he could not conceal from himself that on
religious matters, 'I have no sufficient warrant to presume that
my views are in unison with yours,' he wanted Peel to know
that he had not just given office to a man who differed from
him politically or who had any intentions of challenging his
leadership.

But even those younger Tories who were sympathetic to
Gladstone's religious position did not necessarily draw from it
the same political implications as he did. When Monckton
Milnes published his defence of Newman, *One Tract more by a
Layman*, he included in it a covert criticism of Gladstone's book:

no doctrine [is] . . . less practical for the resolution of difficulties or more beset
with embarrassments than this one of a State Conscience . . . to endow this
State with a conscience is to vivify an abstraction with an unnatural life and to

---

[17] 9 May 1841; *Memoranda*, 136.
[18] *Autobiographica*, 57.
[19] *Diary*, iii, 19 Aug. 1841.
[20] 17 Oct. 1841, Gladstone to Peel, BL Add. MS 44275, f. 19; partially quoted in C. S.
Parker, *Sir Robert Peel*, ii. 514–16.

confound the great problems of the just relations of spiritual and temporal authorities, which our age is in travail to resolve.[21]

Gladstone was quick to take this up. He read the pamphlet on Whit Monday and the very next day wrote Milnes a long letter, mainly of praise, but pointing out that although he had stated the difficulties of a State conscience fairly: 'I do not think you can altogether dispense with the doctrine—in my view if it is anything it is an expression of that which nearly all times and places have recognised though with different degrees of consciousness.'[22]

Perhaps he was right. But what was significant was the inability of his theory to command the support of the very type of man on whose success it depended. If Gladstone could not depend on the Ultras nor convert the leadership he had only the younger generation of Tory MPs to rely upon. And if those who were touched by the Tractarian revival were unable to find in his theory the basis for a common policy, what hope could he have of realizing his vision? It is true that S. F. Wood, Manning's friend, had seen in Gladstone's book 'a standing place whereon to form a Church party in the House of Commons'.[23] Similarly Stafford Northcote, who became Gladstone's secretary at the Board of Trade, thought he saw a small band collecting around Gladstone, ready to fight manfully under his leadership in the impending struggle between good and evil, order and disorder, the Church and the World.[24] But these were straws in the wind. In fact the dilemma went deeper. Gladstone saw the revival of Toryism as the political dimension of the revival within the Church. The one depended for success upon the other. In July 1840 after discussing ecclesiastical matters with Peel, he had written how Peel 'does not take into his calculations that daily growing knowledge of Church principles which is extending and consolidating the broad common ground of faith and discipline upon which churchman can afford to hold in peace their minor differences while even of these they will be in the very best position for getting rid'.[25]

[21] A Layman (R. M. Milnes), 'One tract more, or the system illustrated by the tracts for the times', externally regarded (1841), 14.
[22] Gladstone to Milnes, 1 June 1841, Houghton MSS.
[23] Purcell, i. 150.
[24] A. Lang, Life of Stafford Northcote (1890), i. 65.
[25] 2 July 1840, Memoranda, 127.

This was how Gladstone understood the religious revival of the 1830s. This was what gave him hope for the future. The general quickening of religious life that had its impetus in Oxford was not, he believed, something narrow or partisan. It was, rather, the revival of historic Anglicanism emerging after a century of latitudinarianism and worldliness, a revival complementing and correcting the evangelical revival, and its result would be a renewed Church of England, capable once more of gathering into its communion its separated brethren and thus becoming a truly national Catholic Church, Hooker's ideal become reality.[26]

But in this he was tragically wrong. He did not appreciate the essentially sectarian character of the Tractarian movement, nor its limited social base. He misunderstood the nature of the religious revival completely. The Tractarian leadership in Oxford had despaired of the Conservative party long since. Hurrell Froude had sung his 'Farewell to Toryism' and divided the faithful, like sheep and goats, into Z's: the Establishment-men, and X's, who stood for the Church's spiritual autonomy against the sacriligious encroachment of the State.[27] Between both a deep gulf was fixed. Newman too had little faith in any political party. 'We have nothing to hope or fear from Whig or Conservative governments', he had written to Miss Giberne in 1837. 'We must trust to our own ethos.'[28] Keble, perhaps the most emotionally committed to the Tory party, had opposed Peel in 1829 and his review of Gladstone's book showed that he too no longer trusted in the Establishment nor the traditional alliance between High-Churchman and the Tory party. Pusey also felt the 1830s had ended his Toryism and that he could not be a 'mere Conservative'. 'I could not bind myself or risk the future of the Church on the fidelity or wisdom of persons whose principle it is to keep what they think they can and part with the rest,' he wrote in 1865 looking back on his development.[29]

Not only were the Oxford men disinclined to align themselves with the Conservative party, the revival itself was taking on a

[26] Chapter of Autobiography, *Gleanings*, vii, 142–3.
[27] *Remains* (1838), i. 429; G. Faber, *Oxford Apostles* (1933), 393. For a discussion of Froude's views on Church and State, see C. Dawson, *The Spirit of the Oxford Movement* (1933), 64–76.
[28] Anne Mozley (ed.), op. cit., ii. 241.
[29] H. P. Liddon, *Life of E. B. Pusey* (1894), iv. 99.

character that, instead of consolidating the broad common ground within the Church that Gladstone had described to Peel, was tending rather to destroy it. The publication of Froude's *Remains* had raised the spectre of 'Popery'. The events of the early 1840s, culminating in Newman's conversion, were to shatter Gladstone's hope of a gradual and inevitable permeation of 'Church Principles' and the creation of a national Catholic Church.

The Tractarians were now a definite party within the Church, looked upon with suspicion, the butt of episcopal censure and the concern of the secular authority as well. Peel himself was distressed by 'the progress of the Puseyite doctrines'[30] and in 1841 nominated Dr Gilbert of Brasenose, the chief supporter of the anti-Tractarian candidate in the contest over the Oxford Poetry Professorship, to the see of Chichester.

Catholic Emancipation had already strained the old alliance between High-Churchmen and the Tory party. The emergence, therefore, of a new and vociferous brand of High-Churchmanship, at best lukewarm and increasingly hostile to the idea of Establishment, preferring to assert the Church's corporate identity rather than its dependence on the State, was to weaken the link still further. Instead of making the realization of Gladstone's ideal more likely, the very movement on which he pinned such hopes was to prove one of the major agents in its undoing.

There was one other factor, more mundane perhaps but nonetheless significant, that also undermined Gladstone's early approach to politics. Actual immersion in the day-to-day routine of administration, the down to earth business of government he encountered at the Board of Trade, the sheer unrelenting effort needed to prepare for the tariff revision of the 1842 and 1845 budgets, the railway acts and all the many other practical measures to which Gladstone had to turn his mind in the early 1840s: all this could not but force him to appreciate that politics was rather more than ideas and ideals and that the politician's role was a broader one than he had previously conceived.

At the outset Gladstone had complained bitterly that 'the science of politics deals with the government of men, but I am set

<hr>

[30] Peel to Graham, 13 Dec. 1841, BL Add. MS 40446, f. 189.

to govern packages'.[31] This attitude was soon to change. While he could still write to his father in 1843 that he contemplated political matters chiefly as a means of being useful to the Church,[32] his experience at the Board of Trade was crucial in his political development and marked the effective beginning of that lifelong absorbtion 'in working the institutions of the country'.[33] As Dr Matthew has shown, these years saw Gladstone's growing fascination with the principles and details of administration and though he regretted the curtailment of religious devotions that his work involved, he came to regard it as a necessary part of his vocation and in no way unworthy or second best. By 1845, he was noting the time spent on 'business' in his diary, counting it with study and devotion and time spent in a godly way.[34]

Above all his developing administrative experience made him increasingly aware of the complexity of the social and political order. His analysis of the basis and function of government in the early 1830s had been, he now saw, unrealistic and naïve. Government in itself was no longer capable of much that he had previously regarded as necessary and desirable. In particular it could scarcely hope to fulfil its role as a prime agent for moral and religious progress.[35]

Something of this can be detected in a letter he wrote to Manning from Whitehall in August 1843:

You ask me, when will our Bishops govern the Church? My answer is by another query, When will any body govern anything? . . . Government

---

[31] *Morley*, i. 244.

[32] W. E. Gladstone to J. Gladstone, 28 Oct. 1843, Hawn. P., quoted Checkland, op. cit., 348.

[33] To Sir J. Cowan, 17 Mar. 1894, *Morley*, iii. 535. cf. Sir James Graham's remarks that 'Gladstone could do in four hours what it took any other man sixteen to do, and he worked sixteen hours a day', *Lathbury*, i. 259.

[34] *Diary*, iii, Introduction, xxx.

[35] It would be tempting to say that Gladstone's conversion to free trade played a direct part in his conversion to religious liberty and that his adoption of what Chalmers called 'free trade in Christianity' followed inevitably from his adoption of free trade in the commercial sphere. Shiel's remark after Gladstone's speech on the Dissenters' Chapels Bill (see below) obviously shows that a connection between the two existed in some people's minds. Manning also connected the two: 'In fact it is the question of Free Trade and our existing commerce over again.' Manning to Gladstone, 18 Apr. 1845, Chapeau, op. cit. There is no evidence to my knowledge, however, that Gladstone himself saw the matter in quite this way, though administrative experience undoubtedly modified his conception of the politician's role, and free trade must imply a pluralist view of the State.

altogether is what is vulgarly called *on its last legs*—I mean as applied to all public institutions of compulsory obligation. Thus much it seems to me we may say: the authority of government is still one of the social forces whose combination directs the machine—one of many, not a mere clock-hand but one of the weights that work the pendulum—and the art of the governor, no longer well worthy of his name, at least when he is busied about the higher parts of his vocation, is, to affect the direction of the resultant by the application of his own element of force this way or that.[36]

Gladstone's intellectual pilgrimage away from the position of his book is not difficult to chart. Although Maynooth was the decisive event, it began surprisingly early. Less than a year after the Conservatives had assumed power, on Easter Day 1842, he wrote in his diary that while he still looked in the future for 'the adjustment of certain relations of the Church to the State' he no longer felt that 'the action of the latter can be harmonised to the laws of the former'. 'We have passed the point at which that was possible: and I do not expect to see it recovered. The materials waste away daily.'[37]

But a new possibility was emerging. If Church and State could no longer function in their proper relationship, then the State must allow the Church greater freedom to pursue its task. It would be much, Gladstone felt, if the State honestly aimed at enabling the Church to develop her own 'intrinsic means' and it was to this that he looked in the future.[38]

Perhaps it was the worsening situation in Oxford that prompted these sober feelings. He had rather hoped that his work at the Board of Trade would relieve him altogether from meddling in church matters and that he might derive some benefit from, as he put it to Manners, 'a period of entire intermission, an ecclesiastical fallow'.[39] But this was not what actually happened. Instead, Gladstone had become heavily involved in the struggle surrounding the Poetry Professorship and the Jerusalem bishopric, and 1841 had turned out to be, not a year of tranquility, but 'a year of heart burnings and heart bleedings, a chastening and a humbling year'.[40]

The limitations of politics for effecting the necessary spiritual

---

[36] Gladstone to Manning, 14 Aug. 1843, *Lathbury*, i. 60.
[37] *Diary*, iii, 27 Mar. 1842.
[38] Ibid.
[39] Gladstone to Manners, 17 Dec. 1841, Manners MSS.
[40] Gladstone to Hook, 16 Dec. 1841, BL Add. MS 44213, f. 29.

regeneration of society seem to have become increasingly evident to him. In July 1842 Lord John Manners recorded in his diary how puzzled he had been by a meeting with Gladstone. 'Some days ago,' he wrote, 'I came home from the Duchess of Buccleuch's breakfast with Gladstone. He said he had no faith at all in political remedies; that it all depended on the Church, and on this hope he seemed sanguine: how strange it was to hear the man, who had been gallantly and earnestly battling for his new political creed quietly admitting them to be *nauci, nihili, pili.* Does Peel think the same?'[41] Two weeks later on 20 July, 'reluctant but convinced', Gladstone quietly voted for the Maynooth grant despite having sat through a debate in which the Ulster Tory, Colonel Verner, quoted from his book in denouncing the grant.[42]

1843 saw the great struggle over the educational clauses of the Factory Bill and the victory of the dissenters whose furious agitation effectively destroyed Graham's attempt to promote the claims of the Established church by organizing the schools for the factory children under Anglican control.[43]

During this time Gladstone took his seat in the cabinet. Not, however, without a brief crisis of conscience. He was troubled by possible differences between him and his cabinet colleagues over government policy on a number of issues including the Factory Bill, and he drew up a memorandum for an interview with Peel.[44] He was particularly vexed by the proposed amalgamation of the bishoprics of St. Asaph and Bangor.[45] At their meeting on Saturday, 13 May, Peel discussed this and the other matters with him, reminding him of the necessary compromises and adjustments of opinion that would be necessary to ensure the co-operation of a cabinet composed of fourteen men. Gladstone agreed but pointed out that there were issues

[41] C. Whibley, *Lord John Manners and his friends* (1925), i. 139.

[42] *Hansard*, 3 series, lxv, 387. Gladstone seems to have become convinced that the existing arrangements were just, in that the British parliament had inherited the situation from the Irish parliament; see his letter to Hope, 25 June 1840: 'The discussion two nights ago on the subject of Maynooth College brought out from Shiel more of the historical argument in favour of the pretensions of the contract' (BL Add. MS 44214, f. 94), and the letter to James Lord, 8 Oct. 1841, *Lathbury*, i. 51–2.

[43] O. Chadwick, *The Victorian Church*, i. 336–46; Machin, op. cit., 151–60.

[44] *Memoranda*, 197–8.

[45] By order in council of 1838 these sees were to be amalgamated on the next vacancy in either and Manchester created. The order was rescinded.

involving matters of principle where compromise was impossible and asked for some more time to make up his mind.[46] In fact it was made up for him and after a two hour conversation with Manning and Hope, his 'good angels',[47] the following Monday morning he accepted Peel's invitation and attended his first cabinet meeting.

His first major decision there was to be on the controverted educational provisions of the Factory Act itself. Gladstone had always held strong views on education. He had championed the rights of the Church in the educational battle of 1839 and in a speech made at the opening of the Liverpool Collegiate Institution on 6 January 1843, he could still make a rousing plea for education within a strictly confessional framework:

a great and indestructable principle—namely . . . the principle that education, if it is to be effectual, if it is to be valuable—if it is to be deserving of that name . . . must be a religious education, it must be founded, not upon those vague generalities which are supposed to be common to all men who assume the name of Christians, but upon the definite revelation which it has pleased God to give, and whereby each man among us must hope to stand or fall.[48]

But that was, perhaps, the rhetoric appropriate for such an occasion. By 1843 he was, in fact, far more sensitive to the complexity of the issue and the reality of the political situation. When Graham first presented the Factory Bill, on 8 March, Gladstone found himself in some difficulty. At this point still outside the cabinet, he could appreciate the dissenters' objections to what was certainly the nearest Peel's government had come to helping the Church in an old-fashioned Tory way. Yet he realized their demands could only be met by surrendering the very points that made them valuable to churchmen, and he was well aware that High-Churchmen in particular felt the Established Church should have exclusive control of any national system of education and were unhappy about the conscience clause and the fact that State funds were being used, albeit in a mild way, to aid dissenting instruction.

His position, however, as a member of the government but not a member of the cabinet which was putting forward the measure, imposed its own strains. He felt that anything he might

[46] *Memoranda*, 198–200.
[47] *Morley*, i. 260.
[48] W. E. Gladstone, *Inaugural Address at the Opening of the Collegiate Institution* (1843), 13.

say would be misunderstood and either antagonize the dissenters or arouse the suspicion of his fellow churchmen. 'If I am prepared to support the measures of Government, I may properly speak on them (the education clauses) offhand; if I am not, I think it my duty to lay my objections *first* before them, and not before Parliament,' he wrote to Lord Lyttelton on 24 March, the day of the delayed second reading of the bill.[49] But he was aware that many churchmen looked to him to uphold the Church's position within the government and speak out where necessary. So it was best not 'to utter an uncertain sound upon any controverted Church question, but to be decisive and intelligible'.

This letter to Lyttelton made clear Gladstone's fears. He was not prepared to agree to limit the teaching of the Church in the exposition of scripture in schools and was therefore profoundly disquieted when that very evening in the debate Graham seemed to suggest that it was possible to teach scripture by simply explaining the meaning of the text in a neutral way, thereby avoiding denominational controversy. He was particularly concerned that in the hands of politicans who, however well intentioned, were lacking in any profound understanding of the nature of the Church, a diluted generalized form of religious teaching might be substituted for Catholic truth, and that although this was a measure designed to help the Church it might be better if the Church began to look to its own resources to instruct its members. 'The position of a State and of a society to which such a system is adapted is indeed far from enviable: but I think that, while we have to keep the Church inviolate, our business with respect to the State is to bolster up its practice as well as we can,' he wrote to Lyttelton.[50]

But the need to safeguard the rights of the Church in this matter was now painfully evident, for it was clear both that the strength of dissent could wreck the measure and that a Tory government could not be trusted to act always in accordance with what High-Churchmen in particular regarded as the Church's best interest. The difficulties that hindered the proper action of the State in the high province of religion seemed to

[49] Gladstone to Lyttelton, 24 Mar. 1843, *Lathbury*, ii. 130–1.
[50] Ibid.

increase from year to year, Gladstone informed W. F. Hook, the stalwart Vicar of Leeds. 'We must hope to see them mitigated or removed, but this hope is slender'.[51]

Once inside the cabinet Gladstone could see at first hand how his colleagues approached Church matters. Graham had been obliged to modify the bill to meet the dissenters' objections, but even this compromise did not pacify them and on 15 June he announced that in deference to their criticisms the government would drop the educational clauses.

Gladstone had voted against proceeding. In his *Chapter of Autobiography* he looked back on the whole matter as an anachronistic attempt to give vitality to the old Tory rule that the Established Church should receive exclusive support. 'When I bid it live, it was just about to die,' he wrote.[52]

The rancour of the 1843 debates showed just how unrealistic he had been in the 1830s to pretend that dissenters would leave their dissent at the door of the House. Entry into the cabinet brought home to him how different his conception of the vocation of Anglicanism was from the sincere yet nevertheless essentially pragmatic and erastian viewpoint of men like Peel, Graham and the bulk of the Tory leadership.

In his yearly self-examination on his birthday at the end of December that year he wrote:

Of public life I certainly must say every year shows me more and more that the idea of Christian politics can not be realised in the State according to its present conditions of existence. For purposes sufficient, I believe, but partial and finite, I am more than content to be where I am. But the perfect freedom of the new covenant can only, it seems to me, be breathed in other air: and the day may yet come when God may grant to me the application of this conviction to myself.[53]

The events of 1844 and 1845, the Dissenters' Chapels Bill, the prolonged crisis leading up to Maynooth and his resignation from the government made it seem almost as if that day had, indeed, begun to dawn. Certainly now that he was within the cabinet Gladstone felt more acutely the tensions of his position. To be so directly involved in government decisions could not but be a burden when what he considered the Conservative govern-

[51] Gladstone to Hook, 30 Mar. 1843, *Lathbury*, ii. 133.
[52] *Gleanings*, vii. 116.
[53] *Diary*, iii, 29 Dec. 1843.

ment's real task; the defence of the Church, was obviously neither properly understood nor even central to his colleagues' concerns. For a young man who had seen his political vocation in terms of 'rescuing, rectifying and securing the institutions of the country' so that they could once more become the means of christianizing the social order, the whole drift of politics in the 1840s seemed alarming. Added to this was the consciousness that a peculiar responsibility rested upon his shoulders. 'I know of no one man, not in Holy Orders, on whom the Providence of God had laid so much of the burden of the English Church at this time', Manning had written to him the day after he had joined the cabinet.[54]

The spiritual dilemma this awareness created should not be dismissed lightly. How genuine it was is conveyed perhaps by one small incident that occurred shortly before the end of 1843. On 10 December Gladstone received from Newman a copy of his recently published *Sermons, bearing on Subjects of the Day*. It was a poignant gift. Just over a fortnight before Gladstone had learned from Manning the appalling news that Newman's faith in the *via media* was on the brink of collapse.

The volume contained the since famous sermon on 'The Parting of Friends'. But it was not this that immediately caught Gladstone's attention. Rather it was the sermon preached on a text from Zechariah on the theme 'Feasting in captivity'. Here was a theme that seemed to speak to Gladstone's condition, the need to remain firm to a 'apostolic christianity' in a world where the whole moral, social and political order was in disarray.[55] In a letter of thanks he wrote of the particular acknowledgement he felt he must make for the instruction which it 'conveys at least as pointedly to myself as to anyone that could have heard or may read it'. None he felt could be in more danger of realizing the evil sense of 'feasting in Captivity' than himself.[56]

On 11 February 1844 he was made even more aware of the strong cords that bound him, preventing him from implement-

[54] Manning to Gladstone, 16 May 1843, Chapeau, op. cit.

[55] J. H. Newman, *Sermons bearing on Subjects of the Day* (1843), 381–94. The sermon stressed the joys and dangers of this situation. See D. Newsome, *The Parting of Friends* (1966), 181.

[56] Gladstone to Newman, 12 Dec. 1843, Oratory MSS, Birmingham.

ing this apostolic faith in the political sphere in all its fullness.[57] That evening he read Peel's circular on the Maynooth question suggesting that the grant to the Catholic seminary should be increased and made permanent. Thus began the long and protracted crisis, so decisive for his political and intellectual development, that was to culminate in his resignation from the government a year later. But no sooner had the implications of this begun to make themselves felt than Gladstone was plunged into another issue bearing on Church and State, the Dissenters' Chapels Bill.

This bill, which sought to give Unitarians secure possession of chapels built by their orthodox Puritan predecessors, encountered opposition far greater than Peel or his cabinet had anticipated.[58] Evangelicals, dissenters, and High-Churchmen alike joined in protest. In the House of Commons the opposition was led by Sir Robert Inglis and the evangelical Fox Maule, MP for Kent, who declared that the bill was an insult to the Christian feeling of the country. Gladstone studied the question with his usual thoroughness. He discussed it with Inglis, Manning, Lord Stanley, and Hope and received a deputation of Unitarians. He read widely and delved into the history of Lady Hewley's Trust which had sparked off the matter, and the process by which the Unitarians had separated themselves from orthodox dissent. In the end he was convinced that the bill was just and that, in fact, the Unitarians were the true lawful holders of their chapels. While they did not agree with the opinions of their Puritan forebears, they adhered firmly to the puritan principle that Scripture was the rule without any binding interpretation and that each generation, or indeed each man, could interpret for itself.

Therefore, on 6 June when the bill came before the House for its second reading he spoke and voted for it. He told MPs he was sure that the bill was one which it was incumbent on the House to pass, and then defended his own position. Far from feeling that there was a conflict between his religious principles and

---

[57] The allusion is to his summing up at the end of that year: 'The last years have woven strong cords upon me that I had not before: but my vocation does not seem as yet to struggle against them'. *Diary*, iii, 29 Dec. 1844.

[58] On this see Chadwick, op. cit., 391–5 and Machin, op. cit., 165–9.

those of the legislation before them, he declared that the only use he could make of his principles was 'to apply them to the decisive performance of a great and important act' which, whether its consequences were good or bad, was founded 'on the everlasting principle of truth and justice'.[59]

Looking back on it he wrote: 'This measure in some way heightened my churchmanship but depressed my church-and-statesmanship.'[60] His belief in the authority of the Church as the interpreter of scripture and guardian of true doctrine was confirmed and enhanced by this example of the ultimate deleterious effects of the Protestant principle of private judgement. But his political ecclesiasticism was further undermined in that he had supported an act, proposed by a Tory government, that aided a religious body other than the Established Church and that marked a further extension of the Toleration Act to non-Trinitarians. His action showed clearly the increasing gulf between Gladstone and the more rigorous Tory defenders of the Establishment, a fact not lost on the perceptive Irish MP, R. L. Shiel who, on hearing Gladstone's speech prophesied that 'the champion of free trade, will ere long become the advocate of the most unrestricted liberty of thought'.[61]

Since Gladstone had been forced in his book to justify the apparent anomaly of toleration for dissent in any case, his support for the Dissenters' Chapels Bill was, perhaps, less damaging to his theory than many supposed. The same could not be said for Maynooth which assumed for him a crucial importance. Throughout the remainder of 1844 and into 1845 this issue and its ramifications dominated his mind. From the very outset Gladstone had seen the question as one of principle. The present arrangements whereby St. Patrick's College, founded in 1795 to stop the flow of Irish seminarians to France, was supported by an annual grant voted by the Westminster parliament, could be represented as a legacy from the Irish parliament inherited at the Act of Union. To alter them would be a shock to the religious feeling of the country, would weaken the position of the Established Church in Ireland still further

---

[59] *Hansard*, 3 series, LXXV, 377.
[60] *Autobiographica*, 50.
[61] *Hansard*, 3 series, LXXV, 377.

and would give added encouragement to the supporters of the Voluntary Principle.[62]

He had made it clear at the cabinet meeting of 12 February that in publishing his book he had pledged himself publicly against such an increase and that his mind had not changed. Only 'a great and decisive change of sentiments' could justify his participating in the measure, and no such change had occurred.[63]

By the end of February when it had become clear to him that Peel intended to press the matter, he could no longer disregard the possibility of resignation. But the choice was a cruel one. To remain in the cabinet would go against all that he had written on the matter. Yet to resign would, he believed, give 'a signal for disunion, suspicion, and even conflict in that political party by which alone as I firmly believe the religious institutions and laws of the country are under God maintained'.[64]

He discussed his difficulties privately with Peel and a little later with Lord Stanley. Both found them difficult to understand. They seemed to be the product of too scrupulous a conscience, an incomprehensible commitment to abstract principle, or past pledges, which in any case the public would have forgotten. Stanley suggested that there were times when a politician had to choose between the lesser of two evils. Gladstone disagreed. For him the issue was one bearing directly on his public character and political consistency. 'I am one whose courage has never been tried—I have no position, no rank or state of property in the country—the public may very fairly regard me as a mere adventurer, if I should part company with character,' he told Stanley.[65] To be party to the measure would give the world a right to point at him and say 'that man is not to be trusted—after having written *thus*, and now acting *thus*, no words will bind him'.[66]

---

[62] 11 Feb. 1844; *Memoranda*, 230–4.

[63] Ibid.

[64] 29 Feb. 1844; *Memoranda*, 236–7.

[65] 7 Mar. 1844; *Memoranda*, 247.

[66] 12 Mar. 1844; *Memoranda*, 248. This was not entirely over-sensitivity on Gladstone's part. There were undoubtedly many people who felt he should resign if Peel passed the measure. Hope told him (16 Aug. 1844, BL Add. MS 44214, f. 251) how, in conversation with Mr Lynch, Master in Chancery, Lynch had said it would be impossible for Gladstone to remain in office if such a course was pursued.

In July a way out of the dilemma suggested itself. Peel had for some time been considering re-establishing diplomatic relations with the Holy See. Gladstone was strongly in favour. Indeed he felt such a move was essential if the measures contemplated for Ireland were to have any hope of success. He also believed that it might have a beneficial effect from a religious point of view in providing an opportunity for making the Church of England better known in Vatican circles. Encouraged by Hope, he wrote to Peel on 12 July offering himself as British envoy. It was, to say the least, a surprising request for a cabinet minister to make and in later life Gladstone included it among his 'recorded errors'. He told Peel that if the proposal was unwelcome he would be content to receive no reply. None came.[67]

Throughout the parliamentary recess Gladstone continued to agonize over the situation. He spent the summer, as usual, at his father's estate at Fasque in Kincardineshire. The relative peace afforded an opportunity for reflection on the full implications of the issue both for his own political career and for the relationship of Church and State in England. 'The purpose of Parliamentary life resolves itself with me simply and wholly into one question' he wrote to Hope on 20 August. 'Will it ever afford the means under God of rectifying the relations between the Church and the State and give me the opportunity of setting forward such a work. There must be *either* such a readjustment, or a violent crisis. The present state of discipline cannot be borne for very many years; and here lies the pinch.'[68]

In November it became clear that Peel intended to act. When the matter came before the cabinet at the end of the month, therefore, Gladstone informed his colleagues that he would be unable to take part in the proposals as a member of the government, but mystified them by hinting that he would not necessarily oppose the measure when it came before parliament. A subsequent correspondence with Peel did little to clarify matters, at least in Peel's eyes. But since Gladstone seemed determined to go there was little that he could do, much as he regretted the loss.

At the opening of the new parliamentary session on 4

---

[67] *Morley*, i. 271–2.
[68] Gladstone to Hope, 20 Aug. 1844, *Lathbury*, i. 61.

February, Gladstone delivered his resignation speech.[69] It was too involved to be effective. Designed expressly 'to remove misunderstandings and misapprehensions', it did neither. 'What a marvellous talent is this,' Cobden is said to have remarked to a friend, 'here have I been sitting listening with pleasure for an hour to his explanation, and yet I know no more why he left the government than before he began.'[70] So anxious was he to explain his position fully, to spare Peel embarrassment by stating what had *not* been the cause of his departure and to avoid committing himself either for or against the Maynooth measure, when it did come before parliament he left his audience surprised and confused.

Despite having made it clear in his speech that he was not prepared to join in any opposition to the bill led by the 'No Popery' lobby he was approached on 10 April, two days before the bill's second reading, by Rochford Clarke, the editor of the *Record*, and later by Sir Robert Inglis, to lead the opposition against it. Inglis was quite convinced that the government could be brought down on the issue and hoped that if Peel resigned Gladstone would be sent for. Gladstone listened to him amazed and when Inglis went on to remind him how mistaken they had been in 1829 in not accepting his advice to send the Duke of Cumberland to Ireland with 30 000 men, amazement turned to horror. 'As that good and very kind man spoke the words my blood ran cold,' he wrote of the incident fifty years later.[71]

Gladstone's mind was already made up. He spent the 11 April thinking through the Maynooth question 'which lies heavily on my mind though I have no doubt upon my conscience',[72] and in the evening spoke for just under one and a half hours for the measure: 'I have for myself deliberately arrived at the conviction, that the occasion demands of us all, as a matter of *social justice*, the surrender of something of our rival claims, and our extreme opinions.'[73]

Maynooth split the Tory party twelve months before its more

---

[69] *Hansard*, 3 series, xxvii, 77.
[70] *Morley*, i. 278.
[71] *Autobiographica*, 50.
[72] *Diary*, iii, 11 Apr. 1845.
[73] *Hansard*, 3 series, LXXIX. 551.

fatal rupture over the Corn Laws.[74] At the division on the bills' second reading half the Tory party voted against it and it was passed only with the help of Whigs and radicals. It clearly demonstrated the disaffection felt by many Tories for Peel's leadership. He had pressed on with an attempt to conciliate Irish opinion even though the government was not hostage to Irish votes at Westminster or constituency level. The wounds Catholic Emancipation had inflicted upon the party had not healed. Conservatism was not merely synonymous with the rational moderate philosophy embodied in Peel's Tamworth Manifesto. There remained another conservatism with a fierce and emotional message which united both the Ultras and the evangelicals within the Tory party and which could count on the enthusiastic support of many of the rank and file in the country.[75] 'No Popery' was a potent political force and Peel had erred by underestimating the strength of this ultra-Protestant opposition.

Gladstone's decision to support the bill and not to become involved in the opposition surrounding it was therefore of immense importance. It left the disaffected Tories without a leader of any calibre, unready as yet to follow Disraeli. It was, moreover, further confirmation of Gladstone's deep loyalty to Peel and meant that when the split in the party did occur the following year he met it with surprising equanimity.

But in terms of ecclesiastical politics Maynooth was also profoundly significant. It demonstrated the growing divergence between the older High-Churchmen, firm in their allegiance to the Establishment principle and to the Tory party as a definite Church party, and the younger men influenced by the new mood of the Tractarians, more committed to defending the spiritual integrity of the Church against the increasingly in- different attitude of the State, realizing that it was becoming less possible to depend on the old alliance to succour and sustain it.

---

[74] For the Maynooth question in general see E. R. Norman, 'The Maynooth Question of 1845', *Irish Historical Studies*, XV (Sept. 1967), 407–37; his *Anti-Catholicism in Victorian England* (1968), 23–51; and Machin, op. cit., 169–77.

[75] On this see the tantalizingly brief article by G. A. Cahill, 'Irish Catholicism and English Toryism', *Review of Politics*, xix (Jan. 1957), 62–76, and his 'The Protestant Association and the anti-Maynooth agitation of 1845', *Catholic Historical Review*, xliii (Oct. 1957), 273–308.

For Inglis and others like him in parliament Maynooth was Peel's final apostasy. They were totally unable to accept Peel's claim that no question of principle was involved. Outside parliament conservative High-Churchmen were similarly enraged. William Palmer, the author of the *Treatise on the Church of Christ* and editor of the newly founded *English Review*, a journal representing protestant rather than tractarian High-Churchmanship, was appalled, especially by Gladstone's seeming *volte face*. Maynooth was, he informed Gladstone, 1829 all over again. He implored him to take no further part in 'this *fatal* measure'. 'It will be the death blow of Conservatism. It is as contrary to your own principles as it is repugnant to those of the English people.'[76] 'I address you then,' he begged a month later, 'as a friend of Sir Robert Peel and as a faithful son of that Church which you have in past years strengthened and edified by your admirable writings, and which till this unhappy occasion, I looked up to you as her greatest earthly Hope.'[77]

Two articles in the June edition of his magazine castigated, with a mixture of anger and pity, Peel, Gladstone, Goulburn and the other '*ci-devant* Conservatives' who had voted with them. Gladstone's defection was 'the most severe blow of which the Church had experience'.[78] Nothing could now be hoped from a Conservative ministry. Peel had done none of the things churchmen had expected. 'Has he founded one additional see? Has he given one farthing of the public money to the cause of Church extension, at a time when no less than six millions of our people are destitute of the ministrations of the Church?' It was clear that the 'leaven of Whiggery' had pervaded the whole cabinet. From now onwards Peel's ministry could only be regarded as essentially hostile to the Church.[79]

Shrill though this was, it was the authentic voice of the old High Church tradition. Here was the bitterness and sense of betrayal of men who had hoped for so much and had been given, it seemed, nothing. But Palmer's position was no longer representative of the political thinking of all High-Churchmen. The anti-Erastianism and high ecclesiology of the Tracts had

---

[76] Palmer to Gladstone, 18 Apr. 1845, BL Add. MS 44362, f. 165.
[77] Palmer to Gladstone, 19 May 1845, BL Add. MS 44362, f. 188.
[78] *English Review*, iii (June 1845), 436.
[79] Ibid., 438.

opened up a new path and the political situation and general temper of the times was beginning to force an increasing number of High-Churchmen, not necessarily sympathetic to the Rome-ward theology of the Oxford men, to reappraise their political loyalties and to face squarely the implications for their Church of the stresses which were resulting, if they fully appreciated their cause or not, from the gradual adapting of the Establish-ment to a representative political system. Edward Churton wrote to a fellow High-Churchman, William Gresley, that Palmer's argument that Maynooth would be the ruin of the Conservative party was rather a recommendation in his eyes, 'It has long been so difficult to connect the Conservative party with any definite principles except a silly morbid dread of Puseyism, that any shock which will break them up as a party will be rather a benefit than a misfortune.' Palmer had, he continued, 'leant too much to that very weak principle of making the Church an appanage of the Conservative party. Till the Church is cured of this I see no hope for her.'[80]

Certainly within parliament Gladstone and other High Church Tories, particularly the younger generation, were having to accept a very similar position. Lord John Manners, who had always taken a rather more independent line, voted for Maynooth and used his speech to criticize the Established Church of Ireland itself.[81] Sir Walter James, later Lord Northbourne, countered Inglis' arguments.[82] Besides Glad-stone, other young men who had been influenced by Oxford High-Churchmanship who voted for Maynooth included Sidney Herbert, the Aclands, Roundell Palmer and Lord Lincoln, the son of Gladstone's patron the Duke of Newcastle who, in so doing, precipitated a breach with his father that was not healed until the latter's deathbed.[83]

To these men it was simply impossible to hold fast to the old ideas. It no longer made political sense. 'In the present state of my own mind I do not recognize the picture you draw of it,'

[80] Churton to Gresley, 22 Apr. 1845, Churton MSS, Pusey House.

[81] *Hansard*, 3 series, LXXIX, 833–40.

[82] *Hansard*, 3 series, LXXIX, 1173. See also his interesting letter to Gladstone, 28 Apr. 1845, BL Add. MS 44264, f. 7.

[83] J. Martineau, *Life of Henry Pelham, Fifth Duke of Newcastle, 1811–1864* (1908), 54. 67–70.

Gladstone wrote to William Palmer. He had, he believed, carried on the struggle to adhere even to a mutilated system, of state religion, 'to the extremest point of duty and precedence'. It was the State that had cut the ground from under its own feet. Now the object was to reach a position which promised the Church something like freedom and security from incessant agitation. In the past the Church had 'paid for property in liberty'. Now that process was being reversed and a new chapter in the relationship of Church and State had begun.[84]

What had made Gladstone despair more than anything else was the way in which the Anglican opponents of Maynooth had been prepared to accept the aid of dissenters in common cause against Rome. It was this in particular that seemed to him contrary to social justice. If the State was to follow resolutely a policy of absolute resistance to any further concessions in religious matters then it should be applied to all dissenters equally. There could be no justification for discriminating solely against Romanists and pandering to the 'No Popery' lobby. The anti-Maynooth agitation had shown him the real nature of the national religion he had sought to defend. What pained him, he told Hook, was that 'practically much of the religious life of the country is very nearly associated with the word Protestantism: and it is the form under which the public at large hold in great part their idea of State Religion'.[85] Since this was the case he felt sorrowfully convinced that although the Maynooth measure would mark a further declension in the religious character of the State, his sense of duty compelled him to join in and aid this process; only in this way could the integrity of the English Church be preserved and its Catholic truth safeguarded. On 19 June, as he tried to think through on paper the implications of the last few months, he wrote:

The State will adhere longer longer [sic] to religion in a vague than in a defined form: but I for one am not favourable to tearing up the seamless garment of the Christian Faith in order to patch the ragged cloak of the State.

Keep religion entire, and you secure at least to the individual man his refuge. Ask therefore on every occasion not what best maintains the religious repute of the State but what is least menacing to the integrity of Catholic belief and the Catholic Church.[86]

[84] Gladstone to Palmer, 16 June 1845, BL Add. MS 44362, ff. 242–3.
[85] Gladstone to Hook, 16 Apr. 1845, BL Add. MS 44213, f. 73.
[86] Add. MS 44735, f. 34; *Diary*, iii, 19 June 1845.

'Does the State any longer maintain such a religious character as can be pleased absolutely against the endowment of a religion apart from that of the nation and therefore opposed to it?' he asked himself,[87] No, he answered. The State had done acts, 'great acts, repeated acts, acts becoming more and more frequent, directly in the teeth of it' and there was not the remotest possibility that this would change in the future. The only complicating factor was that in England there was a strong popular sentiment, not against such acts universally but against them being done in favour of a particular community, namely the Roman Catholic Church. This was the dilemma. 'Can we rightly object to do these acts, and avail ourselves of the popular feeling to resist them, upon a plea which we know was contravened yesterday for others, and will be for others again be contravened tomorrow, and would not a refusal upon such grounds both be called by men and be in the sight of God a social injustice to our Roman Catholic fellow subjects?'[88]

Gladstone's own action over Maynooth had shown that for him the answer was no. The year before he had voted with a clear and safe conscience on the Unitarian issue for while its effect was, humanely speaking, to augment 'the means and provisions for the propagation of blasphemy against our Blessed Lord', social justice demanded it. This and the Maynooth measure itself proved that the State no longer had a consistent religious character and that where the principle did survive, it did so only 'in a violent sentiment against the endowment of Romanism'.[89]

I cannot reconcile it to myself to concur with that sentiment [Gladstone wrote on 1 July.] It repudiates social justice by inequality of dealing—while it also repudiates the religious character of the State by placing truth on a level with heresy and schism so it be not Roman schism. Pretending to maintain a conscience in the State and yet systematically contravening it, the one exception from that system has this most miserable effect of inseparably combining the claim to a spiritual character with the determination to contravene it.[90]

Maynooth was the fatal blow to Gladstone's early political creed. The theoretical structure he had laboured to erect in the

---

[87] 19 June 1845, BL Add. MS 44735, f. 41.
[88] Ibid.
[89] Ibid., f. 40, 1 July 1845.
[90] Ibid.

1830s had foundered on the quicksands of political reality. The full implications of the constitutional revolution of 1828–32 for the Church were now making themselves felt. He had clung to the hope that the Conservative party would arrest the steady erosion of the State's confessional basis. His hope had been in vain. To continue now to contend for consistency in the State's profession of religion was useless. It could result only in social injustice or contradiction. To look at the matter in a broader context, what Gladstone was being forced to recognize was the demise of the Confessional State and increasing political pluralism. This was what Maynooth really symbolized. The process could now no longer be halted, far less reversed.

Gladstone realized this. On Whitsunday, 11 May 1845, he wrestled with its implications in a memorandum on the place of the Church in politics.

It was the ancient policy of Christian states to place universal legislation under the control and guidance of religion and religion was understood according to the teaching of the Church. . . . Religion is no longer understood in that sense and the vague notion under which it is conceived in part has lost and in part is losing its power over the conduct of the State.[91]

Revival—and here Gladstone no doubt had in mind the Tractarians—had been commenced in individuals and even in bodies but it was obvious that such revival 'cannot arrest the sinking movement of our public law and policy until it shall have so far raised the general level of sentiment upwards as to meet that movement on its progress downwards'. The State had in a sense, therefore, obtained an emancipation from religion. The voice of the Church had become mingled in the land with many rival voices, 'and the State has no ear for selection, it can only catch their combined result. It has passed from a higher into a lower nature, because those of whom it is composed have become many folds under many shepherds instead of one fold under one shepherd.'[92]

It was this, the essential change now in progress 'from the Catholic to the infidel idea of the State' which was, he later informed Manning, 'the determining element in my estimate of this matter'.[93] For him it necessitated the most painful readjust-

[91] BL Add. MS 44735, f. 34.
[92] Ibid.
[93] Gladstone to Manning, 5 Apr. 1846, BL Add. MS 44247, f. 298.

ment, not simply because he was known as an apologist for the idea of a Confessional State but because he had accepted political life as an essentially religious vocation, his whole object in entering parliament having been to serve the Church. How this vocation could be exercised in a changed situation was now a matter of urgent concern.

But if all this was the result of a change in the nature of the State, what was it that was providing the dynamic for this change? What underlying currents were at work?

To Gladstone the answer seemed clear. 'It is not the decay of the religious life among us,' he had written to Christopher Wordsworth in March 1844, 'but it is the progress of the democratic principle, supervening upon a state of division and disorganization in respect to Church Communion, which becomes, I think, continually more formidable.'[94] Democracy, the abandonment of a paternalist view of the State and the increasing acceptance of the popular will, coupled with the obvious impossibility of the Church of England becoming, in the foreseeable future at least, a truly national Catholic Church embracing the mass of the English people, these were the two factors that had proved the undoing of his cherished ideal.

Yet his theory had always been vulnerable in just this respect and Gladstone was right, therefore, to maintain, as he always did, that in relation to Church and State he had acted consistently.[95] He had entered politics as a reaction against the anti-Christian trends he believed implicit in the Reform Act of 1832. His Toryism had been shaped by his belief in an ethical conception of the State which, contrary to the liberal view, derived its authority not from the will of those governed but ultimately from the will of God. In the *State in its relations with the Church* he had attempted to show that the State so conceived possessed, and historically had exercised, the power to distinguish between truth and error in religion and that it was its duty to fulfil this essentially paternal function by maintaining the one and, passively at least, discouraging the other. On this understanding, therefore, there could be no question of civil equality

---

[94] Gladstone to Dr Christopher Wordsworth, 15 Mar. 1844, *Lathbury*, i. 60–1.
[95] See his memo. 18 Sept. 1845, BL Add. MS 44735, f. 20, where he discusses the matter of his consistency.

for different Churches for this would render the whole idea of a 'state conscience' nugatory.

As he had put it in the sixth chapter:

While government, under whichever of its modes, is viewed in the light of a divine institution, not emanating from the mere will of the society over which it rules, there is nothing incongruous or offensive in ascribing to its rights independent of that will . . . In such a state of things, no constitutional objection can be raised, if the state shall give its preference and support to that religion which it deems best for the country.[96]

But two paragraphs later he made it plain that a different conception of the State would result in a very different attitude to a religious Establishment.

But when it is allowed that government is no more than the representative of the people, the exponent of its will, then all funds committed to the administration of the government are in fact submitted to the will of the people; and government has no duty to perform other than accurately to realise and effectuate in the legislature and in the law the different forces of opinion which act upon it from the country; it has no right to express a preference of its own for any religion as being the wisest or the best; nor to offer a religion to the man who is without one, or a better one to the man who has a worse.[97]

In other words, if the popular theory of government gained ground it would become progressively more difficult for the State to fulfil its paternal function and exercise its conscience. In such circumstances Gladstone's argument for the Establishment would lose its force, for the foundation on which it rested was ceasing to exist. But since Gladstone valued the paternal theory of the State chiefly because it provided a *raison d'être* for Establishment, its demize opened up interesting possibilities. For if the main theoretical argument for the Establishment perished with the Confessional State, so did the main obstacle to Gladstone's acceptance of the popular theory of government. This is what made Maynooth a decisive event not merely for Gladstone's ecclesiastical development in the narrow sense, but for his political development in general. The intellectual basis of his Toryism had been shattered, the way was now open for another advance.

---

[96] *The State in its relations with the Church* (1838), 79–80.
[97] Ibid., 81.

# 5

# REBUILDING THE RUINS: 1845–1859

Although the full implications of Maynooth did not become immediately apparent, the collapse of Gladstone's theory was to have far reaching consequences for his political development. It was not until 1859, when he accepted the Chancellorship of the Exchequer under Palmerston, that he finally abandoned any hope of reunion with the Tories and could be said to have become attached formally to emerging Liberalism. But this step, as `Morley perceived, was not the result of an intellectual conversion; it involved 'a party severance, but no changed principles'.[1] For the real change in principles, which had made possible such a development, had occurred fourteen years before. And it was this change, precipitated by Maynooth, that makes comprehensible, not only the remoulding of Gladstone's career after 1845, but also that fact which Morley found so utterly extraordinary, that 'with a steadfast tread he marched along the High Anglican road to the summits of that liberalism which it was the original object of the new Anglicans to resist and overthrow'.[2]

But this lay in the future. The initial problem in the aftermath of his resignation in January 1845 was a personal one: could he remain in politics and if so, what was the role of a committed churchman in the changing political circumstances of the 1840s? For one who, in adopting a political career, had pledged himself unreservedly to the service of the Church, 'the pole star of my existence', as he had once told James Hope,[3] this was no light matter. Was he in future to support only a policy which maintained the exclusive rights of the Church, or was he to concur or acquiesce in a policy which was 'the best that the condition of the country is capable of bearing in operation?'[4]

---

[1] *Morley*, i. 631; see also *Diary*, v, xxvii.
[2] *Morley*, i. 153.
[3] Gladstone to Hope, 11 Jan. 1839, BL Add. MS 44214, f. 61.
[4] 11 May 1845, BL Add. MS 44735, f. 35.

Gladstone's first reaction was to contemplate retiring from parliament altogether. 'When the time is come for simply bearing witness, that is the witness to be borne', he wrote in May 1845. There was little point, he felt, in remaining in the legislature merely to protest. Continuous and reiterated protest, habitually disregarded, became all too easily like 'the voice of a parrot saying "No, no, no" and not aware nor much caring, whether it be so much as heard'. To preach the absolute demands of Catholic truth to a parliament acting for a nation of all religious colours was like 'resorting to a gambling house to preach against gaming.'[5]

When politics was divorced from religion, and religion from the Church, it was difficult to see political life as an eligible career. He could find, perhaps, 'a secondary satisfaction in the desire to be just, according to the depressed and lowered laws under which the State has now to learn to live, to be just and to be kind, according to the measure of human equity'. But what real spiritual satisfaction could be gained from that? 'Why should we,' he asked himself, 'whose heritage is immortal so bow our necks to a yoke which is not the yoke of the Redeemer, when His unrestricted service is yet open to us elsewhere, when we have the means of the specific devotion of ourselves and our substance to His work and of adapting the whole of our life and agency to His direct unmutilated injunctions?'[6]

This was the predicament. As early as 1842, as his remarks to Manners showed, Gladstone had begun to sense that the State was becoming less capable of fulfilling a specifically religious function. During the factory debates, looking to the floor of the House below, he had told a startled T. D. Acland, 'It is becoming a very serious question whether there is anything left worth contending for here.'[7]

But it was Newman to whom he had unburdened himself when it became clear that the Maynooth issue raised this question in its acutest form. On 3 September 1844, after a long summer brooding at Fasque, he had felt moved to complete a letter to Newman which he had begun nearly seven months

[5] Ibid.
[6] Ibid.
[7] 14 May 1844, A. H. D. Acland, op. cit., 98.

before on 11 February, the day he had read Peel's circular raising the Maynooth issue.

Like his letter to Newman at the end of 1843, this was prompted by a passage in one of Newman's sermons, this time one entitled 'The Church and the World'. In it Newman, alluding (it seemed to Gladstone) to the world of politics, had declared that men were now 'afraid to kindle their fire from the altar of God: they are afraid to acknowledge her through whom only they gain light and strength and salvation, the Mother of Saints'. For Gladstone this was the nub of the matter. How were 'those whose destiny is cast in public life' to kindle their fire at God's altar and do service to His Church? How were they 'to regulate that large portion of their agency in which they are partly (though from year to year in lessening degrees) the directors of a civilised power, made up of almost innumerable and thoroughly heterogeneous wills?'[8]

Clearly the State collectively could no longer perform such a task. While there was no strong voice within parliament clamouring for the separation of Church and State, Maynooth and all that led up to it had been demonstrable proof of the State's moral incapacity to discharge its full obligations to the Church. Division among the various churches within the country rendered the body politic 'radically discordant with itself' in regard to Divine revelation. 'At the same time the authority of revealed religion as a name, to which each class attaches its own meaning, is acknowledged: so that we can neither agree on it, nor agree in renouncing it, we can neither act with it, nor without it.' Likewise the growing strength of democracy demanded that 'the will of the individual subject shall take effect in the acts of the nation'. It was, Gladstone believed, 'quite visionary' to expect any reversal of these trends in the future.[9]

But if the State collectively could no longer perform this task, was it not still incumbent upon the individual politician to do

---

[8] 3 Sept. 1844, Gladstone to Newman, Oratory MSS. The sermon can be found in *Sermons bearing on subjects of the day* (1843), 95–111. It was written in January 1837. As Newman explained to Gladstone: '. . . it was written above eight years ago, when there was far less of open Christian profession to be found in the prominent members or sections of the great Conservative party than exists now'. Newman to Gladstone, 14 Sept. 1844, BL Add. MS 44361, ff. 229–30.

[9] Ibid.

so? On this matter Gladstone could not see his way forward. Should the individual politician attempt to remain unsullied, to refrain from every political act that disowned Catholic truth or compromised the position of the Church whenever it was within his power to do so? Such a course would undoubtedly mean leaving political life, but in his present state this seemed to Gladstone quite as defensible as the alternative, to remain in politics simply in the hope that in God's appointed time national religion would somehow be re-established. For he had always believed, and to Newman he reiterated it, that the restoration of the religion of the State could take place only by the reconversion of individuals by the Church. It must come 'to States through the individuals that compose them, and not to the individuals through States'. It was no more possible 'to reestablish national religion by enacting it, than to change the wind by forcing round the weather cock'.[10]

Yet unsure though Gladstone was of the right course of action, the feeling that he should forsake political life altogether was only a temporary one. In April 1845 soon after the publication of his Maynooth speech he wrote in another letter to Newman that for specific reasons, 'not with an entire conviction, perhaps, but as the better of two alternatives', he had decided not to abjure the work of government.[11] In fact, he had resolved upon a course which to his mind offered the only alternative to that of retirement.

The State had lost its conscience. But in many ways it still continued to act as if it had one. 'The Christian figure of our institutions still remains, though marred by the most incongruous associations.'[12] Because of this there still remained actual relations of the State to religion, relations that offered opportunities for good 'however they may be surrounded with violent moral contradictions'. Therefore, Gladstone wrote, this would be his course of action: 'It is, in all those cases where the State acts *as if* it had a conscience, to maintain that standard as nearly as we can: and in other cases to take social justice according to the lower, but now prevalent, idea for a guide.'[13]

[10] Ibid.
[11] Gladstone to Newman, 19 Apr. 1845, *Lathbury*, i. 73–4.
[12] Ibid., 72.
[13] Ibid.

If it was no longer possible for public policy and law to be moulded according to the Christian model Gladstone regarded as normative, what did he see himself doing in the future? Was he in parliament simply to retard the growing trend of 'indifferentism' in the State's attitude to religion? What were these 'specific reasons' he had hinted at which made remaining a politician the better of the alternatives before him?

Up to a point Gladstone definitely intended to use his position simply to delay this trend. He had never believed that his theoretical conception was wrong. In an ideal State where all the citizens were united with the Church it would be both logical and workable. There was certainly nothing intrinsically good about the movement that undermined it. He viewed its results 'with great alarm'.[14]

But though he had found himself the last man in the ship,[15] he had no right to board the enemy vessel. Or, as he put it later in his *Chapter of Autobiography*, 'It is one thing to lift the anchor; it is another to spread the sails'.[16] His memorandum of 11 May made this clear. If members of parliament, bound by its varied composition to an uncatholic policy, were like gamblers in the gambling house, they were also still found to discharge certain functions for the Church, and could therefore be 'moved and exhorted *quoad* those particular functions, to discharge them aright'. Not all protest need be like that of the parrot: 'protest wisely employed has a power of checking that against which it is directed.'[17]

Yet some compromise would be necessary. No man's protest could or ought to be heeded, Gladstone asserted, if that man simply set his face resolutely against the 'first conditions of the existence and action of the assembly in which he sits'. There must therefore be much acquiescence in order even to make such protest heard. 'It must be seen that such protest and the maker of it has an equitable regard to the actual circumstances and what is practical under them.'

But how was the politician to determine when to resist or how

[14] Ibid.
[15] Ibid. This letter to Newman appears to be the occasion of the origin of this metaphor used later in *A Chapter of Autobiography*.
[16] *Gleanings*, vii. 121.
[17] BL Add. MS 44735, ff. 34-39.

far to concur in uncatholic policies? It was, Gladstone decided, 'a question of degree and of particulars'. But there were certainly two limitations to be placed on the latter alternative. Concurrence with an uncatholic policy could only be allowable 'for the sake of good not otherwise to be attained, and either absolutely or relatively, greater than the mischief'. Secondly, it was not to entail deceit: 'we shall not assent under false colours'.

There was also one other general consideration. 'As Parliament is to the people so are the administration to the Parliament.' The duty of simple representatives was, Gladstone believed, materially different from the duty of men holding governmental office. MPs as a class exhibited the social forces of the country, those who sought to govern were to combine and harmonize those forces. Therefore governors must in their own political language and conduct 'offer to view less of the sharp and violent contrasts, than the forces themselves'. Their office 'partakes fundamentally of the character of mediation'. And, 'a mediator cannot discharge his duty if he be so identified with one party as wholly to exclude sympathy with the other'.

This course of action was worked out with Gladstonian thoroughness. But it was simply a question of tactics, not the whole matter. The 'specific reasons' for his remaining in parliament, to which he had alluded, were not just to retard a process he had already accepted as inexorable; that was merely a negative reason. There was a more positive one: to defend the Church. But not as before; for no longer could the Church hope by parliamentary means to regain its rightful place. No: the task was now to extricate the Church from the more constricting trammels of its attachment to the State in order that it might proclaim more effectively the Catholic truth to which it witnessed.

Gladstone was to stay in parliament 'because the Church fettered this way and that, has not so much left of her original freedom as is necessary for the vigorous and effective prosecution of her work'. When the laws had been so adjusted to place the Church in that condition, then and only then would political life cease to be an obligation to him. But such a conclusion prompted its own set of questions for the future:

And will they ever be so adjusted? Are there now living the men whom God has appointed as His instruments for that work? Will the Church be disorganised by the throes of crude and untrained power within her before the time comes? Or will she take what the State can reasonably give? Or will the State, tyrannical through fear, give what she may reasonably ask? Or will the persons who hope to perform this service for the Church, ever reach the opportunity and power of doing it? Can any man have the confidence of both and unless with the confidence of both can any such operation be effected?

After Maynooth, therefore, Gladstone was without the single, all-embracing ideal that had provided the motive force for his early politics. Never again did he formulate a theory of Church–State relations. From 1845 onwards his approach was characterized by a distinction between, as he put it twenty years later in his letter to John Hannah, 'the abstract and the practical views of the subject'.[18] Although the ideal remained that put forward in his book, it was now clearly impractical given the conditions of the age. England, indeed Europe itself, was in a period of transition from the Confessional to the secular State and the difficulties this raised made it no longer possible to formulate a precise policy on matters relating to Church and State. There were, Gladstone told his father in 1847, many difficulties in the way: 'I have not made up my mind whether they can be got over, nor shall I until the question comes before me in a practical shape.'[19]

In other words, his strategy in future would be to reserve judgement on all such issues and not to commit himself to a particular course of action until circumstances demanded it. Each issue would then be evaluated in both political and religious terms; the political criterion being not mere expediency but social justice, now conceived of as a positive political principle; the religious criterion being not as before, the maintenance of a Christian profession by the State which, in any case, was not seriously compromised, but more importantly, whether or not specific action would assist the Church to gain the freedom from the State that Gladstone believed would become increasingly necessary if it was to fulfil its religious mission.

This approach, 'a sort of general rule, though planted, I grant, upon ground infirm enough', as he told Newman,[20] was

[18] Gladstone to J. Hannah, 8 June 1865, quoted in *Gleanings*, vii. 131. See also *Lathbury*, ii. 7.

[19] W. E. Gladstone to J. Gladstone, 10 July 1847, Hawn. P.

[20] Gladstone to Newman, 19 Apr. 1845, *Lathbury*, i. 73.

essentially that which he had already adopted over the Dissenters' Chapels Bill and Maynooth. Now it was to become the justification for his remaining in political life. Consequently after the crisis of December 1845, when Peel resumed office with the understanding that a further major reconstruction in tariff policy would be carried through, Gladstone accepted the post of Colonial Secretary. But although sufficiently clear in his own mind what his future course of action in regard to ecclesiastical matters would be, and convinced that this both fulfilled his original vocation of serving the Church and was in accord with the Church's best interests, his behaviour was by no means as clear to many of his co-religionists who had looked to him to defend the Church in parliament and for whom his recent action had seemed the most terrible betrayal. For those like Inglis in parliament and Palmer outside it, Gladstone's course of action seemed incomprehensible, disloyal, even blatantly opportunist.

That he ran the risk of such accusations, even the charge of Popish sympathies,[21] Gladstone was well aware. 'I have a growing belief that I shall never be enabled to do much good for the Church in Parliament (if at all), except after having seemed first a traitor to it and been reviled as such', he had written to his wife in October.[22] Although convinced that the Church could no longer cling to its civil privileges and that instead it should use them to purchase its emancipation from the State, 'to give gold for freedom',[23] he realized that there were many who did not see the situation in this way. There were 'so many who will not allow the gold to be touched even though they value freedom and so many more who have the Church to keep all the gold that it may be the price and the pledge of her slavery'.[24] To be scorned by those who had once been his allies was a price he was prepared to pay. The prospects were gloomy and precarious, he wrote to James Hope the day he accepted office, 'but my conviction of duty is clear—I have sought for the best

---

[21] For this see his letter to Lord Lincoln, 28 Mar. 1846, 'there will not be wanting those who will ascribe it [his change of opinion on Maynooth] to a predeliction on my part for the Romish religion'. Lincoln MSS. See also letter to Manning, 5 Apr. 1846, BL Add. MS 44247, f. 299.

[22] Gladstone to his wife, 12 Oct. 1845, *Lathbury*, ii. 266.

[23] Ibid.

[24] Ibid.

alternative, honestly, so far as that term is applicable to any of the operations of my mind. I am sure you will pray for me'.[25]

However, Gladstone's action brought more than misunderstanding from former admirers; it cost him his seat at Newark. The Duke of Newcastle, already appalled by Gladstone's support of the Maynooth grant, could not forgive a man prepared to betray the landed interest. Gladstone therefore decided not to stand for re-election in defiance of the Duke's wishes and for the next eighteen months was without a parliamentary seat.

Worse was to come. On 25 June 1846 the third reading of the Corn Law Repeal Bill was carried without a division and that evening the protectionists took their revenge by joining with the Whigs, Radicals and Irish, to bring down the government over the Irish Coercion Bill. Peel resigned immediately. Within six months of rejoining the cabinet, therefore, Gladstone was not merely without a seat, he was without a party as well.

The disintegration of the Tory party dismayed Gladstone. It left him in a difficult and uncertain position, politically footloose for the next six years and without a definite party affiliation for the next thirteen. But having already made the necessary intellectual adjustments and having mentally denied his party its specifically religious role, the event was, perhaps, less traumatic for him than it might have been. Nonetheless, from a religious point of view it put in power the Whigs under Lord John Russell who could hardly be expected to pursue an ecclesiastical policy favourable to High-Churchmen and left as the alternative the Protectionists under Derby who, besides his stand on tariffs, was in church matters an Erastian incapable of understanding the desire of an increasing number of churchmen for greater ecclesiastical autonomy.

Gladstone's election in August 1847 as burgess for Oxford University, though in many respects an act of good fortune and one much prized by him, also tended to complicate his political and ecclesiastical development.[26] As he told his friend, Robert Phillimore, the members for the Universities 'are in an imperfect

---

[25] Gladstone to Hope, 22 Dec. 1845, Hope-Scott MS, 3642, f. 90.
[26] G. W. E. Russell, *William Ewart Gladstone* (1906), 83. For Gladstone's election to Oxford and his representation of it see J. B. Conacher, 'Mr. Gladstone seeks a seat', *Canadian Historical Association Report* (1962), 55–67.

sense, but still a true one, representatives of the Church in the House of Commons'.[27] And though this undoubtedly enabled him in a difficult period to have a surer political identity and to feel he was in a special way occupying a position of service to the Church, the opposition to his election and his continued stormy relationship with many of his constituents made him profoundly aware that his own desire to work towards a new relationship between Church and State was not shared by all of his fellow Churchmen.

Feared by Low Churchmen as a Tractarian fellow traveller who would use his position only to further the cause of a particular party in the Church, and regarded by Conservative High-Churchmen as unsound in his allegiance to the old principles of the Constitution, the contest at Oxford was bitter. Nor did the controversy or bitterness abate. Despite the tradition that a sitting candidate was not opposed Gladstone faced a contest in Oxford at each subsequent general election, motivated primarily by High Church opposition to his growing commitment to civil and religious liberty, until he was finally defeated in the election of 1865.

*vid. P. 148*

No sooner had he returned to the Commons in December 1847 than the first important test for his new approach to the problems of Church and State presented itself. Faced with the election of Baron de Rothschild as MP for the City of London, Lord John Russell introduced a bill to remove the sole remaining disability against the Jews, their right to take a different oath and thereby sit in parliament. In 1841 Gladstone had spoken against a bill to allow Jews to hold office in municipal corporations, arguing that no broad or clear line could be drawn between their eligibility for that and their eligibility for parliament. When this right was actually granted by Peel's government in 1845 he had taken no part in the proceedings. Now, six years later, Gladstone was convinced that relief must be given. The Church would gain nothing by an obstructive policy. If it was to gain liberty for itself it should not resist the claims of other religious groups, even non-Christians, for liberty. To attempt now sternly to adhere to an exclusive policy would be, he told the Revd J. W. Warter, 'utterly fatal to

---

[27] Gladstone to Phillimore, 24 June 1847, *Lathbury*, ii. 12.

any further beneficial use of the principles of connection between the Church and the State'.[28] And to Phillimore he mapped out what seemed to him the best course of action in the present circumstances. While an attempt should be made to sustain the Church in a national position, it would be sensible to surrender those of its privileges which were 'more obnoxious than really valuable' and in future not to presume too much 'to give directions to the State as to its policy with respect to other religious bodies'.[29]

This was the attitude he now adopted towards the Jews. On 16 December he spoke for just under an hour in support of Russell's motion, despite the opposition of his fellow Oxford MP, Sir Robert Inglis, and a petition against the measure from his own constituents.[30] Unlike his Maynooth speech his argument on this occasion mystified no one.[31] He accepted all Russell's positive arguments in favour of admission and then analysed Shaftesbury's arguments against on the grounds of religious principle, pointing out that the principle for which Shaftesbury was contending had already been forced to give way in the face of 'perpetual conflict and constant change, of progressive movement, all in one and the same direction'.[32] A Church Parliament had given way to a Protestant Parliament, now a final effort was being made to maintain a Christian Parliament. And it would be, he told his opponents, as futile as before. They would be defeated, not unawares nor by accident, but 'owing to profound and powerful and uniform tendencies, associated with the movement of the human mind—with the general course of events, perhaps I ought to say with providential government of the world'.[33]

Since Unitarians had already been admitted to parliament civil justice required the admission of the Jews. This made it,

[28] Gladstone to Revd. J. W. Warter, 21 July 1847, *Lathbury*, ii. 16.

[29] Gladstone to Phillimore, 24 June 1847, *Lathbury*, ii. 13.

[30] He had already, on 8 December, spoke and voted on the Roman Catholic Relief Bill, *Hansard*, 3 series, xcv. 840. 852. This measure, among other things legalized RC religious orders. It was opposed by Protestant High-Churchmen and others.

[31] Thomas Acland warned him not to be recondite, 'in short, *to be as little as possible like Maurice, and more like the Duke of Wellington*'. *Morley*, i. 376.

[32] W. E. Gladstone, *Substance of a speech on the motion of Lord John Russell for a committee of the whole house, with a view to the removal of the remaining Jewish disabilities; delivered December 16, 1847* (1848), 27.

[33] Ibid.

therefore, no matter of mere expediency. It had now become 'in the highest sense' a question of principle.[34] Far from involving disparagement to the religion they professed, or lowering Christianity in the public estimation as some feared, the measure before them was, in fact, an invitation to perform an act of civil and social justice and as such 'one worthy of a Christian legislature to enact, for Christianity recognises no higher, no more comprehensive obligation'.[35]

His stand on Jewish disabilities upset his father and aroused the opposition not only of Constitutionalist 'die-hards' like Charles Wordsworth, Palmer and Archdeacon Denison, but also of moderate High-Churchmen like Samuel Wilberforce and Sir John Taylor Coleridge. To Gladstone's sadness it even lost him the support of Pusey.[36] When he published the speech, therefore, he added a lengthy preface in order both to explain more fully the grounds for his action and to defend himself against charges of inconsistency.

The preface was his first public statement on a matter touching the relations of Church and State since the Maynooth crisis. It was designed primarily to rebut the religious objections to the admission of Jews to parliament. He had made it clear in his speech and he repeated it here, that on purely civil grounds he now regarded the Jewish claim to be a strong one.[37] The religious issues were, however, more complex.

He attempted to counter the religious objections by arguing that the course of action proposed, in no substantive way altered the Christian nature of the legislature. Parliament, he believed, could be described as Christian in several senses; either because all its members professed a specific body of doctrine, or because they accepted the broad designation 'Christian'; or because the

[34] Ibid., 33.

[35] Ibid., 47.

[36] For his father's views see J. Gladstone to W. E. Gladstone, 25 Dec. 1847, Hawn. P. For Charles Wordsworth see Wordsworth to Hope, 1847, *Lathbury*, ii. 373–6. For S. Wilberforce see BL Add. MS 44343, f. 108, 30 Nov. 1847 and Gladstone's reply, 1 Dec. 1847, Wilberforce MSS Bodleian. For Coleridge see BL Add. MS 44138, f. 348, 5 Jan. 1848. For Pusey see the very interesting letter of Gladstone to Pusey, 14 Dec. 1847, where Gladstone talks of preparing to surrender 'the shadow and symbol of a venerable reality', Pusey MSS, Pusey House.

[37] *Preface*, 4–6, especially 5 where he declares that 'the application of the immutable principles of justice to the shifting relations of society must be determined by successive generations for themselves, according to their several diversities'.

vast majority of them were Christians representing Christians in
their constituencies. Parliament had once been Christian in the
first of these senses, it was now Christian in the second, and if
Jews were allowed to enter it would be Christian in the third.
The interval between the first and second of these three states of
what he called 'national or rather legislative Christianity'
seemed to him a wide one, the interval between the second and
third narrow. Therefore the change they were now called upon
to make was in essence a small one, though it seemed great
'because it parts with a symbol, a figure, and an echo of what is
great'.[38]

This symbol, the proposition that all members of a legislature
should be united in the profession of the Christian faith was,
Gladstone contended, undoubtedly a great principle. But he
concluded solemnly:

the proposition that, after they had ceased to hold, or to profess to hold, in
common the distinctive articles of the Christian creed, they should still plead
their uniformity of name in bar and of the civil rights of others, enunciates no
principle that has, so far as I am aware, any adequate ground in history, or in
philosophy or in religion, or in practical utility.

The Christianity of the legislature was not valueless or unreal.
Although incomplete it deserved to 'be held most precious by
every considerate as well as every pious mind'. But it was not the
religion of the Church. As the parliamentary profession of
Christianity had been broadened to include dissenters and even
Unitarians, it was clear that a definite and distinctive creed
uniting members of parliament no longer existed.

It followed, therefore, that since the Christianity of the
legislature now depended mainly on the personal beliefs of the
individual members composing it, the admission of a small
number of Jews would make very little difference. Arguments
from the religious character of the State had lost their force: 'We
have no longer such a theory; and he who plainly announces
this, does not alter facts, but merely discloses them.' He was even
prepared to admit that his own arguments expressed in his book
nine years before had 'unconsciously strained the facts of the
case'.

But to air these considerations, although necessary, was only

---

[38] Ibid., 8; subsequent quotations are from this speech.

part of Gladstone's purpose. The battle for the religious character of the State, at least as regards the exclusive claims of the Church of England, had been fought and lost. What was now more imperative was to awaken his fellow churchmen to the implications of this for the Church's own spiritual integrity.

For to debar the Jew from parliamentary office simply because he could not be called a Christian according to the parliamentary definition was to invest 'legislative Christianity' with an importance which had weighty and alarming consequences. It carried with it the implication that there was a religious unity between the various Christian bodies represented in the legislature which was more important in the civil sense than the laws and tenets which distinguished them. It further implied that this parliamentary definition of a Christian provided a sufficient guarantee of fitness to legislate in matters relating to the distinctive doctrine and discipline of the Established Church.

The elevation of this generalized 'constitutional Christianity' would pose a threat to the faith of the Church itself. Gladstone saw it: 'resolving into more vague and indeterminate forms the well-defined intelligible Christianity of the Church of England, which it is so deeply important, both for the religious and the general interests of the country, to uphold'. Churchmen had not fully appreciated that, as a public institution claiming to be the exclusive handmaid of the State for religious purposes, the Church had been so weakened by political changes and disharmony within that it had surrendered its ancient prerogative of being the sole recipient of the State's bounty while remaining the sole subject of the State's control.

This was the heart of the matter. The principle of endowing different religious bodies which was now becoming the accepted policy of the State made it unjust 'to plead religious opinion in bar of civil privilege'. To continue to do so in the cause of an increasingly diluted Christianity, 'this colourless abstraction', would have the most disastrous consequences for the integrity of that very Church which they were seeking by this means to defend.

Gladstone's defence of his action on Jewish disabilities, therefore, showed not merely that he had become more politically pragmatic and that he had emancipated himself from

the bondage of theory. It showed that he had pondered deeply
what had happened in recent years and was agonizingly aware
of the implications it had for the Church, implications that
many of his fellow churchmen had only dimly perceived, if they
had perceived them at all. And it is this, perhaps, that helps
explain his subsequent political behaviour and the course his
political development was to take. For if, after Maynooth,
Gladstone saw himself in politics both to retard the seculariz-
ation of the State and to work for the emancipation of the
Church from State control, why did he seemingly abandon the
struggle for the former with such apparent haste?

Perhaps this is too stark a description of what happened. But it
is not inaccurate. Only on three occasions in the ten years after
1847 did Gladstone adopt a policy of active resistance to
measures that would as he saw it, widen the gulf between
Church and State further; resistance that showed him at odds
with 'the political temper of the age',[39] to which, in many
respects, he was willing to accommodate himself. In 1849 he
opposed the Deceased Wife's Sister Bill;[40] in 1850 he opposed the
setting up of a Royal Commission to inquire into the affairs of
Oxford University and continued to oppose the abolition of
religious tests; in 1857 he led the opposition in the Commons to
the Divorce bill.[41]

Even here his opposition was not simply motivated by a desire
to shore up the religious character of the State. The Deceased
Wife's Sister Bill and divorce both had, he believed, far-reaching
moral and social consequences independent of the ecclesiastical
issues involved, and he was also opposed to the Divorce bill
because it infringed the liberty of the Church by obliging
incumbents to allow their churches to be used for the remarriage
of divorced persons. His opposition to the Royal Commission is
also explicable given that it was opposed by the bulk of his
constituents, and his opposition to the abolition of religious tests

---

[39] Ibid., 22.

[40] *Hansard*, 3 series, cvl. 616–32, 20 June 1869. Twenty years later he argued for it on
the grounds that it was in the interests of the greatest liberty.

[41] For Gladstone's attitude to the Divorce bill see *Morley*, i. 567–73. In his article in the
*Quarterly* he prophesied a division between Church and State on the marriage question,
and argued that the Church must maintain its rigorist position in spite of the liberalism
of the State. See *Quarterly Review*, clx (July 1857), 283.

is understandable given his belief that the colleges were Church foundations and that religious diversity in a teaching institution might produce confusion or mischief.

It remains true to say, therefore, that despite his profoundly conservative temperament and his intense commitment to the exclusive support of the Church by the State, Disraeli's 'last paladin of principle'[42] embraced with a passion that dismayed so many churchmen, the principle of religious liberty that was totally opposed to all that he had previously stood for.

Was it simply intellectual conviction that drove him forward? Undoubtedly intellectual conviction was important. Gladstone was not a man to argue for a principle without having wrestled with it or considered its ramifications. He believed in religious liberty because he regarded it as a matter of social justice and his commitment to social justice as an end in politics was no affectation. As a school boy he had argued for Catholic emancipation on just this ground,[43] and the necessity of justice in political dealing had been firmly implanted in him through his reading of Aristotle. But his commitment to religious liberty was the other side of his desire for greater autonomy for the Church. By this he did not necessarily mean disestablishment. 'I still think, as firmly as ever, that the connection between Church and State is worth maintaining, and that it both can and should be maintained,' he had written to Phillimore in February 1847. But he was anxious that an end be put to the 'hampering and obtruding the fair demands of the Church upon the State for her own more essential purposes' which he had 'too plainly seen' with his own eyes.[44] What was required was, as he had put it in the preface to his speech on the Jew bill:

the informal but sincere and steady adoption by politicians, whatever be their party, of a rule, or a habit as it may be called, of regarding the general sense and voice of the Church as entitled to great weight, both in respect to laws affecting her internal concerns and to ecclesiastical appointments.[45]

Since the State had made itself, so to speak, external to the Church it was time that the church should also be viewed as, to a

---

[42] Said in the course of his speech on the Maynooth grant (which he opposed), *Hansard*, 3 series, LXXIX, 558.
[43] For this see his letter to W. W. Farr, 22 Nov. 1826, *Autobiographica*, 185.
[44] Gladstone to Phillimore, 15 Feb. 1847, *Lathbury*, ii. 7.
[45] *Preface*, 19.

degree, external to the State. Preferment should be emancipated from 'servitude to political party' and the Church allowed its 'living organs' in order that it might become a faithful exponent of its own system and laws instead of 'echoing back the voice of any section, religious or political, or the notion of the day.[46]

This was the autonomy he believed was necessary. And there were two interrelated reasons why by the late 1840s the need for this autonomy had become imperative for him: the continued strength of Erastianism and the unsettling effect this was having on certain members of the Church, not least his closest friends.

By the late 1840s it had become evident both that the 'good sense and moderation', the 'resolution to resist all temptation to tamper and experimentalize upon our religious system' and 'the honest regard to the laws and formularies of the Church' which he had requested at the time of the Jew Bill[47] had not occurred and that this was one of the prime factors in weakening the faith of some in the *via media*. In the speech itself he had drawn attention to a petition forwarded to him by Archdeacon Robert Wilberforce asking that if the bill was passed and Parliament ceased to be a Christian legislature, the Church should be granted the right to elect its own bishops. He warned that this was symptomatic of a growing desire among the clergy and the more committed laity of the Church for what could be termed 'organic change in the connection between the Church and the State'. Unless there was an increased degree of caution and consideration in the State's dealing with the Church he foresaw the most serious consequences.[48]

He was well aware that the faith of Hope and Manning in the Church of England was no longer as firm as it was. Both men saw the contradictions of Anglicanism as intricately related to its position as an Established Church. 'On the Jewish question my bigotry makes me Liberal,' James Hope had written to Gladstone. 'To symbolize the Christianity of the House of Commons

---

[46] Ibid.

[47] Ibid., 19.

[48] *Speech*, 43. See letter to R. Wilberforce. Charles Wordsworth and Pusey 'are still hugging the phantom—the process is really nothing less wonderful—of political No Popery and declaring that the sensible, the practical course for those who would serve the Church is to adhere to the whole process of twenty years ago, adding to it of course much that it had not but letting slip no jot of what it had'. R. Wilberforce MSS, 10 Aug. 1847.

in its present form is to substitute a new Church and Creed for
the old Catholic one, and as this is a delusion I would do nothing
to countenance it.'[49] Manning went further. From Rome, six
months later, he wrote to Gladstone that the Church had been
deceived into trusting the State too long and thereby seculariz-
ing itself. He was coming to feel more and more that 'Protestantism is heretical and Nationalism is Judaic.'[50]

Instead of handling the Church delicately the State seemed,
to those finely attuned, to be pursuing an even more aggressively
Erastian and latitudinarian policy. Gladstone had been shocked
by the parliamentary opposition to the establishment of a
bishopric at Manchester and the view of bishops as merely State
functionaries put forward by Sir James Graham.[51] All of Lord
John Russell's appointments to bishoprics over the next few
years were either evangelicals or broad-churchmen. Sumner
went to Canterbury, but most notorious was the appointment of
Dr Hampden to Hereford towards the end of 1847. 'If this is the
way in which our bishops are to be chosen the sooner we cut the
cord the better,' Robert Wilberforce wrote to his brother
Samuel.[52] Gladstone himself wrote to the Bishop of London that
he could not in conscience rest contented with such a state of
things and declared himself ready, if he could rely on episcopal
support, to endeavour to secure some sort of legal check on the
Prime Minister's right to appoint bishops.[53]

Then came the Gorham Judgement in 1850. This 'stupen-
dous issue'[54] was one that went, he told his wife 'to the very root
of all teaching and all life in the Church of England'.[55] It was not
simply that it raised the theological question of what doctrine of
baptism was permissible within the Church; more important it
was an extreme example of Erastian intrusion by a lay body into
the Church's spiritual affairs. It was this that ultimately drove

[49] Hope to Gladstone, 9 Oct. 1847, BL Add. MS 44214, ff. 322–3.
[50] Manning to Gladstone, 3 Apr. 1848, Chapeau, op. cit.
[51] See Lathbury, i. 75–9.
[52] 31 Dec. 1847, R. Wilberforce to S. Wilberforce, Wilberforce MSS, Bodleian
Library, D.11, f. 107, quoted in G. I. T. Machin, 'Lord John Russell and the Prelude to
the Ecclesiastical Titles Bill', 1846–51, Journal of Ecclesiastical History, xxv (1974), 279.
[53] Gladstone to the Bishop of London (Blomfield), 31 Jan. 1848, Lathbury, i. 80–1.
[54] Gladstone to Manning, 30 Dec. 1849, Lathbury, i. 96. For the details see Chadwick,
op. cit., 250–71 and Chapter 7 below.
[55] Gladstone to Catherine Gladstone, 25 Feb. 1850, Hawn. P.

the wavering Hope and Manning to Rome. Gladstone himself was profoundly shaken; once more his political vocation was in jeopardy. He wrote to Manning in April 1850:

I have two characters to fulfil—that of a lay member of the Church, and that of a member of a sort of wreck of a political party. I must not break my understood compact with the last, and forswear my profession, unless and until the necessity has arisen. That necessity will plainly have arisen for me when it shall have become evident that justice cannot—i.e., will not—be done by the State to the Church. But it might arise as truly, though less plainly; for I am not to *assume* that, if there be a hope of justice from the State, my continuance in political life is necessarily right in order to do what I can towards improving that prospect. The one thing I hope you understand clearly is that the political life is simply a means to an end, and is to be considered in no other light whatever, and that the abandonment of it may be the best mode of using it.[56]

This naked Erastianism was, Gladstone believed, the fruit of anti-papal feeling that had gained renewed vigour in the wake of Newman's apostasy. 'O Newman! without thee we never should have had a Gorham case showing its face among us,' he wrote to Phillimore. 'But such is the antipapal feeling of the country that, if a man would vent enough of that, he might well nigh preach the Koran.'[57]

Nothing had disturbed Gladstone more at the time of Maynooth than the spectacle of Tory churchmen joining forces with dissenters to beat the 'No Popery' drum. The deep-rooted militant Protestantism of the English people was something that repelled him, despite his own passionate antipathy to Rome. What appalled him more was the fact that Conservative High-Churchmen with their fierce nationalism could also be found on the vanguard of this movement. Though in some respects closer theologically to this churchmanship than to that of more advanced Tractarianism, Gladstone had come to view its political and social dimension with increasing distaste. It was but a contemporary manifestation of that decadent 'High and Dry' churchmanship that had done so much damage to English religion. He had, he had told his father at the time of the Oxford election, many sympathies with Low Churchmen while desiring 'a more firm, a more comprehensive, and vigorous and elevated system than theirs'. But there was one kind of religion with which he had no sympathy whatever:

    [56] Gladstone to Manning, 29 Apr. 1850, *Lathbury*, i. 101.
    [57] Gladstone to Phillimore, 3 Dec. 1849, *Lathbury*, i. 95.

the Protestantism which grew into fashion during the last century and has not yet quite grown out of it [that] lowered and almost paganised doctrine, loosened and destroyed discipline, and much defaced, in contempt of law, the decent and beautiful order of the Church, [that] drove millions into dissent, suffered millions more to grow up in virtual heathenism, and made the Church of England . . . instead of being the glory, in many respects the shame of Christendom. [It was this] false and hollow system of religion, hating all who have disturbed its leaden slumbers, which now unites itself with an honest and vehement fanaticism to raise a cry of No Popery and under that denounces the genuine spirit of the Church of England.[58]

No sooner had the reverberations of the Gorham Judgement begun to subside than the country witnessed perhaps the nineteenth century's most celebrated manifestation of this hysterical anti-Catholicism: the popular response to the 'Papal Aggression' of 1850.[59]

Gladstone left England for Naples shortly after the Papal Brief restoring the new Catholic hierarchy was issued. He was therefore out of the country when Wiseman's, to protestant eyes, inflammatory and insolent Pastoral Letter, *Out of the Flaminian Gate of Rome*, was read publicly on 17 October, and also when, eighteen days later, Lord John Russell added fuel to the fire by his *Durham Letter* which not merely rebuked the Pope but denounced the 'Puseyites' as the secret allies of Rome. However, many friends kept him informed of developments.

Russell's intervention profoundly shocked Gladstone. 'He has behaved vilely', he wrote to Lord Lyttelton on 13 December: 'no man in his position ought to pander to passion as he had done'.[60] The explicit slur on Tractarian clergy was monstrous. He had 'dipped his pen in gall' to smite men 'who not being Papists are such traitors and fools as really to mean something when they say, "I believe in one Holy Catholic Church,"' he wrote to Sir Walter James, a week later.[61]

Although Gladstone lamented the Pope's proceedings, mainly it seems because it was a victory for the Ultramontanes against those moderate English Catholics who preferred the provisional system of government by Vicars Apostolic,[62] he felt

[58] W. E. Gladstone to J. Gladstone, 10 July 1847, Hawn. P.
[59] For this see E. R. Norman, op. cit., 52–79, and G. I. T. Machin, op. cit., 218.
[60] Gladstone to Lyttelton, 13 Dec. 1850, Hawn. P.
[61] Gladstone to James, 20 Dec. 1850, *Lathbury*, i. 122.
[62] See W. E. Gladstone, *Ecclesiastical Titles Assumption Bill* [Speech] (1851), 20–4.

protest was far more appropriate than legislation. To prohibit Roman Catholic bishops from holding titles taken from any territory or place in the United Kingdom, as envizaged by Russell's Ecclesiastical Titles Bill, on the ground that this violated the Royal Supremacy was a nonsense. The Pope had, perhaps, infringed the territorial rights of the Crown, but only in that he had acted without the consent of the territorial sovereign.

He was well aware that the country supported Russell and wanted prohibition on grounds of principle. But, as he wrote to Sidney Herbert, 'I am afraid I for one cannot gratify the country.'[63] On 25 March 1851, therefore, he rose to face a predominantly hostile Commons and, in a speech Morley considered one of his three or four masterpieces, he castigated Russell's bill.

It was a protest against any attempts to meet the spiritual dangers of the Church by temporal legislation of a penal character and a plea that the true interests of the Church of England could not be promoted at that time 'by pretending to place them between any body of our fellow-subjects and the full enjoyment of their religious freedom'.[64] But fundamentally it was a passionate defence of religious liberty: 'We cannot change the profound and restless tendencies of the age towards religious liberty. It is our business to guide and to control their application, do this you may, but to endeavour to turn them backwards is the sport of children, done by the hands of men, and every effort you may make in that direction will recoil upon you in disaster and disgrace.'[65]

Yet the hope of religious liberty was no longer sufficient to restrain Hope and Manning. The outcry against Rome had driven them to a decision. On the morning of Passion Sunday, 6 April 1851, the two men were together received into the Roman Catholic Church at the Jesuit Church in Farm Street by Fr. Brownbill. 'I feel as if I had lost my two eyes,' Gladstone wrote soon after.[66]

---

[63] Stanmore, *Sidney Herbert, A Memoir* (1906), 137.

[64] W. E. Gladstone, op. cit., 4.

[65] Ibid., 29.

[66] C. Wordsworth, 'A Chapter of Autobiography', *Fortnightly Review*, xl (July 1883), 10.

Four months earlier, having just tendered his resignation to his Bishop, Manning had written to Gladstone a moving personal letter, 'the deep conviction of long years of patient silent thought', praying that God might guide his friend 'in this great crisis, on which the faith of England, and of an Empire, wide as the World, may be vitally touched by your lightest word'.[67]

You have by some eighteen years of public life attained a commanding position in Parliament. You represent Oxford; and are the only man into whose hands the effectual power of one side of the House of Commons, under certain contingencies can pass. Let me say what I believe. Parties will from this time form round two centres, the one will be the Protestantism of England protecting or trying to protect, itself and the Church of England, by legislation; the other Political Government, maintaining a powerful neutrality and arbitration among all religious communions.

If you retain your seat for Oxford, and accept the leadership which is approaching you through the old Conservative and Country parties you will take the former as your standing point, which God forbid.

If you take the latter centre to which all our late conferences would lead us without hesitation, you know the cost.

But I believe that is the path of Truth, peace and Christian civilisation to this great Empire.[68]

The political complexities of the 1850s, however, made government and party allegiance depend on factors other than the dramatic clash of religious principle envisaged by Manning. The unsatisfactory nature of the session of 1851, the first in which the Peelites were without Peel, left Gladstone disheartened and depressed. He wanted the group to form a stricter party organization under Aberdeen, but his efforts met with little success. Palmerston's dismissal in December 1851 meant that Russell's fall could not be long delayed unless he gained support from elsewhere. The Peelites were considered but Russell's conduct over 'Papal Aggression' made any rapprochment with them impossible; in any case Gladstone's known sympathy for 'Puseyites' made him unacceptable to many Whigs. The following February Palmerston's 'tit for tat with Johnny Russell' brought down the government on a militia bill and Derby and the Protectionists assumed office.

In this confused situation Gladstone seems to have been

---

[67] Manning to Gladstone, 6 Dec. 1850, BL Add. MS 44248, f. 114.
[68] Ibid., f. 113.

determined to keep his political options open. Three courses lay before the Peelites: Conservative reconstruction, liberal conjunction, or Peelism single-handed. The last he believed to be their least natural position, better that they might be 'liberal in the sense of Peel, working out a liberal policy through the medium of the conservative party'.[69] But though more sympathetic to reunion with Derby than most of his Peelite colleagues, he was still critical of Toryism on two scores: 'Protection and religious liberty', he wrote to Aberdeen on 5 August, 'are the subjects on which my main complaints would turn; shuffling as to the former, trading on bigotry as to the latter.'[70]

Certainly his espousal of religious liberty after Maynooth and his commitment to it thereafter had become one of the decisive elements in his political outlook. During the Christmas recess of 1851 he had written an open letter to Dr Skinner, Bishop of Aberdeen on a question then exercising the Scottish Episcopalian Church, the position and functions of the laity.[71] Although addressed to a specific situation, advocating the right of the faithful laity to constitutional rights and powers in Church government, the letter contained the fullest and most articulate statement of the principle of religious liberty Gladstone had yet made.[72]

It was now impossible to uphold a consistent religious profession in the State, he declared. It was better to accept this and be thankful than to affect a consistency that was deceptive, 'I am jealous of all attempts at consistency in this matter, most of all because I am convinced that they would and must result in the greatest of civil calamities; the mutilation, under the seal of civil authority, of the Christian religion itself.'[73] In the future, freedom must be the bulwark of faith. Against any encroachments on it Gladstone declared that he, for one, would steadily set his face. He would labour to the uttermost for Anglicans and

[69] *Diary*, iv, 25 Feb. 1852, 398.
[70] *Morley*, i. 429.
[71] W. E. Gladstone, *On the functions of laymen in the Church. A Letter to the Rt. Rev. William Skinner, D.D., Bishop of Aberdeen, and Primus* (1851), reprinted in *Gleanings*, vi. 1–46.
[72] As such, vigorously attacked by C. Wordsworth in his *A letter to the Rt. Hon. W. E. Gladstone on the doctrine of 'religious liberty'* (1852); see also *English Review*, xvii (July 1852), and *The Guardian*, 12 May, 313.
[73] *Gleanings*, vi. 6.

non-Anglicans alike to assert the principle, 'vital to us all',[74] of a full religious freedom. Common justice, the sake of religious peace and the maintenance of Divine Truth itself demanded it. When the State had no longer a definite religious character this was the principle 'it is no less our interest than our duty to maintain'.[75]

But it was fiscal rectitude that, in the end, decided the matter. In December 1852 Disraeli produced his budget. His proposals were totally unacceptable to Gladstone. Determined to fight for what he regarded as financial orthodoxy and motivated in no small measure by a personal dislike of Disraeli, he mounted a devastating attack on it in a passionate outburst in the early hours of 17 December. In the division that followed the Government was defeated and that evening Derby tendered his resignation to the Queen.

The new government was a coalition of Whigs and Peelites under Lord Aberdeen. Gladstone was Chancellor of the Exchequer. Brought about more by political circumstances than agreement on political principles and containing both High-Churchmen and Erastians, it was rather an uneasy government from the point of view of the Church. Conservative High-Churchmen, especially Archdeacon Denison, denounced it and regarded Gladstone's joining it yet another monstrous betrayal.

Gladstone himself, however, was reasonably satisfied with the ecclesiastical prospects. He told Sir William Heathcote, his fellow member for Oxford, that he trusted Aberdeen's Church policy as much as Derby's.[76] But despite his hopes Gladstone's membership of Aberdeen's coalition did little ultimately to settle the question of his party allegiance. When the coalition fell therefore, in 1855 over the Crimean War, he faced an unhappy four years which were from a political point of view, extremely unsettled and perplexing. He could, perhaps, have joined Derby in February 1855, but his loyalty to Peelite friends was still too strong.[77] When Derby, Landsdowne and Russell all failed to form a ministry the Queen turned to Palmerstone. The Peelites, with the exception of Newcastle, reluctantly joined and Glad-

*sic*

[74] Ibid., 8.
[75] Ibid.
[76] Gladstone to Heathcote, 28 Dec. 1852, BL Add. MS 44208, f. 33.
[77] See *Diary*, v, 10 ff., 31 Jan.–5 Feb. 1855.

stone resumed office as Chancellor of the Exchequer. But after only three weeks the Peelite ministers resigned. During the next three years Derby made several overtures to Gladstone, but to no avail. In November 1858, having once more felt unable to forsake his Peelite friends and accept office in Derby's new administration, despite the earnest pleading of Samuel Wilberforce,[78] he left England altogether and for three months acted as High Commissioner to the Ionian Islands.

He returned in March 1859 just before Derby was defeated on the question of parliamentary reform. In the election that followed he was returned unopposed for Oxford. Three days after the new session of parliament had begun, Derby's government was defeated and Derby resigned. With Granville unable to form a government, the Queen turned again to Palmerston. Although Gladstone had voted against the Whigs' amendment, he accepted office under Palmerston as Chancellor of the Exchequer in the new ministry, dominated by Whigs, even containing the Benthamite radical Molesworth. His choice of party had, this time, been irrevocably decided. 'How could I', he wrote to Heathcote reflecting on the circumstances that had led him to take the step, 'be the one remaining Ishmael in the House of Commons?'[79]

Gladstone's acceptance of office under Palmerston was interpreted by many, not least by his Oxford constituents, as showing his definite adhesion to the Liberal party then in process of reconstruction. Gladstone himself took a rather different view, justifying his action with a characteristically involved personal and political defence.[80] None the less it was, as Morley said, a 'party wrench'.[81] It brought an end to the possibility of his reunion with the Conservatives and set him firmly on the road to the leadership of the Liberal party and all that this would bring in the 1860s and beyond.

But Morley was undoubtedly correct to point out how mistaken it would be to regard this event as a chief ideological landmark in Gladstone's protracted journey from Tory to

---

[78] G. W. E. Russell, *William Ewart Gladstone* (1906), 62.

[79] *Morley*, i. 627.

[80] See *Morley*, i. 628 and Gladstone's letter to Hawkins in G. W. E. Russell, op. cit., 144–5.

[81] *Morley*, i. 631.

Liberal despite its political import. For on that journey the chief landmarks were those that marked out his conversion to the principle of religious liberty: the fate of his book symbolized by the Maynooth crisis; Jewish disabilities; Gorham; the 'Letter to Bishop Skinner'. It was in this conversion above all that Gladstone's liberalism was born.

Of course it was the complex political developments which followed the disintegration of Peel's Conservative party in 1846 which were eventually to decide Gladstone's political affiliation. It was a political conversion in large measure forced upon him by Tory hostility to Peelite reciprocity. Yet the intellectual origins of his move can properly be traced to the religious crisis of the 1840s. In old age he recalled that Manning had once told him, about the time he was writing his first book, 'The Church is going back into the condition in which it stood before the days of Constantine'. 'Of course this will not hold water as a formula,' Gladstone wrote, 'but it is widely, profoundly and multifariously true.'

The Church came into contact with human nature at every one of the thousand points upon its face . . . There was created an atmosphere of faith, which every one traditionally, it might be unconsciously inhalted. The atmosphere is now in a state of progressive dilution. That grasp of the Church, and with the Church of the faith, and with the Faith of the tradition, upon the individual human creature has been, and is being continually relaxed. . . .[82]

Gladstone's first book had been an attempt to defend the idea of a Confessional State. The political circumstances of the early 1840s, especially the implications of the development of a representative view of government and the failure of the revival of the Church to bring about Christian unity in the nation, convinced him that this was no longer possible. There was no longer a conscience in the State, at least not one capable of recognizing and endowing Catholic truth.

This conviction destroyed the basis of his Toryism. This had always been much more than a matter of party allegiance: it had been a commitment to a religious ideal. The change in Gladstone's political convictions in the late 1840s and 1850s was primarily his response to its collapse. If the Church could no longer demand the exclusive support of the State, then it was

[82] *Autobiographica*, 154.

better that it should give its gold for liberty. To cling to its
Constantinian privileges was to run the risk of mutilating the
faith which it was its solemn duty to preserve. The dilution of the
Christian atmosphere in the State could not be allowed to bring
about any dilution of the faith itself.

But if there was no longer a conscience in the State there
remained the conscience of the individual. To Newman, at the
time of Maynooth, Gladstone had written that there were in
operation 'two great and opposite movements': 'the religion of
individuals rises, the religion of civil societies sinks'. The
capacity of the State to sustain a religious character was
diminishing, yet the 'tone and opinion of our Legislature upon
questions of personal duty improves and . . . the personal
profession of religion increases from year to year'.[83]

The Christian atmosphere in the State was progressively
diluting, but he believed there was at work a counter-process in
individuals, freeing them from the influence of the community
in which they lived.[84] If it was no longer possible, therefore, to
defend a conscience in the State, it was possible, if not essential,
to work towards the emancipation of the individual's conscience. But this was impossible without liberty, religious liberty
to choose Catholic truth, liberty in a more general sense to
enhance the consciousness of moral duty. 'It is liberty alone
which fits men for liberty,' Gladstone told Forster in 1882 when
discussing the problem of Ireland.[85]

If this was the kernel of 'Gladstonian Liberalism' then in a
real sense its origin lay in the intellectual and religious crisis that
followed the fate of his book. Only when he accepted that his
ideal was no longer practical, that the age of the Confessional
State was passing away, was he free to work towards a new
political creed and to rebuild on the ruins of the old.

In this rebuilding many elements, political, economic and
intellectual, converged and combined. As he had told Stanley at
the height of the Maynooth crisis a year before, 'the lower ends
of a State ought to be fulfilled even when the higher ones should
have become impractical'.[86] Indeed these 'lower ends' could

[83] Gladstone to Newman, 19 Sept. 1844, Oratory MSS.
[84] *Autobiographica*, 154.
[85] *Morley*, iii. 58.
[86] *Diary*, iii, 4 Mar. 1844.

now assume a greater importance. As said already, his apprenticeship under Peel was the beginning of that lifelong passionate commitment to working the institutions of government. Administration took on a significance in its own right, accepted in a religious way as a real part of his vocation as a politician.

The same is true of his commitment to free trade and to his view of the right relations with the colonies. To these might also be added his interest in international morality especially as witnessed by his attitude to the Neapolitan government in 1851–2. As Dr Matthew has pointed out: 'To say whether this constituted liberalism is to measure him against an undefined standard.' But on the topics that had become central to his interests, 'he found himself in each case allied with groups which, whatever they were, were not predominately tory'.[87]

But for Gladstone himself, especially in the crucial period from 1845 to 1852, it was the principle of religious liberty that mattered most. It was this that formed the direct legacy of the Maynooth crisis and the fervour with which he proclaimed it, had as its source, the collapse of the Tractarian movement and the religious unsettlement of his friends.

This is why it is not surprising that his journey to Liberalism was along the High Anglican road. The paradox perceived by Morley was more apparent than real. Gladstone's Liberalism had nothing in common with the Liberalism which the Tractarians resisted in the 1830s. That Liberalism was secular, utilitarian, committed to the 'march of mind', hostile to dogmatic faith. It wanted the Church subordinate to the civil power.[88]

If this had remained the only kind of Liberalism then Gladstone's career would never have developed in the way it did. Morley admitted this himself. 'If liberalism had continued to run in the grooves cut by Bentham, James Mill, Grote and the rest,' he wrote, 'Mr. Gladstone would never have grown to be a

---

[87] *Diary*, iii, Introduction, xlii. My indebtedness to Dr H. C. G. Matthew at this point should be obvious. He has discussed these matters fully in his Introductions to Volumes iii and v of the *Diary*.

[88] Cf. Newman's remarks about Froude: 'With Froude, Erastianism—that is, the union (so he viewed it) of Church and State—was the parent, or if not the parent, the serviceable and sufficient tool, of liberalism.' M. J. Svaglic (ed.), J. H. Newman, *Apologia pro Vita Sua* (1967), 46.

N.B.

liberal.'[89] It was because he was a High-Churchman, a believer in the Church's intrinsic spiritual authority and an avowed opponent of Erastianism, that Gladstone saw the danger facing Catholic Christianity. The danger came now, not from the fact that the State was no longer prepared to give its support exclusively to a national Church, but from the fact that, in its place, it was prepared to offer its patronage to an undenominational Christianity, without definite or distinctive historic and dogmatic content.

Faced with this, the maintenance of the purity of Catholic faith was imperative and State patronage was a hindrance, potentially a snare. 'Away,' he wrote in his letter to Bishop Skinner, 'away with the servile doctrine that religion cannot live but by the aid of Parliaments. That aid is a greater or lesser good, according to circumstances, but conditions are also supposable under which it would be a great evil.'[90] The future of Christianity lay with the Christian churches themselves, and in 'the full and free development of their energies from within.'[91] It lay with the acceptance by churchmen of religious liberty, not only for their own Communion but for all other religious bodies, and the vigilant guard against secular interference in their concerns.

Here was the beginning of a different kind of liberalism that accepted the increasing indifference of the State to dogmatic religion and derived from it a more positive valuation of religious liberty and consequently human freedom. In much Gladstone remained a conservative: 'I have never swerved from what I conceive to be those truly conservative objects and desires with which I entered life,' he declared in one of his Lancashire speeches in the 1860s. '. . . But experience has brought with it its lessons . . . I have not refused to acknowledge and accept the signs of the times.'[92] As he told Morley in old age, 'I was brought up to dislike and distrust liberty, I learned to believe in it. That is the key to all my changes.'[93]

And what had forced him to appreciate and accept this?

---

[89] *Morley*, i. 201.
[90] *Gleanings*, vi. 8.
[91] *Gleanings*, vi. 9.
[92] *Morley*, ii. 178.
[93] *Morley*, iii. 474–5.

Surely it was in that confused and troubled period preceding and following Maynooth, in the realization that the State could no longer consistently exercise its conscience, in those years between Newman's apostasy and the Gorham Judgement, faced with the difficulties and dangers besetting the Church, that he was driven to abandon his vision of a Confessional State and to accept the principle of religious liberty. Here was the germ of Gladstone's Liberalism, a Liberalism that developed not from the discarding of his original religious vocation to serve the Church, but from the transformation of it as he journeyed further on that 'high Anglican road'.

# THE OXFORD MOVEMENT: 1833–1851

# 6

# THE OXFORD MOVEMENT: REVIVAL AND
# REACTION: 1833–1845

Gladstone's relationship to the Oxford Movement has not been given the attention it deserves.[1] Political historians have tended to ignore the part it played in his political development and historians of the movement have, until recently, concentrated almost entirely upon the clerical leadership and often simply upon the spiritual biography of Newman himself.

The nature of this relationship, however, needs careful analysis. Gladstone himself always denied that he had been a Tractarian. He had left Oxford before the movement began and his theological development was, he believed, entirely independent of Tractarian influence, at least in a direct way.[2] 'With respect to Tractarianism, it is true, but I suppose of no use to say, that I have not read the Tracts,' he told Phillimore at the time of his election as burgess for the University in 1847. 'If on the other hand anyone had read me, and denounces me as a Tractarian on the ground of what I have written I can say no more: for the argument, from such materials, would last through the next Parliament.'[3]

But in the public mind at least, he was always suspect as a 'Puseyite' and his readiness at times to deny the accusation shows how aware he was that his beliefs, writings, actions, and known sympathies opened him to the charge.

Of course a great deal depends upon how the Oxford Movement is regarded; if it is seen primarily in terms of ecclesiastical politics and partisanship, or in terms of a revival of devotional life and spiritual discipline. With Gladstone we are

[1] Cf. G. Battiscombe's comments, *John Keble: a study in limitations* (1963), 12. For another account see M. J. Lynch, 'Was Gladstone a Tractarian? W. E. Gladstone and the Oxford Movement, 1833–45', *Journal of Religious History*, viii (1975), 364–89.

[2] See Chapter 2, p. 56.

[3] Gladstone to Phillimore, 24 June 1847, BL Add. MS 44276, f. 109; cf. Gladstone's letter to his father, 10 and 22 July 1847, Hawn. P.

fortunate in having enough material not only to analyse his outward behaviour but also his inner spiritual life. Thus we are able to see how his religious practice altered as a result of becoming a High-Churchman, especially through his connection with Tractarianism. Indeed, Gladstone's response in this respect is particularly fascinating because of his being a layman. Despite so much written about the influence of the Oxford Movement on clergy and public worship, little or no attempt has been made to explore the religious life of the Tractarian laity and though Gladstone's experience was not perhaps typical,[4] it does shed some light on the nature of lay piety in the first half of the nineteenth century.

Gladstone firmly believed the Oxford Movement had been particularly beneficial in deepening the spirituality of the nation. In old age he took A. W. Hutton to task for treating Tractarianism as merely retrogressive. 'If the business of Christianity be the formation of Christ in the souls of men, it was surely progressive, and England at this day bears witness, among many opposite signs, to its progressiveness,' he wrote in 1892.[5]

But Gladstone was certainly never an advanced Anglo-Catholic and the more extreme Roman Catholic habits of devotion had little appeal for him. In fact, in his spiritual as in his theological development, a more Catholic outlook tended to be superimposed upon an evangelical base. Although his theological understanding of the eucharist undoubtedly deepened as a result of becoming a High-Churchman, he had always been a frequent communicant. Regular reception of the sacrament was stressed by many evangelicals and did not denote a particular type of churchmanship. Similarly the habits of private prayer and Bible reading he had formed early in life were not much altered by his ecclesiastical development. Nor was there a change in his keeping of Sunday. It remained always a day for church attendance, usually twice, and for spiritual reading.

---

[4] For a discussion of Gladstone's involvement with the lay Tractarian 'engagement', and for dealings with the prostitutes and the 'sexual crisis' of his middle-age, I refer the reader to Dr Matthew's account which has placed the whole matter in the context of Gladstone's religious and family life, *Diary*, iii, Introduction, xliv–xlviii.

[5] Gladstone to Hutton, 21 Apr. 1892, BL Add. MS 44215, f. 256.

In some respects, the evangelical strain remained. His self-examination, thorough and regular, did not develop into the practice of sacramental confession. More must be said of this later. Gladstone also retained a strong sense of Providence, not an exclusively evangelical emphasis obviously, but one more often associated with evangelicalism. He felt God could speak to him through the Bible, and found the Psalms, in particular, a source of help in times of difficulty or decision.[6]

The way in which his evangelicalism was subtly altered by his High-Churchmanship can be illustrated best by his attitude to family prayers. Evangelicalism was pre-eminently the religion of the home. By the late 1830s, however, Gladstone was anxious to relate this domestic religion to the Church's liturgy. His House Rules for religious observance at 13 Carlton House Terrace, in the early 1840s, show that the family and servants assembled in the dining-room daily for prayers at 9.15 a.m. and that the servants were expected to attend Church at least twice on a Sunday: in the morning and either in the afternoon or evening. Two pews were rented for this purpose in St. Martin's Church. The rules also contained the direction that 'It is earnestly hoped that they [the servants] will attend the Holy Sacrament. It is administered every Sunday as well as Good Friday and Christmas Day.'[7]

Gladstone clearly attempted to centre these household religious observances on the Prayer Book. In 1845, for example, he published *A Manual of Prayers from the Liturgy arranged for family use*, which had the explicit purpose 'of providing the very best materials for family devotion, and of bringing that description of worship into harmony with the temper and system of the Church'.[8] It was also his custom to preach a short homily on Sundays and Holy days, the majority of which tried to explain in a simple and direct way parts of the prayer book service or the meaning of the day itself.

As regards public worship Gladstone discovered his ideal at the Margaret Chapel in London's West End, the forerunner of All Saints' Margaret Street. He visited it first in the company of

---

[6] e.g. *Diary*, iii, 14 May 1843; *Diary*, iv, 9 May 1854.
[7] Among the papers at Hawarden.
[8] *A Manual of Prayers from the Liturgy, arranged for family use* (1845), iv.

Joseph Anstice in the mid-1830s when William Dodsworth was minister and the churchmanship still evangelical. He became a frequent attender, however, from 1841 onwards. Two years before this Frederick Oakeley had been licensed as priest-in-charge. With his assistant, Upton Richards, Oakeley soon transformed a small and rather dingy chapel into the main centre of Tractarian worship in London.[9]

The services were not ritualistic in the later sense of the word, but Oakeley introduced the daily office with eucharists on Sundays and Holy days conducted with reverence and re-strained dignity. Gladstone became a frequent attender of the Sunday evening service from 1841, and attended regularly in Lent and Holy Week. What impressed him was the atmosphere of devotion that pervaded the chapel. In April 1842, for example, after attending both the morning and evening services he wrote in his diary of 'the reality of earnest concurrence in the work of holy worship' there, which 'I know not where else to look for'.[10] A few months later he wrote to his wife after the morning eucharist that he could 'scarcely recollect to have seen a service which throughout derived such solemnity from the earnestness and demeanour in general of those engaged in it'.[11]

It was about this time that he began writing his 'Secreta Eucharistica', a form of personal devotion for the communion service in English and Latin. He revised it during his life, but it belongs mainly to the 1840s and shows both how central the eucharist had become in his spiritual life and that he had by this time attained a catholic understanding of the sacrament.[12] From the early 1840s onwards he received communion at least weekly unless circumstances made it impossible.

By the early 1840s he was also trying to keep Lent strictly. The busy pressures of political life sometimes made this difficult and he felt something of a conflict between the claims of professional life and devotion. On Easter Sunday 1842, looking back, he described his Lent as 'more deficient in outward means even

---

[9] For the history of the chapel see W. A. Whitworth, *Quam Dilecta* (1891) and Gladstone's letter to Whitworth, *Lathbury*, i. 408–9.
[10] *Diary*, iii, 10 Apr. 1842.
[11] Gladstone to his wife, 10 Aug. 1842, Hawn. P.
[12] A version can be found in *Lathbury*, ii. 421–7.

than the last', and wrote that 'business confuses my sense of the periods of this season'.[13]

His remedy was to attempt, in 1845, a rule as regards time spent in sleep, eating, and recreation. Certainly he recognized that it was impossible to be too stringent while under the obligations of political life. He accepted the fact that his work prevented him from attending daily services except in Lent and Holy Week. He also abandoned the idea of fasting, again except for a time immediately preceding Easter.[14]

Nevertheless, his devotional life was disciplined and thorough. He might not have been able to attend the daily office in church, but he usually said it privately in addition to family prayers. The diptych of prayer on the flyleaf of his diary, following 13 April 1848, shows how seriously he took the work of intercession. Sunday was always kept as a day free for religious employments. Undoubtedly, with Gladstone's temperament, his spiritual exercises helped to give him a stability that he would otherwise have lacked. 'Devotion is by far the best sedative to excitement,' he wrote to Manning in 1846.[15]

Gladstone also joined a secret fraternity of lay High-Churchmen in 1845. The idea of an association of laymen pledged to a common rule seems to have been suggested by T. D. Acland in 1844. The rule itself was drawn up by Keble and included the necessity of regular communion, observance of the feasts and fasts of the Church, prayer at particular times during the day, the undertaking of a regular work of charity, and the giving of a definite portion of income (one-tenth was suggested as a minimum) in alms and offerings. Once a year, near St. Barnabas' day, the members were to meet in London to compare notes on their progress during the previous year and to make plans for the next. A record of their activities was to be kept in cypher.[16]

By March 1846 it consisted of fifteen members, all professional men, including the Aclands, Frederic Rogers, Roundell

[13] *Diary*, iii, 27 Mar. 1842.
[14] See his letter to Manning, Purcell, op. cit., i. 436–8.
[15] Ibid.
[16] *Diary*, iii, 23 Feb. 1845, and Keble's letters to John Taylor Coleridge, Bodleian MS Eng. lett. d.134, ff. 221, 226.

Palmer, and the architect William Butterfield. But it does not appear to have been a particularly stable association. Its members represented different shades of High-Churchmanship, and were not, therefore, entirely in agreement about some of the forms of devotion. Gladstone appears to have had scruples regarding prayer for the dead. There was disagreement in late 1846 about the use of Roman Catholic devotional books and some withdrew. One of the members, William Monsell, eventually became a Roman Catholic, and one or two others may also have done so.[17]

Its main problem, however, was that its demands were individual rather than corporate. Although Keble and Coleridge habitually referred to it as 'the Brotherhood', it was not sufficiently tightly knit to be regarded as a form of Tractarian freemasonry. As the members met together only once a year, there was little possibility of engendering much corporate spirit. Nor did the rules require anything particularly distinctive. They demanded little more than might be expected of any pious churchman.

Unable to attend the meeting in June 1849, Gladstone wrote to Acland voicing his fears.[18] Members had only a slight knowledge, or even no knowledge at all, of one another. He felt there was little possibility of it working better unless they met together more frequently and undertook some sort of reciprocal duties. He had the previous winter suggested that the members should be grouped into 'sections' and a greater attempt made to sustain each other in the religious life and, to an extent, supervize each others' conduct. None of this, however, was taken up and the Brotherhood ceased to exist in the early 1850s.

One of its rules had been that members 'consider with a practical view the direction of the Church concerning confession and absolution'.[19] Gladstone did not, however, adopt the practice of sacramental confession or seek the advice of a spiritual director. This is, perhaps, surprising and it shows how wary one must be of describing Gladstone as an Anglo-Catholic. He certainly contemplated going to confession. In 1840, for

[17] Bodleian MS Eng. lett. d.134, ff. 295, 458.
[18] Gladstone to T. D. Acland, 10 June 1849, Bodleian MS Eng. lett. d.89.
[19] Rule 9.

example, he wrote in his diary that although it was probably unnecessary for many consciences, 'for mine it is a question to be pondered'.[20] He appears to have considered it quite seriously again in November 1844 when he joined the Brotherhood.[21] But in the end he decided against it. His letters to Manning in 1847, where he attacked compulsory confession, especially when linked to spiritual direction as a 'blow at man's freedom', will be mentioned later.[22] In old age he put on paper some reflections on the practice. There he acknowledged that confession to a priest had an uncontestable place in Anglican formularies and had been practised by some of the Reformers. He also admitted that as a spiritual exercise it had an undoubted effect in 'bracing . . . the mental process of repentance'. Nevertheless he believed 'The healthy soul ought to be able to discharge its burdens at the foot of the great throne without the assistance of an intermediate person.'[23]

This teaching seemed to him the authentic teaching of the Prayer Book and he declared that of all the works he had read on the subject, that nearest the point was a pair of sermons by George Wilkinson, Bishop of St. Andrews. It is interesting, perhaps, in view of Gladstone's own spiritual development that this should be the case. Wilkinson was one of the greatest exponents of what has been termed 'Catholic Evangelicalism', a synthesis of the evangelical emphasis on personal conversion and Catholic sacramentalism.[24] Gladstone became very close to Wilkinson in his last years and it was Wilkinson who ministered to him during his last painful illness.[25]

One further point should be mentioned. At Fasque in Kincardineshire, to which Gladstone's father retired and where Gladstone often spent the summer, an episcopalian chapel dedicated to St. Andrew was erected in the mid-1840s. It was Gladstone's idea and since it could hardly be said to meet the needs of the presbyterian inhabitants, its purpose was plainly to

---

[20] *Diary*, iii, 25 Dec. 1840.
[21] Gladstone to his wife, 24 Nov. Hawn. P.
[22] See below, Chapter 7, p. 197.
[23] 17 December 1893, BL Add. MS 44790, ff. 89–95; *Autobiographica*, 158–61.
[24] For Wilkinson and the phenomenon of Catholic evangelicalism, see Dieter Voll, *Catholic Evangelicalism* (1963).
[25] G. W. E. Russell, *Mr Gladstone*, 281–2.

meet his own.[26] He had always taken a tender interest in the tiny episcopalian remnant in Scotland and though he would attend presbyterian services if no other were available, he much preferred to worship in the Scottish Episcopalian Church. Indeed, Scottish episcopalianism with its caroline ethos, and its communion office based on Laud's Scottish Liturgy, probably approximated most closely to his own ideal of Anglicanism as both Catholic and reformed.

In the early 1840s, with James Hope, he had founded the episcopalian boarding-school, Trinity College, Glenalmond, in Perthshire, with the intention of spreading episcopalian principles among the Scottish middle class and providing future priests for the Church.[27] St. Andrews, Fasque, however, met a more personal need. It was in a real sense Gladstone's own private oratory and although a priest came to celebrate the sacraments, Gladstone would himself conduct the daily office. Perhaps, here, in the little chapel at Fasque, he found compensation for abandoning a priestly vocation for the vocation of a politician.

In terms of his spirituality, therefore, Gladstone could be described as an adherent of the Oxford Movement. However, it is not difficult to see why he maintained he was never a Tractarian, for to most people that meant not a particular sort of devotional life so much as membership of an ecclesiastical faction. And if the Oxford Movement is viewed in that way then Gladstone was indeed right in denying that he was a Tractarian. For Gladstone never regarded himself a member of a Church party. Indeed the very idea was always abhorrent to him. When by the late 1830s hostility to the Oxford men had crystallized and they were regarded as a definite party within the Church, Gladstone told Hope as 'one who will not misapprehend me', that 'if there be such a party I am no member of it, not only for the reason that I cannot allege concurrence in its distinctive opinions, but also because the whole basis of party seems to me to be uprooted and abolished by the first principles of catholicity in religion'.[28]

[26] *Diary*, iii, liii; 15, 19 Aug., 20 Oct. 1844; 18 Oct. 1846.
[27] Ornsby, op. cit., i. 207–15.
[28] Gladstone to Hope, 13 Feb. 1840, *Lathbury*, i. 233.

This is important to grasp, for unless Gladstone's conception of the movement is appreciated, his own relation to it is likely to be misunderstood. For, as already noted, Gladstone saw the Oxford Movement as part of a much greater spiritual revival in English religious life, a reaction against the laxity and worldliness of the Hanoverian Church and a reassertion of traditional Anglican doctrines of the Church and sacraments after a century of Latitudinarianism and neglect.[29] For him it was never a movement preaching new doctrine. Rather it was the complement to the Evangelical Revival of the previous century, which had so forcefully reasserted the doctrine of grace and the centrality of Christ's atonement, but had, in its Calvinistic form at least, fallen below the standard of the Prayer Book and articles in relation to ecclesiology and sacramental teaching.[30] 'I am entirely convinced', he wrote to Hope in 1839, 'that in substance the movement termed evangelical, and that falsely termed Popish, are part of one great beneficent design of God: and that in their substance they will harmonise and cooperate.'[31]

Moreover, in the early stages Gladstone firmly believed that this revival would result in a renewed Church that would win back the love and allegiance, not only of the masses who were falling into irreligion, but also of the non-conformists outside. The Church of England seemed poised to become, what it had always claimed to be, a truly National Church.

This was the hope, over-sanguine as he later admitted,[32] that provided the inspiration for his first book. The union of Church and State made perfect sense if the Church was, in reality, the nation at prayer. The movement in Oxford, therefore, was both evidence of and a contribution to this national resurgence. Indeed, one of his reasons for writing the book was to impress this upon those Oxford men who, he felt, seemed to have become cool in their desire for the maintenance of a religious establishment.[33] Establishment was not necessarily Erastian: it did not

[29] *Gleanings*, vii. 141–3.
[30] Ibid., 207.
[31] Gladstone to Hope, 11 Jan. 1839, BL Add. MS 44214, f. 63. The Oxford men would, he believed, be as helpful to religion as Cambridge men were in the previous generation.
[32] *Gleanings*, vii. 142.
[33] Gladstone to Hope, 13 Feb. 1840, BL Add. MS 44214, f. 84.

have to threaten the Church's undoubted spiritual independence. No conflict between Church and State was necessary if
the Establishment was put upon a proper basis and understood
in the right way. As if to underline the point Gladstone inscribed
the book to the University of Oxford 'in the belief that she is
providentially designed to be a fountain of blessings . . . to the
present and future times; and in the hope that the temper of
these pages may be found not alien from her own'.

Gladstone's understanding of the movement was, therefore,
rather different from that of the men who became its leaders,
and from the view of it held by the public at large. By the time
Gladstone had written his book on Church and State, Newman,
Keble, Pusey, and the bulk of their young followers were no
longer much interested in seeking a better accommodation to
the State; the theology of his *Church Principles* was far closer to
that of the older High-Churchmen who were becoming increasingly aware of their growing divergence from the more advanced Oxford men.

Despite their more general community of interest in defending the Church and reasserting its apostolic claims, there were
political and theological differences separating Gladstone from
those who were to control the future of the movement, which
became clearer as its controversial character became more
apparent. Moreover, these differences were reinforced by the
fact that Gladstone's focus was the House of Commons, the
defence of the Church in parliament, and his concern to bring
his own party to a better understanding of its religious mission.
As a politician he became increasingly aware of the tensions
between ideal and reality and from the early 1840s onwards he
was conscious, as most of the clerical Tractarians were not, of the
difference between adherence to dogmatic principle, and the
tactical flexibilities necessary in political and ecclesiastical life.

Living in London, Gladstone did not know the direction the
movement was taking until the late 1830s. From May 1834 until
April 1841 he never visited Oxford and his knowledge of the
movement came from the press and from his friends. He received
occasional letters from sympathisers in Oxford, like Benjamin
Harrison and Walter Kerr Hamilton, gaining information
second hand from Hope, Manning and no doubt others, but his
own personal contact with the leadership was extremely limited.

He knew Pusey from his time at Christ Church and began corresponding with him on Church matters early in 1833, six months before Keble's Assize Sermon.[34] But it was not until the crisis over subscription and the proposed admission of dissenters to the University, that Pusey began to make common cause with the Newman group; and not until much later that he could be said to occupy an unambiguous position within the Tractarian party.

Gladstone, unlike Hope, never fell under Newman's personal influence. Although he profoundly admired Newman's sermons, and never underestimated his contribution to the life of the Church of England, he declared in old age that Newman was never 'an instructed English Churchman', meaning that Newman had never entered into the spirit of Anglicanism as exemplified by the Caroline divines.[35] With Keble, that 'sweet singer of Israel',[36] Gladstone had no direct contact until 1840, when, after Keble's review of his book, Gladstone began a fairly irregular, though amicable, correspondence.[37]

This helps to explain Gladstone's increasing ambivalence to the movement in the period up to Newman's conversion. In the early years when the defence of the Church was uppermost, and when the movement appeared to be simply reasserting Church principles acceptable to the broad mass of High-Churchmen, Gladstone looked upon it enthusiastically as confirmation that his hopes of a regeneration of National Religion were not misplaced. After the publication of Froude's *Remains*, and more especially after Tract XC, it became clear that the theological basis was shifting. He then became increasingly concerned, though still anxious to defend the Tractarians from public attack. In the early 1840s when conflict intensified, he saw it as his mission to mediate, feeling that a protestant reaction would set back the real cause, the revival of authentic Anglican theology and discipline, doing more harm than good. The emergence of a distinctly pro-Roman party horrified him and his hope of a united movement, soundly based, and with it the steady permeation of Catholic principles throughout the

---

[34] Gladstone to Pusey, 15 Feb. 1833, Pusey MSS, Pusey House.
[35] Gladstone to R. H. Hutton, 6 Oct. 1890, *Lathbury*, i. 406.
[36] *Gleanings*, vii. 141.
[37] The correspondence began on 11 January 1840. Between 1840 and 1865 Gladstone sent Keble 23 letters: Keble MSS, Keble College.

Church, was shattered. But he still continued to defend even the more advanced Oxford men on the grounds of justice, since he was not prepared to have men hounded from the Church for stretching Anglican theology in one direction when no similar witch hunt was conducted against those who stretched it in the other. Newman's conversion, however, at much the same time as his own crisis over Maynooth, convinced him that his wider hopes for the movement had been in vain. Although it had played its part in reviving religious life, it had, rather than increase unity within the Church, proved a source of division. The break-up of the movement in these years, and the loss of many of its followers to Rome was, therefore, a potent factor in his own realization of the impracticality of his early political creed and the abandonment of his theory of Church and State.

As a devout young man of obvious promise and occupying a strategic position, it was not surprising that the Tractarians should look to Gladstone as a potential ally. In October 1833, soon after the publication of the first Tracts, Newman wrote to his young friend Frederic Rogers: 'As to Gladstone, perhaps it would be wrong to ask a young man so to commit himself.'[38] But six weeks later to J. W. Bowden, listing some of the movement's new supporters, he included Gladstone's patron the Duke of Newcastle, Sir William Heathcote, Joshua Watson, and Gladstone himself.[39]

It seems likely, however, that the impetus to approach him came from Gladstone's old undergraduate friend Benjamin Harrison, who was still in Oxford and now a keen follower of Newman. In early November he had sent Gladstone a pamphlet suggesting the formation of an 'Association of Friends of the Church', and told him that Newman would very much like him to come to Christ Church to discuss matters.[40] It was clearly Harrison who overcame Gladstone's initial wariness and convinced him that there was nothing irregular in the proposed association. It was from Harrison also, that Gladstone received the first Tracts.[41]

*Benj. Harrison*

[38] 23 Oct. 1833, A. Mozley, op. cit., i. 404.
[39] Ibid., 13 Nov. 1833, 424.
[40] Harrison to Gladstone, 2 Nov. 1833, BL Add. MS 44204, f. 35.
[41] Harrison to Gladstone, 15 Nov. 1833, ibid., f. 38.

Gladstone was, therefore, wrong to say later that he had never read the Tracts, but probably right that they had not decisively influenced him. By late 1833, he had already moved considerably from his early evangelicalism and his progress towards a High Church theology seems to have been the result of his own experience and reading which the Tracts, such as he read, can simply have confirmed. He would obviously have been sympathetic to any group concerned with Church defence in those troubled years and the Tractarians themselves were quite aware of the usefulness of having committed men in parliament. When in 1834, for instance, the question of allowing marriages to be solemnized in dissenting chapels arose, Gladstone and Sir Robert Inglis were consulted by the Oxford group.[42] Gladstone was also consulted, principally by Pusey, on the proposals to relax subscription and allow dissenters into the University, in the hope that he would rally churchmen in parliament against the proposal.[43]

Gladstone's growing commitment to the Tractarian cause in those early years is most evident in his attitude to the nomination of Dr Hampden to the vacant Regius Chair of Divinity, by Melbourne in 1836. Hampden was a marked man for the Tractarians on account of his supposedly heterodox opinions and his conviction that subscription to the Thirty-nine articles should be relaxed and dissenters admitted to the university, which he had put forward in a pamphlet in 1834. In the hostile reaction that followed, 'the first outbreak of Tractism, and its success the great strengthener of the party', as Whately later described it,[44] Gladstone lined up squarely with the Oxford men, an action he later regretted.[45]

Pusey brought the affair to Gladstone's attention.[46] Rumours were already rife about the new appointment early in February and when news of Melbourne's choice leaked out on February 7, Pusey immediately began to marshall the opposition.

Gladstone followed the controversy intently. On 15 February

[42] A. Mozley, op. cit., ii, 26.
[43] Gladstone to Pusey, 21 Apr. 1835, 14 May 1835; Pusey to Gladstone, 5 May 1835, Pusey MSS.
[44] Quoted in H. Hampden, *Memorials of Bishop Hampden* (1871), 51.
[45] See his letter to Hampden, 9 Nov. 1856, H. Hampden, op. cit., 199–200.
[46] Pusey to Gladstone, 2 Feb. 1833, Pusey MSS.

he read Hampden's pamphlet *Observations on Religious Dissent*, with the postscript Hampden had added in the following year. Five days later he put his thoughts on paper in what was obviously intended to be a pamphlet of his own. Anxious to deal with the subject in a manner 'above the region of party disputation' and 'to touch exclusively upon the dogmatic principles' rather than the personal character of the individual concerned,[47] Gladstone had come, nevertheless, to the conclusion that there were opinions, expressed in Hampden's pamphlet which appeared 'likely to operate most unhappily upon the discharge of the duties belonging to the Regius Professorship of Divinity'.[48] They were not, Gladstone believed, necessarily proof of personal heterodoxy. Rather, Hampden held views without, perhaps, realizing that the grounds on which they were based and the manner in which they were framed were fundamentally erroneous. The charge he would want to bring against Hampden was that, 'his deliberations of truth are such as to ordinary minds must prove shadowy and impalpable: that he has been bewildered in the subtleties of his own metaphysical enquiry, and in pursuing them with enthusiastic zeal has forgotten the relation which they ought to bear to the practical purposes of religion'.[49]

Hampden's appointment by a Whig government was, Gladstone told Manning early in March, 'an act of infatuation', though its evil consequences would be compensated and perhaps more, by the orthodox reaction it would provoke. It would create in the future 'a spirit of tenacious adherence to truth of doctrine'. None the less, its immediate effect was lamentable. It would embitter political strife by introducing a religious element, widen still further the gulf between the different parties in the Church and put yet another difficulty in the way of that unity 'which still remains the amiable chimera of some minds'.[50] With Pusey supplying information, Gladstone considered organizing parliamentary protests.[51]

[47] 20 Feb. 1836, BL Add. MS 44726, f. 306. Gladstone did not read Hampden's *Bampton Lectures* and he read only Newman and Pusey's hostile pamphlets. This is perhaps why he later regretted his action.

[48] Ibid., f. 307.

[49] Ibid.

[50] Gladstone to Manning, 4 Mar. 1836, BL Add. MS 44247, f. 7.

[51] Gladstone to Sandon, 9 Mar. 1836, BL Add. MS 44355, f. 31.

Nothing came of this plan, but Gladstone certainly intended going to Oxford to vote for the statute condemning Hampden and he was only prevented from doing so by his desire to vote on Buxton's motion on Negro Apprenticeship on 21 March.[52]

Yet despite his eager condemnation of Hampden, it would be unwise to conclude that Gladstone was so committed to the Tractarian cause by the mid-1830s that he had surrendered his independence of mind or action, still less that he had become absorbed into the group. After all, the opposition to Hampden also included evangelicals like John Hill of St. Edmund Hall, who genuinely believed that the new professor was a heretic, unfit to teach the young.

The Tractarians were to be constantly made aware that Gladstone would go his own way. Newman, for example, was less than enthusiastic about Gladstone's speech on the Irish Church in 1835, and told Rogers so.[53] Pusey felt Gladstone was far too concerned to satisfy everyone's point of view. He was not pleased by Gladstone's behaviour over the Metropolis Churches Fund in June 1836,[54] and was very disappointed that Gladstone did not take a stronger line, initially, over the proposed use of lay agents by the Church Pastoral Aid Society. His letter to Acland on this matter was, Pusey informed Harrison, without 'a trace of Church Principle, but just as he was about the Metropolis Church Society, carving out, on this side and that, how you might satisfy all people's unreasonable desires, and with scarcely any definite views except finding a sop for each of the mouths of one hundred headed Cerberus'.[55]

This independence of mind became more pronounced as the movement began to excite more heated opposition in reaction to what, for Gladstone, were its increasingly 'morbid tempers'. He read the first instalment of Froude's *Remains* 'with repeated regrets'.[56] But the growing divergence from historic High-Churchmanship and what Gladstone understood by Church

---

[52] *Diary*, ii, 21 Mar. 1839.

[53] A. Mozley, op. cit., ii, 86. This was the speech on the Irish Church delivered on 31 March 1835 containing the germ of his ideas on Church and State; see Chapter 2 above.

[54] The Metropolis Churches Fund, with Gladstone on its committee, was created in 1836 to provide for the building of churches in London.

[55] Pusey to Harrison, 28 Dec. 1838, Pusey MSS. For the dispute in general, see Chapter 2 above.

[56] *Morley*, i. 306.

principles, was to produce an intense conflict of loyalties for him. On the one hand he was becoming more apprehensive about the direction the movement was taking, but on the other he still felt it necessary to defend the Oxford leaders from public attack. When in July 1838, in the course of a debate on the Maynooth grant, Lord Morpeth used the occasion to denounce the Tractarians as crypto-papists and then read extracts from the *Remains*, Gladstone felt it incumbent upon him to protest. To suggest that Roman Catholic principles were being inculcated in the University of Oxford was, he declared, a 'vulgar calumny'. He tried to defend the publication of the work on the grounds that in the preface the editor had expressly guarded himself against entertaining the opinions of the author, stating that he gave it to the world 'as the singular production of a remarkable mind'.[57]

Gladstone's own book *Church Principles* clearly aimed to state, or perhaps restate, the theology of the revival in its broader sense, to show that these principles were moderate and in no way contrary to the Anglican tradition. It was imperative, he told an old university friend, Lord Arthur Hervey, that 'the general principles relating to the nature and function of the Church . . . should be kept carefully apart from the private opinions, the ambiguous or more than ambiguous theories, and the partial infusion of morbid tempers with which they have been associated by some of the writers at Oxford'.[58] Fortunately Froude's work had not appeared to have 'many or any imitators of such extravagances as it contains respecting the English Reformation'. Gladstone took comfort in the fact that the generation of clergy who would replace Newman and his friends were, as far as he knew, less likely to succumb to this morbid spirit. 'They will be less of cloistermen, and will have more I think both of the wisdom of the serpent, and of real ingrained moderation.' It would have been surprising, given human experience, if the chief movers of so great a reaction in the English Church, had mixed nothing of inferior quality with the truths for which they were standard bearers.[59]

[57] *Hansard*, 3 series, xliv, 818–19.
[58] Gladstone to Lord C. A. Hervey, 11 Nov. 1840, Bodleian MS Eng. lett. c 297.
[59] Ibid.

Perhaps because he was so unacquainted with the actual situation in the University, Gladstone had profoundly misjudged the temper of the rising generation. Far from displaying 'ingrained moderation', it was the younger men, W. G. Ward, Frederick Oakeley, William Palmer of Magdalen, John Brande Morris, and others, who were beginning to force the movement into a more extreme and pro-Roman direction. Gladstone could not understand, still less sympathize, with this trend. For him the object of the revival was what it had been at the beginning: the revival of caroline theology to meet the exigencies of the times. By the late 1830s his theological position was more or less fixed, and as *Church Principles* showed, fixed firmly in the tradition represented by the conservative wing of the movement led by William Palmer of Worcester. This position satisfied him as historic, balanced, and well able to withstand the buffets of Roman Catholic polemic. He was unmoved by the problems that had begun to disturb Newman: the implications of the appeal to antiquity; the need to repudiate the Reformation and remould the Church of England on the basis of primitive tradition; the need to strive for reunion with the centre of Unity, the see of Peter.

Despite his hostility to ultra-Protestantism, Gladstone was, even before the secession of his sister and friends, a resolute anti-Papalist. While yearning for Christian unity, he was convinced that the Church of England possessed an unshakeable claim to an authentic apostolic title and, having seen the workings of the Roman system at first hand in Italy and elsewhere, he was sure that if the charge of schism could be laid against Anglicanism, still more could the charge of idolatry be laid against Rome.

Having learned in Italy from Hope of the scheme to erect a memorial to the Reformation martyrs, he subscribed, even though he realized that it was meant as a distinct protest against the Tractarians and as an act of adhesion to the principles of the Reformation, repudiated by Froude.[60] In 1838 Newman published his *Lectures on Justification* dealing with one of the tenderest points at issue between Catholic and Protestant. This also caused Gladstone 'the greatest apprehension'.[61] While not

[60] W. E. Gladstone to J. Gladstone, 22 July 1847, Hawn. P.
[61] Gladstone to Hervey, ibid.

certain that he had entirely grasped Newman's subtle meaning, he saw in the work the spectre of human 'merit', and a sermon in the fifth volume of Newman's *Sermons* published in 1840 had, he told Manning, staggered him exceedingly.[62]

Even in 1841, however, Gladstone was still prepared to accept these pro-Roman tendencies as an aberration, a temporary phase through which the movement was passing. When in late February, therefore, Newman published Tract XC, Gladstone met it with surprising equanimity, despite the fact that many opposed it as the most blatant example of the Romeward direction of the movement that had yet appeared. 'Newman has again burned his fingers,' he wrote to Lyttelton, comparing the Tract to the publication of Froude's *Remains.*[63]

He felt the terms in which Newman had characterized the present state of the Church of England in his introduction were 'calculated to give both pain and alarm', and that 'the whole aspect of the tract is like the assumption of a new position', though the proposition for which Newman argued was manifestly correct. The fact that the Thirty-nine articles were not meant to bind all men to a particular interpretation and were designed to keep as many Catholic sympathizers as possible within the reformed church seemed to him 'an ABC truth, almost a truism, of the history of the reign of Elizabeth'. The most serious feature to his mind was that, in an attempt to restrain his disciples from defecting to Rome, Newman had occupied their point of view exclusively and in so doing had 'placed himself quite outside the Church of England in point of spirit and sympathy'. But even in this he has acted, Gladstone believed, 'with very honest intentions' and in his *Letter to Jelf* seemed to have reoccupied some of his old ground.[64]

Gladstone had not attempted to participate directly in the controversy surrounding the Tract.[65] He did not even read it until 12 March, four days after the four tutors had published their *Letter* and practically on the eve of the proceedings of the Hebdomadal Council. Even then he did so at the suggestion of Sir Robert Inglis. He seems to have decided not to intervene

[62] Gladstone to Manning, 22 Apr. 1841, *Lathbury*, i. 235.
[63] Gladstone to Lyttelton, 18 Mar. 1841, *Lathbury*, i. 233.
[64] Ibid., 234.
[65] See Chadwick, op. cit., 181–9.

when the popular press took up the matter. But by the end of 1841 he was forced to lay aside detachment and commit himself to the fray.

The two matters that prompted this direct action were the problems of the Jerusalem bishopric in the autumn and the controversy surrounding the election of a new Poetry Professor at Oxford. The Jerusalem bishopric was of rather wider importance, but with particular implications for the Tractarians. Although it had the support of some High-Churchmen, Newman regarded it with utter horror, writing in the *British Critic* of the English bishops becoming 'the august protectors of Nestorians, Monophysites, and all the heretics we can hear of'.[66] Gladstone later maintained that it was this that 'snapped the link' which bound Newman to the English Church.[67] This was, perhaps, too simple a view, but as Newman himself wrote: 'It brought me to the beginning of the end.'[68] The Poetry Professorship on the other hand, was a more exclusively Oxford affair, a trial of strength between the Tractarians and their opponents, which resulted in their first defeat as a party.

Gladstone's real involvement in the Jerusalem bishopric began only after the scheme had been officially sanctioned by the British government. On the 28 October he was invited to become one of the Trustees of the endowment fund.[69] The invitation clearly embarrassed him. Despite having dined a fortnight earlier with the King of Prussia's special envoy, Chevalier Bunsen, to celebrate the foundation of the bishopric, he was not entirely happy with it. But he was worried lest his refusal be interpreted as open hostility to the whole project.[70]

His own view, initially, seems to have been that the bishopric

---

[66] *British Critic*, July 1841, quoted *Lathbury*, i. 229.

[67] Ornsby, op. cit., ii. 282.

[68] M. J. Svaglic (ed.), J. H. Newman, *Apologia pro vita sua* (1967), 136.

[69] Gladstone to Blomfield, 28 Oct. 1841, Bishop of London, *Lathbury*, i. 236–8. For full details of the scheme see Chadwick, op. cit., 189–93 and R. W. Greaves, 'The Jerusalem Bishopric, 1841', *English Historical Review*, lxiv (July 1949).

[70] *Lathbury*, i. 236–8. Gladstone had first met Bunsen in Rome in 1839 at the suggestion of Hamilton: Hamilton to Gladstone, 20 Feb. 1839, BL Add. MS 44183, f. 182. He later felt that the whole project of an Anglican bishopric in Jerusalem had been 'the child of Bunsen's fertile and energetic brain', Ornsby, op. cit., ii. 282. In 1846 he informed his wife that Ashley was hand in glove with Bunsen 'who in my opinion has done the Church of England more mischief than any man alive', 1 May 1846, Gladstone to his wife, Hawn. P.

was acceptable provided it was understood as a means of providing for Anglicans in the area, for members of other Protestant churches who might wish to place themselves under its jurisdiction and as a centre for missionary work among Jews and Druses. He was therefore alarmed to discover that some of the evangelical proponents of the scheme, and perhaps Bunsen himself, saw it as a means of absorbing the ancient local churches and even as a device for proselytizing. He was also concerned at the proposal to retain the Augsburg Confession alongside the Thirty-nine Articles, a proposal which he informed Bunsen, seemed to him 'a virtual and substantial adoption by the English Church of *a new Confession*'.[71]

Further letters to Bunsen and a breakfast party with him and the Prussian theologian Abeken on 5 November did little to clarify matters in Gladstone's eyes.[72] The arrangements still seemed insufficiently worked out and the whole scheme lacked definitive ecclesiastical sanction.[73] The next day he wrote to Hope asking for advice.[74] But, although unhappy, he did attend the consecration of the new bishop, Dr Alexander, on 7 November.

Hope, who had been called in during the summer to help frame the parliamentary bill necessary for the consecration of a bishop exercising spiritual jurisdiction over Anglican congregations in a foreign country, was violently against the scheme. By now close to Newman, he tried to make Gladstone aware of the opponents' point of view. The scheme was, he told him, 'a perfect act of communion' with Lutheranism which would have disastrous consequences among Anglicans and 'disparage us with other Catholic Churches'. Moreover it was a plan for constructing a new 'catholicity of extent' against the Church of Rome, a plan for 'gathering up the scraps of Christendom and making a new Church out of them'.[75]

By this time Gladstone needed little persuasion, although he did not feel 'driven to the length of sinister conclusions' that

[71] Gladstone to Bunsen, 3 Nov. 1841, *Lathbury*, i. 241.
[72] *Diary*, iii, 5 Nov. 1841.
[73] Gladstone to Bunsen, 5 Nov. 1841, BL Add. MS 44111, f. 194.
[74] *Lathbury*, i, 242–3.
[75] Hope to Gladstone, 19 Nov. 1841, BL Add. MS 44214, ff. 177–9, cf. his letter to Newman, Ornsby, op. cit., i. 304–6.

Hope did.[76] An article in the *Globe*, extracted from the *Allgemeine Zeitung*, which declared that by accepting the scheme the Church of England has proclaimed its distinctive institutions of secondary importance and had united its ecclesiastical system to that of Germany, depressed him immensely. He wanted Hope to use his influence with *The Times* to get a firm protest entered against it. 'I am ready individually to brave misconstruction for the sake of union with any Christian man, provided the terms of union be not contrary to sound principle,' he write on 20 November, '. . . but to declare the living constitution of a Christian Church to be of secondary moment is of course in my view equivalent to a denial of a portion of the faith.'[77] The scheme was 'ill digested' and 'full of hazards'.[78] The previous Sunday he had read the Augsburg Confession. Its eucharistic teaching and avowal of the doctrine of Catholic consent, rather than the principle of private judgement, pleased him. He was, however, worried that 'it seems to declare that extraordinary doctrine that it is a sin not to have an absolute certainty of personal forgiveness and acceptance'.[79]

Although prepared to press on with the scheme, he was more and more struck by Hope's remark that the whole matter should be thoroughly examined by competent theologians before it received final consideration by the bishops.[80] So, on the 23 November he went to Cambridge to see Dr Mill, the Hebrew scholar, who said he would be prepared to undertake such an examination, if called upon;[81] this came to nothing. On 27 November Gladstone learned from the Bishop of London that delaying the execution of the Trust until the scheme had been sanctioned by a meeting of the entire episcopate was 'out of the question'.[82]

Deeply shocked, Gladstone returned the deed of trusteeship unsigned and requested 'an authoritative and distinct declaration of the nature of the scheme'.[83] The affair had been, he

---

[76] Gladstone to Hope, 21 Nov. 1841, BL Add. MS 44214, f. 183.
[77] Gladstone to Hope, 20 Nov. 1841, ibid., f. 180.
[79] Ibid., f. 186.
[80] Gladstone to Hope, 20 Nov. 1841, ibid., f. 182; 21 Nov. 1841, ibid., f. 187.
[81] Gladstone to Hope, 25 Nov. 1841, *Lathbury*, i. 247–9.
[82] Ornsby, op. cit., i. 296–7.
[83] Gladstone to Blomfield, 30 Nov. 1841, *Lathbury*, i. 251.

confessed to Manning, 'one of the saddest and most anxious' in which he had ever been engaged.[84] On receiving the bishop's letter he felt the ground had been cut from under his feet. He had been betrayed: 'It is impossible that the Church of England can continue to be delivered over bound hand and foot into the hands of any knot of prelates—such an idea gives not a foundation broad enough for the august fabric of Catholicism.'[85] For the first time he had felt really alarmed for the Church's unity. The danger could still be averted but 'if Newman lighted the flame of discord by Tract 90 on one side it is a strange way, instead of extinguishing, to rival it by a yet brighter glare in another quarter of our close beleaguered camp'.[86]

Gladstone's attitude to the Jerusalem bishopric demonstrated both his moderation and his desire to keep both sides together by some sort of mediation. Despite declining the trusteeship, he refused to take Hope's extreme view of the proceedings. He still retained, he told Bunsen, 'a sincere belief that the Bishopric of Jerusalem might be so constituted as to produce highly beneficial results, without any sacrifice of principle'.[87] Newman's protest, which Hope had sent him, seemed 'a premature adoption of the worst possible interpretation that the scheme can bear'.[88] He had cherished a real hope that the idea of submitting the scheme to competent theologians would prove an effective way forward. This hope had been dashed. But, none the less, he refused to be dismayed. He told Manning he could not believe that the Church had been 'saved through great and portentous crises from its foes and from its friends to fall beneath a momentary freak', or that the pillar of cloud had conducted her this far in order that 'she may utterly perish in the wilderness before she touched the land of her rest'.[89]

The essential moderation and desire for a just compromise to

[84] Gladstone to Manning, 30 Nov. 1841, BL Add. MS 44247, f. 103.
[85] Ibid., f. 106.
[86] Ibid.
[87] Gladstone to Bunsen, 6 Dec. 1841, BL Add. MS 44111, f. 217.
[88] Gladstone to Hope, 30 Nov. 1841, BL Add. MS 44214, f. 206.
[89] Gladstone to Manning, 30 Nov. 1841, BL Add. MS 44247, f. 107. In 1843 Gladstone put together material for an article on the Jerusalem bishopric surveying the different attitudes to the matter and putting forward his own feelings. BL Add. MS 44683, ff. 92–106.

preserve the Church's unity was demonstrated most clearly, however, in the struggle over the Poetry Professorship.[90] In October 1841 Keble had retired as Professor of Poetry and the fellows of Trinity put forward his friend Isaac Williams as their candidate for the vacant chair. Williams was a gentle man, respected as the author of some pleasing religious verse. But he was also the author of three Tracts, two of which, dealing with reserve in communicating religious knowledge, had excited particular criticism from Tractarian opponents. Brasenose had put forward a rival candidate called Garbett.

Pusey, perhaps inadvertently, turned the whole election into a theological trial of strength. He issued a circular asking for support for Williams on the ground that his known religious views would ensure that the office of Poetry Professor would be used to minister to religious truth. Gladstone regarded Pusey's intervention as unfortunate, liable to prejudice Williams' cause. He felt that if the opposition to him was due to his connection with the Tracts, then it would have been better for some independent person, a fellow of Williams's own College perhaps, to have stated so publicly.[91] But he did not believe that it was right to exclude someone from public office in the university for holding theological opinions that had not been formally condemned by the Church. Therefore when Badeley, one of Williams's committee, wrote requesting his support, Gladstone assured him of it.[92] Gladstone had, however, heard of a proposal, that both Williams and Garbett might withdraw in favour of another candidate. In the same letter he expressed his earnest hope that this proposal might be accepted. Nothing would be more calamitous for the Church, he told Badeley, than the spectacle of Oxford divided against itself upon matters of theology.[93]

Convinced that Williams was likely to lose, the withdrawal of both candidates seemed to Gladstone to offer the best solution. On 3 December he wrote an impassioned letter to Frederic Rogers, one of Williams's London committee, deploring the

---

[90] See Chadwick, op. cit., 202–5.
[91] Gladstone to Hope, 27 Nov. 1841, BL Add. MS 44214, f. 201.
[92] Gladstone to Badeley, 30 Nov. 1841, *Lathbury*, i. 266–8.
[93] Ibid., 267.

blow to Catholic principles which Williams's defeat would imply.[94]

But Gladstone was wrong in assuming that an offer for mutual withdrawal existed. Indeed, far from abating, the strife was becoming more bitter. Early in December, Roundell Palmer, the chairman of Williams's committee attempted to solicit Ashley's vote. Ashley refused on the grounds that the tract on Reserve was open to grave objections and that Keble had used his position as Poetry Professor to publish 'sundry poems of admitted talent and disputed theology'.[95] He then accepted the invitation to become chairman of Garbett's committee and issued a circular making it clear that, as far as he was concerned, the contest hinged on theological considerations.

Gladstone wrote to Viscount Sandon urging him to beg that Ashley avoid the scandal of a contest for the sake of the Church. To pass judgement upon Williams's opinions in this way would, he wrote, have much the same effect as a sentence by the church on the question of baptismal regeneration would have had twenty-five or thirty years before: 'the great mass of the best and most useful clergymen then in the Church must infallibly have been cast out'.[96]

Feeling that he was not alone in wanting to avert a crisis, Gladstone set about organizing his own scheme for a joint withdrawal. Assured of Manning and Hope's support, he wrote to several people in an effort to form an intermediate body that would propose to the committees of both candidates that they should withdraw in favour of some third person.[97] A circular, calling for an address by members of Convocation, went out on 23 December, the nine signatures headed by that of Lord Devon, the High Steward, with Gladstone's at the bottom.[98] Eleven days later the address followed, bearing the names of 244 non-resident members of Convocation, five of them bishops, and including the signature of Bagot, the Bishop of Oxford himself.[99]

---

[94] Gladstone to Rogers, 3 Dec. 1841, BL Add. MS 44358, ff. 205–12.

[95] See E. Hodder, *The Life and Work of the Seventh Earl of Shaftesbury, K. G.*, (1886), i. 389 ff.

[96] Gladstone to Sandon, 14 Dec. 1841, BL Add. MS 44357, f. 287.

[97] Gladstone to Manning, 18 Dec. 1841, BL Add. MS 44247, f. 115.

[98] A copy is in BL Add. MS 44247, f. 130.

[99] Gladstone to Hope, 3 Jan. 1842, *Lathbury*, i. 269.

Gladstone was particularly hopeful that the bishops' signatures would carry weight with Williams's committee. Indeed he felt that the bishops themselves, especially the Bishop of Oxford, would feel their position and authority compromised if the contest continued.[100]

In fact, Bagot's intervention proved decisive, but caused considerable embarrassment to Gladstone. No sooner had he signed the address than Dr Gilbert, the Principal of Brasenose, put out a letter declaring that he had no intention whatsoever of withdrawing his candidate. Faced with this, Bagot wrote to Gladstone informing him that, given a declared rejection of the compromise, he felt it was best, both for the University and the Church, if Williams withdrew unconditionally.[101] After a short exchange of letters between Gladstone and the bishop, this proposal was put to Williams's committee, much to the distress of Keble.[102]

Williams himself was quite prepared to accept Bagot's request. But the President of Trinity, Ingram, was jealous of the bishop's interference in university affairs. Before Williams resigned, therefore, an agreement was made for a comparison of pledged votes. This gave Garbett 921 to Williams's 623 and on 20 January 1842, a week before the election, Williams withdrew his name.[103]

The Tractarians were naturally vexed by this turn of events. Pusey blamed Gladstone and told Newman that he was 'sacrificing us to his own views' and 'taking too much upon himself'.[104] Keble was also disgusted, though Newman tried to sooth him:

I do not agree with Gladstone, but I think he hopes that if no collision takes place, Catholic opinions will gradually gain the ascendency. Again, his great object is the religionising of the *State*; you must recollect this. He thinks that even a division of opinion in the Church, though real, does not hinder that up to a certain point.[105]

This was true, but Gladstone had never intended the issue to end

---

[100] Ibid.
[101] Bagot to Gladstone, 1 Jan. 1842, BL Add. MS 44359, f. 2.
[102] Ibid., 16 Jan. 1842, f. 46.
[103] G. Prevost (ed.), *The Autobiography of Isaac Williams* (1892), 145.
[104] 18 Jan. 1842, Liddon, op. cit., ii. 267.
[105] 6 Jan. 1842, A. Mozley, op. cit., ii. 343.

this way. Hope informed Newman that when he had first put forward his scheme, Gladstone had every reason to suppose it would be successful. The bishop had made his subscription conditional on it being understood that his intervention would not be ineffectual. The origin of the proposal for Williams's sole withdrawal had come from him. It was one which Gladstone himself had never contemplated till he had received the bishop's answer and, even then, he had done no more than acquiesce in what the bishop proposed.[106]

By early 1842, therefore, Gladstone had twice attempted to use his influence to keep the opposing sides together and maintain the Church's unity. While sympathetic to the Tractarians, he was motivated by broader considerations than they, and his object was not the furtherance of their cause in any partisan way. Despite some bad feeling from individual Tractarians, they mostly accepted this. 'Everyone must admire a man like Gladstone, in spite of his Tylerising,' Newman wrote to Hope in February.[107]

Gladstone's defence, however, did not stop there. The possibility of an official condemnation of Tractarian principles by Church leaders worried him increasingly. No sooner had the struggle over the Poetry Professorship drawn to a close, than he learned from Philip Pusey and Hope of the concern in Oxford that the bishops might make some move of this sort at their forthcoming meeting in London.

Convinced that if this became generally known it would provoke demands for severe measures to be taken against the Tractarians and, as he told Hope, 'to deter sober minded men from joining in the hue and cry', it seemed to him that some indication should be given 'of the immense hazards that will be run'.[108] He therefore proposed to send an anonymous letter to *The Times* on the matter.

As it happened, Gladstone's plan came to nothing since Delane, the editor, refused to publish the letter on the grounds

---

[106] Hope to Manning, 20 Jan. 1842, Oratory MSS.

[107] 9 Feb. 1842, *Correspondence of John Henry Newman with John Keble and others, 1839–1845*, edited by members of the Oratory (1911), 183. By 'Tylerising' Newman meant that Gladstone was not a good party man.

[108] Gladstone to Hope, 30 Jan. 1842, Hope-Scott MS 3672, ff. 169–70.

that it touched on 'controverted points of theology'.[109] None the less, the letter provides further evidence of Gladstone's own attitude to the movement at this rather critical juncture.[110] In it he made clear, against what he termed 'the professors of Ultra-Protestantism', that the doctrines commonly associated with Puseyism, 'those great Catholic principles which distinguish our Church from many other Protestant bodies', were in fact the doctrines found in Anglican formularies. These doctrines were held by men such as Palmer, whose Treatise was dedicated to the Archbishop of Canterbury, Dr Hook, and even the examining chaplains of the Archbishop of York and the Bishop of London. All this proved how insufficient were 'the newspaper definitions of Puseyism', and how 'ignorant of the history, spirit and constitution of the Church' were those persons who 'are too apt to denounce under that title her unequivocal and holy teaching'.

It went on to sound a note that was to become increasingly evident in Gladstone's defence of the Tractarians: the injustice of a one-sided censure. Would the bishops also condemn Dr Arnold's views, or Baptist Noels's? The 'palsy of a century' had lain upon the Church. Was the 'exuberance of zeal' more worthy of sharper handling than 'the languor of decay', 'the lethargy of worldliness' or 'the pestilence of heresy'? 'Some ears are itching for language such as this from the Anglican Episcopate, but they are mere dreamers who can seriously expect to hear it.'

He concluded with a solemn warning. How would those who were the objects of this coming censure react? It was the business of those who professed Catholic truth to be not where they liked or where they chose, but to be 'where they have the promise of the Spirit'. When the character of Catholicity is erased, 'the Church leaves them, and not they the Church'. If the ill-omened hour should come when the spiritual life of the English Church shall be found 'too faint to animate a Catholic system', their duty could not be denied, 'athough the struggle go to dividing bone from marrow, and to the rending asunder flesh from spirit'. In other words there would be sucession from the Church, and *Sic*

[109] Delane to Gladstone, 31 Jan. 1842, *Lathbury*, i. 279.
[110] The letter is reprinted in *Lathbury*, i. 270–8.

in such circumstances, Gladstone appeared to argue, secession would be justified.

At this time, however, he was still largely unaware of the existence of an increasingly pro-Roman element within Tractarianism. On 31 July 1842 he walked back from evensong at the Margaret Chapel with Robert Williams, a former Tory MP and himself a sympathizer with the more extreme group, in the hope of learning from him 'the general view of the ulterior section of the Oxford writers'.[111] What he learned startled him; they looked not merely to the renewal and development of Catholic teaching within the Church of England, but considered the main condition of that development 'to be reunion with the Church of Rome as the See of Peter'.[112] This was a shattering blow for Gladstone, not least because it came so soon after the upheaval caused by the reception of his own sister Helen into the Roman Catholic Church by Dr Wiseman.[113]

Helen's conversion was a considerable source of pain and embarrassment to him, especially as he was now more in the public eye. He tried to convince himself that he was not to blame and that the conversion was, in any case, 'a temporary and artificial amelioration' which did not 'seem to reach far or to pierce deep'.[114] But with this, and the revelations of Williams, he felt increasingly vulnerable. Early in the New Year he drafted 'a sort of protest on Church affairs', in reality an address to the Archbishop of Canterbury, written 'because in connection with our published works or otherwise we have been publicly accused at various times and with more or less urgency of having contributed to produce or prepare the way for such secessions'.[115] In the end the address was never sent. Manning felt it more than the situation demanded and that it 'might encourage the evil by assigning to it too much importance'.[116]

---

[111] *Diary*, iii, 31 July 1842.

[112] Ibid.

[113] For this, see *Diary*, iii, 11 June 1842, and Checkland, op. cit., 329–30.

[114] Gladstone to his wife, 16 Aug. 1842, Hawn. P.

[115] BL Add. MS 44732, f. 15; *Diary*, iii, 14 Jan. 1843. In *Protestantism or Popery* (1843), Edward Young cited Helen Gladstone as one whose apostasy was due to the Romanizing tendencies of *Church Principles*. Gladstone protested that she was unacquainted with the book. BL Add. MS 44359, f. 250.

[116] Gladstone to his wife, 13 Jan. 1843, Hawn. P. On 29 December 1842 he had tried to formulate again his own religious beliefs in the form of 'Twenty Seven Propositions relating to current questions in theology', *Autobiographica*, 236–45.

Gladstone, however, was not deterred from defending individual Tractarians when he felt they had been treated
unjustly. When in May 1843 Pusey was suspended from
preaching for two years by a Vice-Chancellor's court for a
sermon in which he had affirmed the Real Presence, he wrote to
Pusey expressing his surprise and regret.[117] With other non-
resident members of Convocation he signed an address to the
Vice-Chancellor, protesting at the course adopted. Although he
would have preferred non-interference in an ordinary case, he
told Manning, 'I thought too much was at issue in this
instance.'[118]

Despite this, Gladstone was still much troubled by the
romanizing elements within the movement which had taken
control of the *British Critic* and were using it as a mouthpiece for
its views. While at Fasque in the summer, he drafted an article
on 'Catholic development in the Church of England', which was
later published in the October edition of the *Foreign and Colonial
Quarterly Review* under the title 'Present Aspect of the Church,
1843'.[119] Its object was to vindicate what he considered the
original object of the movement, the revival of Church principles. The growth, among a portion of the Oxford divines, of a
disposition to fraternize with the Church of Rome 'in a manner
as well as a degree which I cannot but think objectionable and
dangerous' had made him, he told his father, anxious to separate
'that section and its tendencies in the public view from the
general body of those who hold that which my conscience
assumes me are the true and genuine principles of the English
Church'.[120]

His aim was, in fact, remarkably similar to that of William
Palmer who, in the late summer of 1843, published his *Narrative
of Events connected with the publication of the Tracts for the Times*, an
attack on the pro-Roman party in an effort to save the
movement by rallying the old High Church wing and the
moderates.[121] Palmer sent it to Gladstone, who read it on 13
October. Three days later he wrote Palmer a letter of thanks. It

[117] Gladstone to Pusey, 30 June 1843, Pusey MSS.
[118] Gladstone to Manning, 26 June 1843, BL Add. MS 44247, f. 163.
[119] *Diary*, iii, 2 Sept. 1843 reprinted in *Gleanings*, v. 1–80.
[120] Gladstone to John Gladstone, 28 Oct. 1843, Hawn. P.
[121] See W. Palmer's remarks, *Contemporary Review*, xliii (May 1883), 636–59.

was, Gladstone declared, another important service Palmer had rendered the Church.[122]

No sooner than Gladstone's article had appeared, he received most disturbing news: Newman had lost his faith in the Catholicity of the English Church. In the article, Gladstone had written of his basic confidence in Newman's allegiance to the Church, his conviction that Newman would reject 'with abhorrence the temptation to apostatise'.[123] Now he learned that he had been mistaken.

On 24 October he received from Manning a letter, enclosing a note that Newman had sent Manning, a letter explaining his recent resignation from St. Mary's. Gladstone read it 'with pain and dismay'.[124] He could only suggest that Newman had broken down under the strain. But four days later he received another letter, enclosing a second note from Newman in which Newman declared that since the summer of 1839 he had believed that 'the Church of Rome is the Catholic Church, and ours not a branch of the Catholic Church because not in communion with Rome'.[125] Gladstone was appalled. He replied immediately: 'I stagger to and fro, like a drunken man, and am at my wits end.'[126] Newman's account of his views was 'more like the expressions of some Faust gambling for his soul, than the records of the inner life of a great Christian teacher'.[127] He urged Manning to write to Newman telling him that he could not accept the letter as it stood, its real meaning was too difficult to grasp, its ideas did not seem to hang together. What construction would be put on his words if the letter was made public? It would irrevocably damage his authority and character. Men would say, 'He whom we have lost is not the man we thought.'[128] Shaken, Gladstone refused to abandon hope. He still believed Newman would not forsake the Church. If he had

---

[122] Gladstone to Palmer, 16 Oct. 1843, *Lathbury*, i. 280.

[123] *Gleanings*, v. 67.

[124] Gladstone to Manning, 24 Oct. 1843, *Lathbury*, i. 281–3; *Diary*, iii, 24 Oct. 1843. Newman had resigned from St. Mary's on 18 September. Before this he had issued a formal retraction of his violent language against the Roman Church. The letters to Manning are printed in the *Apologia*.

[125] *Diary*, iii, 28 Oct. 1843.

[126] Gladstone to Manning, 28 Oct. 1843, *Lathbury*, i. 283.

[127] Ibid., 284.

[128] Ibid., 285.

carried 'this fatal conviction' for nearly five years in the hope of its being changed, then 'perhaps he may still wait, and God's inexhaustible mercy may overflow upon him and us'.[129]

But Gladstone realized that this hope might, as before, prove illusory. Assuming that Newman was lost to the Church and his apostasy imminent, he felt that he should resurrect his idea of a declaration by those associated with Newman, of their loyalty to the English Church and their resistance to the actual system and claims of Rome. Without waiting for Manning's reply he began another letter two days later suggesting that Manning, Pusey, and Palmer might draw up such a document. The Church of England had the right to expect, even from those whose beliefs afforded no reasonable ground for complaint, something positive and emphatic, adapted to 'the greatest crisis and the sharpest that the Church has known since the Reformation'.[130] For as Gladstone made clear, this was how he regarded the apostasy of a man 'whose intellectual stature is among the very first of his age, and who has indisputably headed the most powerful movement . . . that the Church has known, at least for two centuries'.[131]

In the midst of writing it, he received Manning's reply warning against precipitous action. Nothing should be done that might goad Newman to a hasty act. Gladstone saw the logic of this, but he was convinced Newman had to be made aware of the dreadful consequences of his secession. He left the next course of action in Manning's hands.[132] Gladstone's anxiety for Newman continued. Towards the end of November, Manning sent him a letter he had received from Pusey counselling calm and blaming the current unsettlement of the extreme Oxford men on the 'painful condition of our Church' and the conduct of the bishops. Gladstone found much to agree with, but felt Pusey's letter 'one sided'. No vigorous effort to stop defection could be expected from him.[133]

Every approach should be used to save Newman, but there was a need for sensitivity. 'What is wanted is that cords of silk

[129] Ibid., 284.
[130] Gladstone to Manning, 30 Oct. 1843, *Lathbury*, i. 286.
[131] Ibid., 287.
[132] Ibid., 287–8.
[133] Gladstone to Manning, 22 Nov. 1843, *Lathbury*, i. 288.

should one by one be thrown over him to bind him to the Church,' he wrote to Manning at the end of the year. 'Every manifestation of sympathy and confidence in him, as a man, must have some small effect.'[134] He hoped Manning might use his influence with some of the bishops. Their charges had 'overshot their mark in the Protestant sense'. Could this not be moderated and an attempt made not to open 'fresh sores'? He was even tempted to use the opportunity afforded by Newman's present of his recently published sermons to open a correspondence with him himself.[135]

So, from the end of 1843, Gladstone was aware of Newman's crisis of faith. But such was his respect for him, and so fearful seemed the consequences of his secession, that he could not bring himself to admit Newman as lost to the Church of England. The year 1844 was to be one of crisis for Gladstone himself, and it was to Newman, perhaps deliberately, that he turned to share his feelings, as Maynooth forced him to accept the impossibility of his cherished political ideals. It was as if he wished Newman to realize that he too was racked with doubt and unsure of the way forward.

Despite this knowledge and his own political anxieties, Gladstone continued to defend the Tractarians when they appeared the victims of unjust attack, fighting for the movement's original purpose in the face of the Romanizing wing and still attempting to restrain them from their Romeward course. In May 1844 he considered publishing an account of the proceedings against R. G. Macmullen, a young Tractarian zealot whom Dr Hampden had prevented from proceeding to the BD degree, in order that the Church at large might be made more fully aware of them.[136] It was a matter of vital importance, Gladstone told Hope, a further instance of one-sided condemnation. Was a policy of 'stern compression and repression' to be pursued on one hand, 'in conjunction with a policy of licence and laxity on the other'?[137]

The most important event in the Tractarian struggles of 1844

---

[134] Gladstone to Manning, 31 Dec. 1843, *Lathbury*, i. 291.
[135] Ibid. This was the origin of his letter to Newman about 'Feasting in captivity', see Chapter Four, p. 110.
[136] For details of this affair, see Chadwick, op. cit., 205.
[137] Gladstone to Hope, 16 May 1844, *Lathbury*, i. 302.

was the publication in June of W. G. Ward's *Ideal of a Christian Church*. Written as a reply to Palmer's *Narrative*, it made clear to all that for one section of the Tractarians at least, the Ideal was now to be found in the Roman Catholic Church of the Counter Reformation. Gladstone read Ward's book at Fasque in September and immediately determined to answer it. In December his review appeared in the *Quarterly*.[138] It was a stringent criticism of Ward's method and conclusions and of Ward himself in his position as a priest of the Church of England. It focused on four areas: Ward's view of the Reformation; his charges against the contemporary English Church; his philosophy of the supremacy of individual conscience; and the whole question of Ward's ecclesiastical allegiance.

On the first Gladstone denounced Ward for attempting to evaluate the Reformation on philosophical rather than properly historical grounds, a thrust that was both important and fair. On the second he criticized him for performing his task not in a calm minded or equitable way but in the spirit of 'railing accusation'.[139] His argument for the supremacy of conscience resolved itself, Gladstone maintained, into a purely subjective theory of truth. Mr Ward was 'strangely bitten . . . with the spirit of the age'. He owed 'far more of his mental culture to Mr. John Stuart Mill than to the whole range of Christian divines'.[140]

The final part of the review dealt with the 'very grave questions of ecclesiastical allegiance' and the disturbing effects the books would produce in various quarters.[141] Whatever Ward's private beliefs, he and those like him were not, Gladstone contended, released from their obligations to continue in the communion of the English Church. Although their private judgement might prefer the religious system of the Roman Church, so long as they could not deny that the Church of England was their 'spiritual parent and guide ordained of

---

[138] *Quarterly Review*, lxxxv (Dec. 1844); the full version is in *Gleanings*, v. 81–172. Lockhart wished to alter it substantially; see *Purcell*, i. 296, BL Add. MS 44237, f. 371 ff. and *Lathbury*, i. 305 ff.

[139] *Gleanings*, v. 108. See also W. Ward, *W. G. Ward and the Oxford Movement* (1889), 297–302.

[140] Ibid., 141.

[141] Ibid., 150.

God', they owed to her 'not merely adhesion, but allegiance'.[142]

The fact that some members of the Church desired to import the Roman system was indeed, a matter of 'the deepest grief and pain'.[143] But this was an entirely different matter from the contention that such people should, as a matter of consistency, quit the Anglican for the papal communion. Such views as theirs could be held as private opinions within the English Church. It was the duty of churchmen to resist every effort by individuals to draw the bonds of communion tighter than present ecclesiastical formularies permitted.[144]

Although criticial of Ward, Gladstone's review was primarily an attempt to undercut any efforts to eject the pro-Roman element from the Church. It had not been his purpose, he informed Newman, to write against Ward's main propositions. Rather he wished to 'intercept the discussion of them' on account of the 'fatal prejudice which would attach in the general mind' to the true and important things he had said by their association with such 'unrestrained licence of expression, and a precipitancy and cruelty of judgement . . . almost wholly overleaping evidence'.[145]

This explains Gladstone's attitude to the attempt begun in December 1844 by the Heads of Houses in Oxford to deprive Ward of his degrees and to institute a new religious test whereby the Vice-Chancellor should have the power to require a member of the University to subscribe to the Thirty-nine Articles interpreted in a Protestant sense.[146] Gladstone regarded the new test as ridiculous. It was, he told Samuel Wilberforce, no guarantee against Wardism, because it was part of Ward's theory that he was acting wholly within the theory of the promulgators. In any case, precisely what sense the framers of the articles intended could only be known by historical study. He was himself disposed to believe that it was a sense very liberal to the Church of Rome.[147] The Censure of Tract XC, which the Heads proposed on 4 February after withdrawing the idea of a

---

[142] Ibid., 152.
[143] Ibid., 155.
[144] Ibid., 152 ff.
[145] Gladstone to Newman, 23 Jan. 1845, Oratory MSS.
[146] For the details see Chadwick, op. cit., 208–10.
[147] Gladstone to S. Wilberforce, 29 Dec. 1844, W. Ward, op. cit., 323–4.

test, he considered disgraceful. Much as he deplored the recent changes in Newman's views, the proceedings meditated at Oxford were, he told Pusey, 'enough to make the heart burst to witness them'. It was a proposal 'to treat Mr. Newman worse than a dog', and act of 'incredible wickedness'.[148] He wrote to Hawkins, the Provost of Oriel, urging that the matter be delayed.[149]

But it was to no avail. On 13 February, accompanied by Manning and Hope, Gladstone went to the Sheldonian where nearly 1,200 members of Convocation had gathered to vote on the proposals. The *Ideal* was condemned by 777 votes to 386 and Ward deprived of his degrees by 569 to 511. Gladstone voted in the minority in both divisions. When the third proposition, the censure of Tract XC, was put, the two proctors, Guillemarde of Trinity and R. W. Church of Oriel, declared *non placet*, amid cheers and hisses.[150]

Standing with Ward in the rostrum was Frederick Oakeley, who had publicly associated himself with Ward's opinions. Shortly afterwards, he challenged the Bishop of London by claiming the right to hold (though not to teach) Roman Catholic doctrines, while retaining his licence to minister at the Margaret Chapel, where Gladstone often worshipped.

'Oakeley has sadly complicated these vexed affairs,' Gladstone wrote to Manning.[151] He felt unable to subscribe to the fund opened by Hope to meet Oakeley's expenses during the prosecution.[152] But he discussed the matter with Blomfield and, at the end of February, sent the bishop a letter in which he praised Oakeley's personal character and wrote that he could scarcely exaggerate the personal debt he owed him 'as a restorer of the inward life and spirit of Divine worship among us'.[153] Cited before the Court of Arches, Oakeley was suspended; in September he was received into the Roman Catholic Church.

The Tractarians were now in open disarray and the move-

---

[148] Gladstone to Pusey, 7 Feb, 1845, Liddon, op. cit., ii. 430.
[149] *Lathbury*, i. 314 ff.
[150] But Gladstone declined to sign the address thanking the proctors for their action on Tract XC printed in the *English Churchman*, *Diary*, iv, 21 Feb. 1845.
[151] Gladstone to Manning, 17 Mar. 1845, BL Add. MS 44247, f. 257.
[152] Ornsby, op. cit., ii. 58.
[153] Gladstone to Blomfield, 24 Feb. 1845, *Lathbury*, i. 335.

ment on the verge of collapse. After Ward's degradation, Manning had turned to Gladstone and said: 'So begins disaster'.[154] Hope felt much the same. 'This looks like the beginning of the end,' he had written to Gladstone on 10 March.[155] But Gladstone himself, despite the overshadowing of the Maynooth crisis, and possessed of a deep foreboding, refused to be dismayed. Though in the midst of the 'most painful oppression of heart' he wrote to Hope, he was still convinced of the 'great opportunities, the gigantic opportunities of good or evil to the Church', which the course of events would open up. To be ready and alert to serve the Church as the need arose, this was their duty.[156]

To fulfil it might mean a struggle against 'pain, depression, disgust, and even against doubt touching the very root of our position'. But Gladstone was sure in his own mind that such doubt was unjustified. Despite all that had occurred there were grounds of optimism in regard to both the Church of England's present position and its future hopes. Devotional life was increasing. Ascetic institutions were beginning to be restored. Those who had left England for missionary work showed that there was no want of heroic self-devotion. They had 'left all for their Lord's sake in as true and as high a sense as the Church has ever known'.

The Church's foundations were secure. There were no compelling reasons for believing that they were cut off from 'the body of our Lord'. He countered one by one the doubts that had been raised; the rejection of the Pope's jurisdiction, the Reformation, the charge of schism. As for the Church of Rome, it was 'the very best and the very worst of all the Churches of Christ', capable of forming exalted spirits and performing glorious deeds, but beset by 'the most frightful evils'.

He could well conceive 'a far more perfect system than that of the English Church as it was on paper'. And yet if a man could rely on inward and spiritual facts, he felt he could say with 'immovable conviction', that, 'even amongst her mutilated institutions', the Church of England had 'large and free access to

---

[154] Purcell, op. cit., i. 299.

[155] Hope to Gladstone, 10 Mar. 1845, BL Add. MS 44214, f. 261.

[156] Gladstone to Hope, 15 May 1845, *Lathbury*, i. 363, from which the following quotations are taken.

our Lord and a communion with Him sufficient to form in ourselves . . . all the lineaments of His Divine Image'. If this was so, 'how *can* things be right if, while we drink the blessed life-giving stream, we disown the channel that brings it, and suffer our hearts to wander and our hands to be slack?'

It might be that the hopes of realizing the Catholic system within the Church of England would come to nothing. Heresy might thrive, the harvest of unbelief ripen, defection increase. But only two things really disturbed him, Newman and the future action of the Church of Rome.

He could scarcely bear to contemplate what might happen if Newman abandoned the English Church. The extent of the evil that would follow was 'an awful secret of the future'. How appalling it would be if 'the fairest hopes that these three hundred years had yielded, not only for religion in England, but for the ultimate reunion of Christendom', were to be blighted by the agency of the man who was the principal instrument in calling them into existence. Even now, he refused to regard it as certain.

Nor would it be 'less mysterious and wonderful', he wrote, if the Roman Catholic church 'which at this moment quakes in every country where it is dominant . . . shall display among us a power for evil which she cannot evoke for good, and shall destroy us while she is engaged in a struggle of life and death, but not a triumphant struggle, with unbelief abroad'.

These two desperate fears apart, he retained an over-all confidence. 'Our sphere is small,' he concluded, 'our strength is but weakness, our hopes are only in the bud, and yet they are such that it is no presumption, I think, to declare it proved by experience that they are beyond the reach of fatal harm from every other quarter.'

Though Gladstone had refused to accept its inevitability, Newman's apostasy was not long delayed. On 9 October he was received into the Roman obedience by Father Dominic the Passionist at Littlemore. In view of all that he had said and written, Gladstone took the news with surprising calm. His diary makes no mention of it. At the time he was in Baden, ministering to the hysterical Helen. From there, on 29 October, he wrote Manning a letter, the restraint of which contrasted markedly with that of his letter to Hope five months before. He expressed the hope that Manning might persuade Pusey to issue a declaration of loyalty to the Church that would settle men's minds. He hoped also that any more secessions would happen quickly. The feverish excitement which would result if the process was prolonged would destroy confidence and make it harder for people to concentrate on their duties.[157]

But he remained tranquil, looking steadily to the future with a quiet confidence:

Then the conviction always returns upon me that, as the Church of England, being a reality, is not dependent upon this or that individual, the immediate duty is, when one secedes, simply to think of the supplying his place, as a rear rank man steps forward when his front-rank falls in battle. And what does England and its Church want? Certainly nothing of all that ordinary powers and appliances of human nature can supply: nothing but the development of spiritual gifts, and of the Divine Life within us. Have we men ready to devote themselves in mind and body and all that they have to the work of God? If not, it is all over with us—but if so, then every question that remains is subsidiary, and every difficulty surmountable.[158]

---

[157] Gladstone to Manning, 20 Oct. 1845, *Lathbury*, i. 349.
[158] Ibid.

# 7

# THE OXFORD MOVEMENT: THE PARTING
## OF FRIENDS: 1845–1851

With Newman gone, Gladstone looked to others to fill the breach.[1] It was clear, to him at least, that Pusey could not be relied upon. 'One-sidedness as to the Church of Rome' was becoming an 'article of faith' with Pusey, Gladstone had written to Manning early in August.[2] There remained James Hope. At the end of October Gladstone had written to him from Baden of the great crisis facing the Church. She had 'come to the birth, and the question is, will she have strength to bring forth?' He was convinced it was written in God's decrees that she should and that after 'deep repentance and deep suffering a high and peculiar part remains for her in healing the wounds of Christendom'. There was no man, he assured Hope solemnly, whose portion in her work 'is more clearly marked out for him than yours'.[3]

It was Manning, however, who seemed the obvious successor. In November Gladstone wrote asking him if he might consider answering Newman's *Essay on the Development of Christian Doctrine*.[4] This piece of weighty apologetic had been completed two days before Newman's reception. Gladstone had written to his wife from Germany that he supposed many were waiting for its publication before making up their minds whether to convert or not.[5] He received it himself on 28 November at Hawarden and spent the next four days reading it.

It would have been surprising had it unsettled him. He was anxious to learn its argument but, as he told E. L. Badeley the

[1] For the background to this chapter, see D. Newsome, *The Parting of Friends* (1966), especially 313–69, to which I am greatly indebted.
[2] Gladstone to Manning, 1 Aug. 1845, *Lathbury*, i. 348, cf. his remarks seven months later in Purcell, op. cit., i. 316.
[3] Gladstone to Hope, 30 Oct. 1845, Ornsby, op. cit., ii. 69–70.
[4] Gladstone to Manning, 21 Nov. 1845, BL Add. MS 44247, f. 275; partially quoted in Purcell, op. cit., i. 313–14.
[5] Gladstone to his wife, 22 Oct. 1845, Hawn. P.

ecclesiastical lawyer, it was only as argument that it concerned him. For five or six years Newman had lost, to his mind, 'that sort of authority which depends upon judgement as apart from argument'.[6] The *Essay* itself he saw more as a threat to belief in a definite objective revelation than to the Church of England itself.[7] 'Newman's book interests me deeply, shakes me not at all,' he wrote to Manning. 'I think he places Christianity on the edge of a precipice; from whence a bold and strong hand would throw it over.'[8] Had Bishop Butler been alive, he would have been able to tear the whole argument into shreds.[9]

Manning was keen to undertake such a task. He had for some time, he informed Gladstone, been working in the direction of Newman's book. It had deeply impressed him. No other book had so held his attention. It was as if 'the doubts, difficulties, and problems of the last ten years were suddenly brought into focus'.[10] It threw down a challenge. 'Newman's book seems to me to demand of us a higher theology, as the public events of the last 15 years demand a new church organisation.' Yet, like Gladstone, he was not unsettled by it. It had not advanced the debate further: in the end, 'I feel where I was.' His faith remained secure. Some things transcended reason and survived all objections. Of the former was, he felt, the invocation of God; of the latter, the reality of the English Church.[11]

Gladstone was delighted. 'I augur that you will find your confidence grow as you proceed,' he wrote in reply.[12] But Gladstone was wrong. Unknown to him, Manning had reached a decisive turning-point in his religious life. In the course of 1846 his confidence in the Church of England gave way. He had already decided not to rally the broken remnant of the Oxford party. 'I feel I have taken my last act in concert with those who are moving in Oxford. Henceforward I shall endeavour, by God's help, to act by myself, as I have done hitherto, without any alliance,' he had recorded in his diary in November 1845.[13]

[6] Gladstone to Badeley, 16 Nov. 1845, Hope-Scott MS 3679, f. 32.
[7] See his letter to W. Palmer, 12 June 1846, BL Add. MS 44528, f. 58.
[8] Gladstone to Manning, 23 Dec. 1845, BL Add. MS 44247, f. 277.
[9] Gladstone to Manning, 28 Dec. 1845, ibid., f. 279.
[10] Manning to Gladstone, 26 Dec. 1845, Chapeau, op. cit.
[11] Ibid.
[12] Gladstone to Manning, 28 Dec. 1845, BL Add. MS 44247, f. 279.
[13] Purcell, op. cit., i. 324.

In December he declined the invitation to become Sub-Almoner to the Queen, a post that would have made his elevation to the episcopate almost certain. He felt it would curb his freedom of speech and action and make more difficult a calm and objective assessment of Anglican claims. Besides, he feared the snare of wordly ambition.[14]

In March 1846 the King of Prussia nominated Samuel Gobat, a Swiss missionary thought to hold unsound views, to the vacant bishopric of Jerusalem. High-Churchmen protested, but in vain.[15] In late April Manning's sister-in-law and her husband, George and Sophia Ryder, were received into the Roman Catholic Church while in Italy.[16] In June, as the political situation worsened, he became more pessimistic for the Church. If the Whigs came to power it would precipitate a crisis. The Protectionists were no better. They were deeply Erastian. He had heard they were ready to transfer the clergy from the rent-charge to the Consolidated fund.[17] The Church was quite unprepared 'spiritually and maturely' for changes of this kind.[18] If public events forced them on her 'there is no hope of holding long together', he informed Gladstone. Extensive spiritual unity could only come from a united episcopate. 'I can only shelter by shutting my eyes, and hoping.'[19]

Gladstone had often told him there was in parliament an increase of personal religion among individuals and a decrease of ecclesiastical principle corporately. Manning saw the same in the Church, but it was this lack of corporate improvement that unsettled him. 'I have a fear amounting to a belief that the Church of England must split asunder, the *diversa et adversa*

---

[14] Purcell, op. cit., i. 277–84; Newsome, op. cit., 316–17.

[15] Manning wrote to Gladstone that the Jerusalem bishopric was assuming 'a decidedly worse aspect', 17 Apr. 1846, Chapeau, op. cit. For the matter in general see Pusey's letter to Gladstone, 9 Apr. 1846, Liddon, op. cit., iii. 71–2. Gladstone's reply is in *Lathbury*, i. 351–2.

[16] Newsome, op. cit., 308–13. Manning to Gladstone, 17 Apr. 1846, Chapeau, op. cit.

[17] This would have made the clergy the paid servants of the State and enable the State to employ only those clergy whose views it favoured (thus driving out the Tractarians completely without open persecution). Though many Protectionists would have liked to do this it seems unlikely that they had any concerted plan to do so as they were only in the course of formation as a party in June 1846. I owe explanation of this matter to Dr G. I. T. Machin.

[18] Manning to Gladstone, 12 June 1846, Chapeau, op. cit.

[19] Ibid.

*contientes* must be absorbed by a higher unity or parted. Absorbtion seems impossible and the passive traditions of the Established Church are broken as green swaths,' he wrote in August.[20]

Gladstone did not appreciate the extent of Manning's crisis of faith. Or rather, he misunderstood it. So convinced was he of the essential soundness of the Anglican position, he did not realize that it was Manning's faith in the Church's Catholicity that was disintegrating. He assumed that it was only the Protestant and Erastian elements within Anglicanism that were unsettling him and that if these could be purged, as he felt they would, Manning's fears would be set at rest.

The Church would not split asunder, he told Manning. Nothing was more firm in his own mind than the very opposite. Jansenist and anti-Jansenist had been in conflict within the Roman Church for longer than puritanical and catholic principles had been in conflict within the Church of England. It was the impact of the French Revolution and the hostility of State and Church that had brought about an ultimate fusion in France. The same could happen in England. The Church would live through her struggles. She had 'a *great* providential destiny before her'.[21] And he ended by reminding Manning how confident he had been six or seven months before. Gladstone was convinced that there was no matter of magnitude on which the two of them could differ.[22]

Gladstone, therefore, misconceived Manning's dilemma. Theologically they had begun to drift apart without Gladstone realizing it. Gladstone did not appreciate the attraction the devotional ethos of Roman Catholicism had begun to have for Manning. As a priest Manning was a strong sacerdotalist. His pastoral experience had done much to mould his ideas. Yearning for sanctity, he now saw little hope for the English Church without a revival of ascetical theology and especially confession and spiritual direction. For him the Erastian and Catholic elements within the English Church were locked in a deadly struggle. There was no possibility of co-existence, one or other would triumph, and he feared the worst.

[20] Manning to Gladstone, 28 Aug. 1846, Chapeau, op. cit.
[21] Gladstone to Manning, 31 Aug. 1846, *Lathbury*, ii. 352.
[22] Ibid., 353.

Gladstone, though distressed, was not alarmed by the existing situation. He was sustained by a deep sense of God's providence working through the Church. The present troubles were a testing, a baptism of fire from which she would emerge revived and renewed. His own experience of the actual workings of the Roman system had often left him scandalized. He was convinced that the opposing elements within Anglicanism could co-exist, even co-operate. For over three hundred years the English Church had comprised almost every shade of opinion from absolute Romanism to 'the naked scheme of Geneva'.[23] In some ways the spirit of Puritanism and that of Catholicity were contradictory, but not in all things. They had never been found in their 'abstract existences', but always as modifications 'developed by the human heart'.[24] It was no 'overweening paradox', he felt, to suggest that a Church grounded in Catholicism might find a place and use for a puritan spirit. There was no sufficient reason for concluding that the Church of England must either lose its Catholicity or eliminate its Puritanism.[25] 'If Catholicity can exist where idolatry is countenanced, it does not seem much to claim that it is possible it may flourish where puritanism receives toleration and connivance: and with joy should we find ourselves in a condition to deny that idolatry is as traceable within the Roman pale as puritanism is within that of the Church of England.'[26]

Manning would not have been able to accept such sentiments. On 1 December 1846 he wrote to Gladstone that he saw 'a visible increase in the activity and antagonism of two irreconcilable elements in laity, Priesthood, and Episcopate'. He could no longer maintain that this contradiction was in the region of opinion as distinct from faith, 'Our Ecclesiastical, and Social Church System has duration in it, but our theological and spiritual activities . . . are disengaging themselves rapidly.'[27]

This was the nearest Manning came in 1846 to a frank explanation of his real difficulties to Gladstone. He had, in fact,

[23] BL Add. MS 44733, f. 150, a memorandum written on 12 November 1845, viewing the situation in the light of Newman's conversion.

[24] Ibid.

[25] Ibid., f. 151.

[26] Ibid., f. 152.

[27] Manning to Gladstone, 1 Dec. 1846, Chapeau, op. cit.; Gladstone's reply is in *Lathbury*, ii. 353–4.

found it impossible to reply to Newman.[28] The work had led him to question his own assumptions expressed four years earlier in the *Unity of the Church*. As early as May he had written in his journal of an extensive change in his feelings towards Rome, 'It seems to me nearer the truth, and the Church of England in greater peril. Our divisions seem to me to be fatal as a token, and as a disease . . . Though not Roman, I cease to be Anglican.'[29]

His letter of December did not put matters so directly. Gladstone still had the impression that Manning's anxieties stemmed chiefly from the position of Anglicanism as an Establishment. The letter was Manning's first communication with him since the end of August. It had begun with a confession of Manning's failure to write as promised, 'the first time I have broken my word with you'. The subjects which they had discussed in their last letters had been so important, and their importance seemed to grow, so that he felt 'less inclined to try the impossible feat of conjuring them into a letter'. He was aware that what he had now written seemed to contradict what he had written six months before. But he could no more repent of it 'any more than Aneas Sylvius did when he was made Pope'. The letter ended, 'Now as you are strong, be merciful.'[30]

Perhaps Manning wished to spare Gladstone obvious distress. He may well have thought it wrong to make plain his feelings, even to one of his closest friends. He remained a priest of the English Church, an archdeacon, a man with a public position and a trust that should not be abused. The outcome of his inner struggle was still unclear. Perhaps he felt Gladstone would sense the extent of his fears, how fundamental his doubts about the position of Anglicanism had become. He had often told Gladstone how great the crisis facing the Church appeared to him. It seemed as if 'the Will of God is that we should be brought to an issue of first principles', he had written in April.[31] Before that, in December, when he had taken up the challenge to answer Newman, he had warned Gladstone that he could not

[28] See his remarks two years later to his curate Laprimaudaye, Purcell, op. cit., i. 318–19.

[29] J. Fitzsimons, *Manning: Anglican and Catholic* (1951), A. Chapeau, 'Manning the Anglican', 19–20.

[30] Manning to Gladstone, 1 Dec. 1846, Chapeau, op. cit. Gladstone's reply is in *Lathbury*, i. 353–5.

[31] Manning to Gladstone, 17 Apr. 1846, Chapeau, op. cit.

'do things for the nonce, or patch an inconsistent theory'. He was seeking an ultimate position in which he could stand for life.[32]

Gladstone misunderstood this. Nor did he appreciate the significance of Manning's serious illness in February and March 1847. *Timor mortis* had the effect of weakening still further Manning's confidence in the Church of England. He felt himself overwhelmed by a sense of sin, the failures of past years reared before him. On 18 March he made his first confession to his curate Laprimaudaye.[33]

This widened the gulf still further. At this very time Gladstone, in an effort to reassure Manning and convince him that his picture of the religious prospect was too sombre, had written that members of the English Church had a position far more in accord with the laws and will of God than was given to those in the Church of Rome. She had aimed 'a deadly blow at man in his freedom'.[34] By this Gladstone meant, as Manning rightly surmised, the confessional.[35] Compulsory confession and the system of spiritual direction that often accompanied it, Gladstone explained in a further letter written the very day before Manning made his own confession, was one of the many indictments against the Church of Rome which it seemed to him 'a most positive and pressing duty to keep alive'.[36] He told Manning he was going to discuss this in an article in the *Quarterly*.

Manning was naturally distressed and wrote back to Gladstone outlining his view of its necessity. For him it was the lack of auricular confession that made the Church of England's claim to be part of the Church Catholic questionable.[37] Gladstone brushed aside their differences. It was not the first time they had approached questions from different sides, and because of that 'have expressed ourselves very differently when our real mean-

---

[32] Manning to Gladstone, 26 Dec. 1846, Chapeau, op. cit.
[33] Chapeau, op. cit., Purcell, op. cit., i. 330–9.
[34] Gladstone to Manning, 15 Mar. 1847, BL Add. MS 44247, f. 325.
[35] Manning to Gladstone, 16 Mar. 1847, Chapeau, op. cit.
[36] Gladstone to Manning, 17 Mar. 1847, BL Add. MS 44247, f. 326. Gladstone's attitude to this differed from many supporters of the Oxford Movement.
[37] Manning to Gladstone, 18 Mar. 1847, Chapeau, op. cit., and 23 Mar. 1847. Though here again Manning argued the matter without perhaps drawing out the full implications this had for his view of the Church of England.

ings were not far apart'. His own convictions on the matter were, in any case, 'in an immature and half-developed state'.[38]

But here, as before, Gladstone misjudged the situation. The two men were further apart than he imagined. Manning's ties to the Church of his birth were loosening daily. He could no longer justify the Anglican position intellectually. The Church of England's theology seemed chaotic, its devotional system deficient, its unity disintegrating yearly. Yet he could not bring himself to deny completely its spiritual validity. The Holy Spirit still seemed present in the Church.[39] His heart overruled his head.

Recovered from his illness, he resolved to visit the continent and spend the winter in Italy. Before leaving he celebrated Holy Communion in his church at Lavington. Nothing reveals more clearly the poignancy of his dilemma: 'I never felt the power of love more: nor so much bound to my flock. It is the strongest bond I have. I believe it to be of the reality of the Catholic Church. And yet it will bear no theological argument except a denial of visible unity altogether—which is self-evidently false.'[40]

Manning's continental journey of 1847–8 was of immense importance to him.[41] During it he drank deep of the spirit of the Roman Church. In Rome he visited churches, witnessed the ceremonies, discussed matters with Roman ecclesiastics. Before he left in May he had an audience with Pio Nono. What he saw greatly affected him. 'Things seem to me clearer, plainer . . . more harmonious: things which were only in the head have gone down into the heart,' he wrote to Robert Wilberforce at Christmas.[42]

Shortly before he reached Rome he read the news of Hampden's confirmation as Bishop of Hereford, despite ecclesiastical protest. 'I am left without defence,' he wrote. The event had brought out the miserable truth: the civil power was the ultimate judge of doctrine in England, 'a principle which is not more heretical than atheistical'.[43]

---

[38] Gladstone to Manning, 20 Mar. 1847, *Lathbury*, ii. 277.

[39] See his letter to Robert Wilberforce, 9 June 1847, Purcell, op. cit., i. 341.

[40] Ibid., 342, 5 July 1847.

[41] For the details see Purcell, op. cit., i. 343–417.

[42] Fitzsimons, op. cit., 25–6.

[43] From a letter to Robert Wilberforce, 12 Feb. 1848, Purcell, op. cit., i. 509–10.

In January he wrote to Gladstone eager for news. The Hampden business deeply disturbed him. He had heard also of Gladstone's support for the removal of Jewish disabilities. It was, he felt, the end of England as a Christian nation. But this would weigh more heavily with Gladstone than with him. No longer could parliament legislate for the Church. All legislation for the Church, unless sanctioned by the Church 'is null and void and of no force to bind a christian man'. In future, 'the Church must obey Parliament as she would Nero; for no other reasons, and no further'. It was a hastening on of the period of which he and Gladstone had foreseen, when a son of the Church could serve her no longer in parliament. The days were coming when the Church would have to go into the wilderness.[44] It was a theme to which he returned three months later in his next letter.

Manning returned to England on 18 June. On 9 July Gladstone visited him. They discussed Gladstone's position in politics and Manning's in the Church. The conversation ended with Gladstone convinced of Manning's full allegiance to the Church and his increasing disposition 'to dwell on her Catholic and positive character rather than on what is negative, or peculiar, or external viz. the Protestant and the national aspects'.[45]

[44] Manning to Gladstone, 20 Jan. 1848, Chapeau, op. cit.
[45] *Diary*, iv, 10 July 1848. That Gladstone believed this is clear from his diary. Whether he had correctly understood Manning's position is a matter of dispute, see Purcell, op. cit., i. 583. In his own copy, now at Hawarden, Gladstone has pencilled against the sentence 'Manning, for instance, disputed the accuracy of Mr Gladstone's memory as to what passed in the memorable conversation between them on Manning's return from Rome, in 1848', the words 'But never stated his own version?'
  In old age Gladstone certainly believed that Manning had deliberately misled him about his actual position during these years. Manning was undoubtedly during this period confiding more fully in Robert Wilberforce than Gladstone. Gladstone was deeply pained to discover this later; see his remarks in Purcell, op. cit., i. 569. On p. 464 where Purcell has written 'To make statements on grave matters of faith to one person or set of persons in contradiction of statements made to others, is only a still stronger proof of a sensitive mind, perplexed by doubt, losing for the time being its balance', Gladstone had written 'ma' (meaning 'but') and in the other margin the words 'and to conceal from each'.
  It would appear, however, that what Manning actually meant on 9 July was that he did not believe the Church of England had ceased to be a means of grace, a position that he still believed (as did James Hope, Purcell, op. cit., 525) until 1850. On 23 January 1850 Manning wrote to James Hope. 'In the summer of 1848 when I came from Italy I told Gladstone that I did not feel any point in the Roman system to have a 'coercive

In the summer of 1848, therefore, it still seemed to Gladstone that Manning's faith in the Church of England as a Church, rather than as an Establishment, remained secure. He did not, perhaps could not, appreciate that Manning now found it impossible to distinguish the two. The Establishment and its workings seemed utterly Erastian and the Church's Catholicity totally compromised. The Hampden affair had revealed the full extent of the Church's subservience to the secular power. By participating in Hampden's consecration the entire Episcopate shared in his heterodoxy. They had separated themselves 'from the whole episcopate under heaven', he had written to Robert Wilberforce.[46]

Gladstone's own remedy: patience, confidence in the gradual but inevitable spread of the Catholic ethos within the Church, the call for greater freedom to rule and order itself in doctrinal matters, was now inadequate to quell Manning's fears. While Gladstone, though distressed, still looked with hope for a gradual improvement in the situation, particularly some sort of corporate action by the Episcopate, Manning felt such a hope illusory.

Although in his charge in July he took refuge in the fact that Hampden had never been formally condemned as a heretic by any tribunal of the Church and that until such a pronouncement was made he ought publicly to be treated as orthodox,[47] he felt inwardly that the fort had already been betrayed.

When Gladstone wrote to him early in January 1849 that if the Episcopate would not act, the laity must be organized to do battle, he replied that while that was true, little could in fact be expected from the laity. Looking at the Church as it was, he saw 'the Church of England party', the aristocracy and country gentlemen, were nine-tenths Erastian and opposed to all that he

jurisdiction' over my conscience—meaning that I did not feel a fear of dying in the Church of England, or compelled by my claim or conviction to submit to the Church of Rome. This has long been my feeling: and I have held to the Church of England not through repulsion from Rome but from love and a belief such as you express that the means of salvation are with us.

I must now admit to myself that the reversing of my sincere belief in our Ecclesiastical status weakens, as you say, my foundation'. Hope-Scott, MS 3675, ff. 66–7.

[46] Manning to R. Wilberforce, 12 Feb. 1848, Purcell, op. cit., i. 509.
[47] Purcell, op. cit., i. 478.

and Gladstone stood for. The middle classes were hostile. The only laity upon whom the Catholics within the Church could rely were a few individuals among the upper strata of society and the poor.[48]

Unaware of Manning's real position, Gladstone was more concerned for James Hope. He realized that Hope had been greatly influenced by Newman and that since the creation of the Jerusalem bishopric had taken an increasingly pessimistic view of the Church's situation.[49] His letter in May 1845, with its emotional reminder of Hope's solemn promise five years before to co-operate with him in furthering the welfare of the Church, with no limit placed on the extent of such co-operation; the confession that the withdrawal of this promise would increase his sense of desolation which, as matters then stood, 'often approaches to being intolerable'; the space given to countering, one by one, the objections to the Anglican position; all this suggested that Gladstone feared for Hope's safety.[50]

He was concerned that Hope seemed to have withdrawn from the public activities in which, before, he had been so conspicuous. Did this not place him in a false position, Gladstone asked? Was such withdrawal favourable to religious inquiry?[51] Whether Gladstone appreciated how deeply the Hampden business had shaken Hope's confidence is impossible to say.[52] He certainly hoped that his marriage, in August 1847, would give him greater stability.[53] But Hope was almost as far from Gladstone as Manning, and had resolved to play no further part in Church affairs. In October 1847 he wrote to Gladstone supporting his stand on Jewish disabilities, adding that with parliament now no longer Christian the Church must claim 'those rights and that independence which nothing but the pretence of Christianity can entitle the legislature to withhold

---

[48] Gladstone to Manning, 9 Jan. 1849, BL Add. MS 44248, f. 1; Manning to Gladstone, 12 Jan. 1849, Chapeau, op. cit.

[49] As early as 1843 Hope had begun to feel himself closer to Newman than to Gladstone, see the controversy over the 'Lives of the English Saints' edited by Newman and especially Hope's letter to Newman, 5 Dec. 1843, quoted in Ornsby, op. cit., ii. 32–3.

[50] Gladstone to Hope, 15 May 1845, *Lathbury*, i. 335–42.

[51] Gladstone to Hope, 7 Dec. 1845, Ornsby, op. cit., ii. 70–2.

[52] See his letter to Newman, 23 Apr. 1846, Ornsby, op. cit., ii. 76–7, where he admits that with his present doubts he has ceased to be Anglican, without yet becoming Roman.

[53] Gladstone to his wife, 20 July 1847, Hawn. P.

from it', and concluding he had now withdrawn from Church politics and had never had any interest in merely secular political activities.[54]

Had Gladstone realized how close to Rome his two friends had come, he would have been appalled. His attitude to the Roman Church had, if anything, hardened in the years following Newman's apostasy. 'The temptation towards the Church of Rome of which some are conscious,' he wrote to Dr Hook in June 1846, 'has never been before my mind in any other sense than as other plain and flagrant sins have been before it.'[55]

He treated all conversions with the same unsympathetic horror he had displayed towards that of his sister Helen.[56] His diptych of prayer, written in his diary in September 1847, contained a special category of intercession: those to be prayed for on account of spiritual trial, danger or fall. It included twenty names.[57]

Would-be converts who wrote to him for advice received short shrift. 'Stavordale, I grieve to say, wrote to me to say that he is again unfixed, and likely to go to the Church of Rome, but yet uncertain, and he was then waiting to see whether Dr. Pusey could say anything to keep him back', he wrote to his wife in July 1847. 'I could not help writing him a strong letter. God knows whether rightly or wisely.'[58]

In fact, Gladstone was not at all convinced that Pusey was using his influence to its full extent or in the right way. He wrote to him in May 1847 that there was a feeling abroad that he was rather too lenient in this matter. He appeared to be advising people to remain in the Church of England rather 'as on the whole safe and proper than as a matter of imperative obligation'. He did not seem to take a very strong view of the positive

[54] Hope to Gladstone, 9 Oct. 1847, BL Add. MS 44214, f. 323.

[55] Gladstone to Hook, 30 June 1847, BL Add. MS 44213, f. 102.

[56] In 1847 Gladstone had still not come to terms with this. He told Hope that Helen had attached herself to the Church of Rome 'not on grounds of a religious change but as a powerful means of excitement'. Gladstone to Hope, 7 Dec. 1847, Hope-Scott, MS 3673, f. 126.

[57] *Diary*, iv, 13 Apr. 1848. The list contains the names of Keble and Pusey. Hope and Manning were prayed for as friends, though as Gladstone made clear, 'Some of the persons are prayed for in mixed regards'.

[58] Gladstone to his wife, 21 July 1847, Hawn. P. Lord Stavordale was the thirty-year-old son of the Earl of Ilchester.

evils and dangers to which, quite apart from the act of desertion, people joining the Roman Church exposed themselves. Gladstone felt Pusey should make his hostility to the secessions more widely known.[59]

His own most public outburst against the Roman Church in this period was a review of the book *From Oxford to Rome*, which appeared anonymously in the *Quarterly* in June 1847. This book with its sub-title, 'and how it fared with some who lately made the journey', was written by an anonymous Roman convert as a warning to others.[60] Gladstone was much taken by it. He began it on 13 February and finished it in three days. 'It is a most remarkable book, most eloquent, beautiful and touching as well as full of instruction,' he recorded in his diary.[61] The next day he wrote to its author, and to Lockhart, the editor of the *Quarterly*, bringing it to his attention.[62] In the next few weeks he mentioned it often to friends. He was intrigued to discover that Manning knew something of its background but would not reveal it, though he hinted that it was unsavoury.[63]

The review itself contained a great deal of comment both about the secessions (or 'defections' as Gladstone called them), and the errors of the Roman Church. He boldly declared, with a sense of national fervour acceptable to the most ardent holder of 'No Popery' opinions, that the English character made impossible a widespread acceptance of 'the rankness of the Papal system'.[64] Englishmen had strong instincts towards loyalty, obedience, order, tradition, 'but these are effectively balanced by an energetic love of freedom'. The Roman obedience could perhaps 'repel us and scatter us as a people' but could never attract or unite us, until she had unlearned 'the depraving lessons of her pride, and shall have returned to the spirit of her first love in its simplicity and its freedom'.[65]

---

[59] Gladstone to Pusey, 3 May 1847, Pusey MSS, Pusey House.

[60] It was written by Elizabeth Harris who, having become disillusioned with the Roman Catholic Church, took the paradoxical step of remaining in it and writing books about it as a warning to others. See R. Chapman, *Faith and Revolt: Studies in the Literary Influence of the Oxford Movement* (1970), 119 ff.

[61] *Diary*, iii, 14 Feb. 1847.

[62] Ibid., 16 Feb. 1847; the letter to Lockhart is among the Lockhart MSS 1556 f. 144, National Library of Scotland.

[63] Manning to Gladstone, 12 Mar. 1846, 16 Mar. 1846, Chapeau, op. cit.

[64] *Quarterly Review*, lxxxi (June 1847), 151.

[65] Ibid.

He went on to catalogue her evident vices and terse
vehemence:

She offers us a sealed Bible; a mutilated Eucharist; an arbitrarily expanded
modern creed; a casuistry that 'sews pillows to all arm holes', and is still open to
the reproach of Pascal, that while it aspires to the service of virtue it does not
disdain that of vice; a scheme of worship involving constant peril of polytheistic
idolatry; a doctrinal system disparaging scripture, and driving her acutest
champions upon the most dangerous and desperate theories; and a rule of
individual discipline which offends against duty even more than against
liberty, by placing the reins of the inward and outward life, given by God to
conscience, in the hands of extraneous person under the name of a Director.[66]

Nothing reveals more clearly the gulf separating Gladstone
from Manning and Hope than this fierce diatribe.

By 1849 the unity of belief and purpose that had bound these
three friends in the 1830s was on the point of disintegration, with
Gladstone still only partially aware of the full extent of the
divergence between them. The 1840s had proved a decisive
decade for all three. Manning's and Hope's faith in the *via media*
had been tried and found wanting. Gladstone, though still firm
in his commitment to the Church of England, had been forced,
after a period of agonizing self-appraisal, to abandon the theory
of Church and State that had provided the *raison d'être* of his
parliamentary life. While Manning and Hope waited in dread
for the final call to abandon the Church, Gladstone was
attempting to find, again, a role for himself as servant of that
Church in parliament.

Looking back over a distance of nearly forty years, the then
Cardinal Manning nostalgically recalled their respective paths.
Their friendship had opened in the period of their books:
Gladstone's on Church and State, his own on the Unity of the
Church. 'The next years were spent by us in testing our
experiments. You found yours impractical, and I found mine
untenable.'[67]

It was the Gorham Judgement that brought the parting of the
ways. In August 1849 the refusal of the Bishop of Exeter to
institute the Revd G. C. Gorham to the living of Brampford
Speke on the grounds that he was unsound on the doctrine of
baptismal regeneration was upheld by the Court of Arches, and

[66] Ibid.
[67] Manning to Gladstone, 20 Sept. 1887, BL Add. MS 44250, f. 246.

Gorham appealed to the Judicial Committee of the Privy Council which, since 1833, had been the final court of appeal in matters ecclesiastical.[68]

For High-Churchmen the issue presented two grave problems. The first was doctrinal. If a Calvinist interpretation of the articles on baptism and the reception of the sacraments in general was permitted, it weakened further the Church of England's claim to teach the Catholic faith. But more fundamental was the question of authority. The whole issue was being decided by a secular tribunal, thus demonstrating that the Royal Supremacy could determine the doctrine of the Church.

For Manning and Hope the Judgement was the final and unequivocal demonstration of the essential Erastianism of Anglicanism. The appointment of Hampden had violated the divine office of the Church in respect to its discipline, the appeal to the Judicial Committee of the Privy Council violated its divine office in respect of doctrine. Until this point Manning had tried to convince himself that the Royal Supremacy was simply civil and in no sense spiritual or ecclesiastical. Its function was merely to protect, uphold, and affirm the Church's doctrine and discipline.[69]

Hope had already gone beyond this. The Gorham appeal was no different in principle from all previous appeals. The ultimate jurisdiction in ecclesiastical matters had, since the Reformation, lain with the Crown. The Gorham appeal merely demonstrated what had been implicit in the Royal Supremacy from the beginning. His letter to Manning on 29 January 1850 attempted to make this plain. He quickly won Manning over.[70]

Gladstone did not see matters in this way. For him the crucial issue was doctrinal. If Gorham's views were upheld then, he told Manning, 'not only is there no doctrine of Baptismal regeneration in the Church of England as State-interpreted, but there is

---

[68] See Chadwick, op. cit., 250–71.

[69] See Manning's letter to S. Wilberforce, 24 Jan. 1850, quoted in Newsome, op. cit., 350.

[70] If Manning had not already changed his mind. His letter to Hope of 23 Jan. 1850 (Hope-Scott MS 3675, ff. 64–5) suggests that between his letter to Hope on the 31 December 1851 with its enclosure (a paper stating Manning's theory of the Anglican ecclesiastical position), he had done so. Hope appears to have written his letter of 29 January 1850 (quoted in Purcell, op. cit., i. 524–7) without reference to this letter of 23 January.

no doctrine at all, and Arians or anybody else may abide in it with equal propriety'.[71] But though he felt the Church must speak out, he feared an open conflict with the State. The Church was not yet ready for it, still less for disestablishment, which might be its outcome.

Newman's secession was too fresh in the public mind. More years of faithful work in spreading Catholic principles within the Church were needed. In any case, connection with the State was not wholly without benefit. He could conceive of several matters—the Colonial Church for instance, or alterations in the system of Church Rates—where parliamentary action would be of immense value to the Church. Whether the State of its own free will might grant the Church greater liberty, especially if the Church was prepared to surrender some of her temporalities in exchange, was another matter deserving investigation.[72]

This again, reveals the difference between Manning and Gladstone. With the collapse of his theory of Church and State, Gladstone was now attempting to serve the Church by extricating her, as each crisis arose, from her subservience to the civil power. A consistent profession of Catholic truth by the State was no longer possible. But a completely secular State was still far off, and in England with its widely diffused Christian ethos, it would develop more slowly than in most states of Europe.

In this changing situation Gladstone had found himself a role. But for Manning with his intense allegiance to dogma, his hatred of Erastianism and his conception of the Church as an almost mystical Absolute, the choice was now starkly defined. Nothing shows this more clearly than his Charge in 1849. 'The true and perfect idea of Christendom is the constitution of all social order upon the basis of faith and within the unity of the Church,' he declared.[73] The sacredness of the State was completed by its incorporation with the Church. The jurisdiction of the State in matters of religion was either an endowment

---

[71] Gladstone to Manning, 30 Dec. 1849, *Lathbury*, i. 95–6.
[72] Ibid., 96.
[73] H. E. Manning, *A Charge delivered at the Ordinary Visitation of the Archdeaconry of Chichester*, July 1849 (1849), 42. This charge appears to have been overlooked by both Newsome and Purcell.

conferred upon it by the Church, or the action of the Church itself, through the forms and procedures of the civil order.[74]

In recent times the State had made religious indifference its central principle. By so doing it had dethroned itself from its true elevation in the Kingdom of God. It had reduced itself to its natural and unconsecrated rudiments.[75] Now a new path of duty was re-opening for the Church. It must resume its sole and independent action. It must not lament the past, nor dream of the future, but accept the present.[76] The civil and spiritual powers throughout the world were parting asunder. Church-men were standing in suspense; 'but everyone must soon choose his side'.

Men are wearied out with a sort of heart-sick sense that there is no firm ground in public life or in political theories: they are falling back upon the supernatural power, which, as it regenerated and has preserved society these eighteen hundred years, and has again and again interposed to restore falling states and to recover wasted civilisation, so now it is the one only certainty for the intellect, the one only home for the heart, the one only foundation of faith. 'On this rock will I build my church.'[77]

On March 1850 judgement was given. The Judicial Commit-tee declared that Gorham's opinions were not 'contrary or repugnant to the doctrine of the Church of England, as by law established', with one lay member and one ecclesiastic, Bishop Blomfield of London, dissenting.[78]

Manning and other High-Churchmen immediately con-vened a meeting for the following Monday evening, 11 March, in the vestry of St. Paul's, Knightsbridge, to consider what should be done.[79] It was decided to draft a declaration condemning the Judgement. Gladstone was prevented by illness from attending the meeting.[80] But the following evening Manning, Robert Wilberforce, Badeley, the Bishop of Exeter's advocate in the case, and others came to tell him of the proposed declaration and ask for his support. Although he concurred in

[74] Ibid., 43.
[75] Ibid.
[76] Ibid., 43. 71.
[77] Ibid., 45.
[78] Liddon, op. cit., iii. 229.
[79] Manning to Dr W. H. Mill, 8 Mar. 1850, Lambeth MS 1491 f. 29, marked *Confidential*.
[80] *Diary*, iv. 11 Mar. 1850.

the proposal, he informed them that 'strong and special reasons' delayed him from attaching his name.[81]

It was hoped that as many as possible would sign. Keble and Pusey, however, were unhappy at its wording. At James Hope's suggestion, therefore, another meeting was held at Gladstone's house on Thursday morning to redraft it.[82] Since they were unable to reach agreement, it was decided that all proposed amendments should be sent to Archdeacon Denison and another meeting called the following week.[83] Four days later, in the evening of Monday, 18 March, Pusey and others met at Gladstone's house to sign the amended declaration. Gladstone was not present.[84] Why he refused to sign is not entirely clear. It was not, as Manning's recollections in Purcell suggest, because of his Privy Councillor's oath.[85] The most likely explanation is that he would not commit himself initially because he wanted to wait until he had seen the Bishop of London the following day.[86]

What took place at that meeting is unknown. Blomfield may have given Gladstone to understand that he, and perhaps other bishops, intended to take some sort of action repudiating the Judgement in the near future and that over-hasty protests of the wrong sort would be unhelpful. What is certain, however, is that when Gladstone met Manning privately that afternoon his

[81] *Diary*, iv. 12 Mar. 1850; Manning to Dr W. H. Mill, 13 Mar. 1850, Lambeth MS 1491, f. 33: 'The enclosed paper was agreed to and signed last night. And I am directed urgently to request that you will send authority to attach your name. We propose to publish it in *The Times* of Monday next. And we hope by that time to obtain Mr Gladstone's name. He entirely concurred but strong and special reasons delay his attaching his name.' This was clearly the meeting that Manning later remembered (Purcell, op. cit., i. 530). It was not, therefore, as Purcell suggests, the *final* meeting concerned with the declaration but the second, and the first at which Gladstone was present. Manning was not present at the final meeting. He left London early on Thursday (14 March) for Lavington, and a meeting of the archdeacon on Tuesday (19 March) prevented him from returning for the final meeting on Monday (18 March). His name was affixed to the declaration, on his instructions, by Hope; see his letters to Hope, 14, 15, 16, 17, and 20 Mar. 1850, Hope-Scott MS 3675, ff. 68–81.
[82] Hope to Gladstone, 13 Mar. 1850, Bl Add. MS 44214, f. 337; *Diary*, iv. 14 Mar. 1850.
[83] Purcell, op. cit., i. 529.
[84] *Diary*, iv, 18 Mar. 1850.
[85] Gladstone took strong exception to this, see Gladstone to Purcell, 14 Jan. 1896, *Lathbury*, ii. 338–41: 'I entirely disavow and disclaim Manning's statement *as it stands*.'
[86] Blomfield had written to Gladstone the day of the proposed meeting at St. Paul's, requesting he call on Wednesday, 13 March, at 1 p.m.; Blomfield to Gladstone, 11 Mar. 1850, BL Add, MS 44369, f. 60.

objections to the declaration had increased.[87] He was now thinking of organizing an address to the Bishops instead. On the following Saturday with Hope, Pusey and several MPs, including Sidney Herbert, he drafted such a document.[88]

After this he seems to have decided to have nothing more to do with the declaration.[89] Before the final meeting on Monday, 18 March, he sent a letter to the Revd W. Maskell, Phillpotts's chaplain, explaining why he proposed not to attend. It was not because he disagreed with the declaration or felt its language too strong. Indeed, the delay in framing it had arisen, he informed Maskell, from a desire on the part of some of those concerned 'to adopt the language least likely to make any brother in the Church an offender, or a stumbler'.[90] Though he did not feel the amendments had diminished its force.

As for himself, however, he did not intend to pursue the consideration of them that evening: 'First because the pressure of other business has become very heavy upon me, and secondly, and mainly, because I do not consider that the time for any enunciation of a character pointing to ultimate issues will have arrived until the Gorham Judgcmcnt shall havc taken effect.'[91] So long as Gorham had not been inducted, the Judgement was liable to be called in question, in which case it would be null and void. He felt this was not merely possible but likely, likely enough to have brought him to the conclusion that 'the time for very decisive steps has not yet come'. At the same time he had taken part in preparing an address which denounced the Judgement and pointed to its remedy, action by the episcopate.[92]

---

[87] Manning to Hope, 14 Mar. 1850, headed 'Brighton "in transition"', Hope-Scott MS 3675, f. 68.

[88] *Diary*, iv, 16 Mar. 1850.

[89] From Manning's unpublished letters to Hope in the Hope-Scott MSS it is clear that he was more concerned to secure Pusey's name. He was prepared to fall in with Gladstone's proposal of an address to the bishops, 'unless something intolerable be annexed as a condition'. Indeed, if Gladstone would sign he preferred embodying the resolutions in an address to the Bishop of London. 'I prefer acts which terminate on a person—not in the air' (16 Mar.).

But the address and declaration were kept separate. The declaration appeared in *The Times* on Wednesday, 20 March, and Gladstone's address on 28 March; see also Purcell, op. cit., i. 522–33.

[90] Gladstone to Maskell, 18 Mar. 1850, BL Add. MS 44369, f. 87.

[91] Ibid.

[92] Ibid., f. 88.

The address itself, in the form of a letter to the Bishop of London, appeared in *The Times* on 28 March. It was signed by sixty-three eminent laymen, including eleven peers and eighteen MPs. It declared the Church was in danger, the judicial committee unfit to pronounce on doctrinal matters, and called on Blomfield to take counsel with his fellow bishops.

Gladstone's decision to sign the address and not the declaration showed his desire to approach the matter as a churchman in politics rather than associate himself too closely with a purely ecclesiastical, or clerical, protest. But the tensions were great.

In late February he had written to his wife that the Gorham Judgement might impose duties upon him that would separate for ever 'my path of life public or private and that of all political parties'.[93] Three days after absenting himself from the final meeting about the declaration, he had a conversation with his friend T. D. Acland.[94] He told him that his chief aim in the present circumstances was to keep everyone together. The worse evil would be the acquiescence of the Church in the Judgement. It would be degrading and demoralizing. It would allow a clergyman to interpret the articles in a non-natural sense, to sign one thing and preach another. It would ruin the whole principle of an ecclesiastical Establishment and open the way for the Privy Council to assume greater power over doctrine. The second evil was that it would drive men to Rome; the third, the formation of an independent 'quasi-Scotch' communion. But the greatest problem was personal. He felt that if he lifted his voice in favour of the separation of Church and State, his political life would be at an end. Yet, such was the crisis, he felt he might have to sacrifice all private feeling and throw himself into the breach.

He felt himself, he told Manning early in April, 'between a variety of distinct obligations, the harmony of which is not easy to discern at certain given points'.[95] The main question was, should he try 'to act for the Church *in* the State or *on* the State'. He was sure Manning would appreciate all the change of a single letter implied. The decision of Sidney Herbert not to sign the address because he was a member of the Government was an

---

[93] Gladstone to his wife, 25 Feb. 1850, Hawn. P.

[94] *Diary*, iv, 21 Mar. 1850; the conversation is recorded in a letter of Acland to his wife written shortly afterwards, op. cit., 163.

[95] Gladstone to Manning, 4 Apr. 1850, BL Add, MS 44248, f. 36.

indication that he might have to quit parliament and serve the Church from outside, 'for the reluctance of other men in politics to commit themselves in any degree of course must tend to drive me forward as the keeping in company with them would tend to hold me back'.[96]

Manning's advice was uncompromising. The ecclesiastical consequences of the Constitutional Revolution of 1828–32 were only just making themselves felt. Churchmen should loose themselves from the State for their own well-being. The time for doing anything for the Church in parliament was past. 'We want Truth and Principles to which the reason and heart, the whole soul in man can respond,' he wrote to Gladstone. These had no voice or life in Anglicanism.[97]

But Gladstone did not take so extreme a view. He could not forsake politics until it was clear there was nothing more for him to do. That time had not yet come. The Judgement had still not been implemented. The Episcopate could still repudiate it. Phillpotts had already done so in an open letter to the Archbishop of Canterbury at the end of March.[98] There was still Blomfield.[99]

In an effort both to clear his own mind and in the hope it might help others, he began to investigate the nature of the Royal Supremacy itself. By late April he was writing to Manning that he felt: 'better pleased with the Reformation in regard to the Supremacy than at former times, but also much more sensible of the drifting of the Church since away from the range of her constitutional securities, and more than ever convinced how thoroughly false is the present position.'[100]

The result of these investigations was his *Remarks on the Royal Supremacy as it is defined by reason, history, and the constitution: a letter to the Bishop of London*, published early in June 1850.[101] Written by

---

[96] Ibid., f. 37.

[97] Manning to Gladstone, 6 Apr. 1850, Chapeau, op. cit.

[98] Chadwick, op. cit., 263.

[99] Blomfield had in February attempted, before the Judgement was announced, to introduce a bill to reform the final court of appeal. Chadwick, op. cit., 258. At the end of April, Gladstone was still sure 'the great majority' of the bishops were 'disposed to try for a settlement', Gladstone to his wife, 30 Apr. 1850, Hawn. P.

[100] Gladstone to Manning, 29 Apr. 1850, *Lathbury*, i. 101.

[101] Reprinted in *Gleanings*, v. 173–285, from which subsequent quotations are taken. See also M. D. Stephen, 'Gladstone and the Composition of the Final Court in Ecclesiastical Causes, 1850–73', *Historical Journal*, ix, 2 (1966), 191–200.

one who felt the Church should not abandon her legal privileges 'until she actually sees that the hour appointed for her to make that choice, is at hand', it was an attempt to vindicate the Royal Supremacy as set forth in the Reformation Settlement, while showing that the present composition of the appelate tribunal in regard to doctrine was 'unreasonable, unconstitutional and contrary to the spirit of the Reformation Statutes'.

His view of the Supremacy remained much as he had expressed it in the fourth chapter of the State in its relations with the Church. In itself it involved no violation of the integrity of the Christian faith. At the Reformation the reformers may have conceded too much to the civil power, but this was explicable given the exigencies of the time. The Church had not 'sold herself for gold'. The reasons for a close amalgamation of ecclesiastical and civil authority were strong. The King had resorted to the ancient regal jurisdiction and abolished one that had been usurped. This no more involved the surrender of the Church birthright than the supremacy exercised by Constantine or Justinian. The idea that the Pope was the source and centre of ecclesiastical jurisdiction was 'false in history and false in Law'.

But the Supremacy was not despotic. Its power in regard to the legislative office of the Church was a power of restraint. The jurisdiction the Crown exercised was subject to the maxim that laws ecclesiastical were administered by ecclesiastics. The creation of the Judicial Committee of the Privy Council in 1833 as the final court of appeal in ecclesiastical matters was an illegitimate development that violated the original intentions of the Reformation Settlement. It was a 'pseudo-ecclesiastical' court which had no right to pronounce on doctrinal matters. The real scandal of the Gorham Judgement had been that the Archbishops had supported it. The letter ended by giving support to Blomfield's parliamentary bill with its proposal to separate the 'spirituality' from the Judicial Committee and require that doctrinal questions be submitted to the Episcopal Bench for decision.

If Gladstone hoped his letter would have much influence he was disappointed.[102] Although Blomfield's bill was backed by

[102] That he hoped it might restrain some people, otherwise likely to secede can be seen from his letter to Hawkins, 8 Sept. 1850, Hawkins MSS, Oriel.

Samuel Wilberforce, Bishop of Oxford, the Lords rejected it by eighty-four votes to fifty-one. Having failed there, it stood little chance in the Commons.[103] Manning had written off the bill even before it was introduced. 'It seems to me to be a total and vital failure,' he told Robert Wilberforce on 22 May.[104]

Since January, Manning had taken a far more critical view of the Supremacy than Gladstone. He found Gladstone's pamphlet 'insular'.[105] The Supremacy could only be acceptable if it was reduced to what it was in Common Law before 1530. His own conviction was that the Tudor Statutes went beyond the Common Law in the vital point and that, 'Sir Thomas More lost his head between the edges of the old and new Supremacy.' What was now needed was the restoration of the Common Law supremacy ('to which, I believe, Pius IX would make as little objection as Pius II'), and the readmission of Catholic authority in doctrine and discipline as an active and sustaining principle of the Church of England.[106] In July he published his own views in an open letter to the Bishop of Chichester, declaring that the whole jurisdiction of the Episcopate over the teaching and discipline of the Church lay 'prostrate at the foot of the Civil Power'.[107] He sent proofs to Gladstone for his comments. Gladstone could not accept its constitutional and historical argument which, he told Manning, 'greatly weakens the authority which your Tract is in other respects so well fitted to carry'.[108]

With Robert Wilberforce and Dr Mill, Manning drew up another declaration, denying the Crown the power of 'hearing and deciding in appeal all matters, however purely spiritual, of discipline and doctrine',[109] which was circulated to every beneficed clergyman and layman who had taken the Oath of Supremacy. On the 23 July, after hesitations swept aside by

---

[103] See Gladstone's comments, *Diary*, iv, 3 June 1850.

[104] Purcell, op. cit., 538.

[105] Manning to Gladstone, 15 June 1850, Chapeau, op. cit.

[106] Ibid.; see also his letter to Gladstone, 19 June 1850, BL Add. MS 44248, f. 58 ff., and the letter of 25 June 1850, Chapeau, op. cit.

[107] H. E. Manning, *The Appellate Jurisdiction of the Crown in Matters Spiritual. A Letter to the Bishop of Chichester* (1850), 38.

[108] Gladstone to Manning, 9 July 1850, *Lathbury*, i. 112.

[109] Purcell, op. cit., 541.

Gladstone, he spoke at the meeting called by the Church Union at St. Martin's Hall, in London.[110]

But though the meeting repudiated the Judgement, only one bishop, the aged Bagot of Bath and Wells, was present. It was becoming increasingly evident that the bishops were unwilling to take corporate action. Manning's circular attracted only 1,800 signatures.[111] On 10 August, despite Phillpotts's threat that he would excommunicate anyone who instituted and inducted Gorham, he was admitted to the living of Brampford Speke.

Secessions had already begun. In June, William Maskell, Phillpotts's chaplain and Mrs Robert Wilberforce were received into the Roman Catholic Church. On 30 August, Viscount Feilding who had helped preside at the meeting on 23 July, joined them. In mid-September T. W. Allies and Henry and Mary Wilberforce were also received.

It was the step Gladstone had dreaded. In his conversation with Acland in March he had spoken with contempt of those 'having the superstition to suppose they must join the Church of Rome to save their souls and desert their calling to work out the destiny of Englishmen, and all God has called the Church of England to'.[112] In an attempt to maintain unity he proposed a covenant, or engagement, whereby all who could not accept the Judgement would solemnly bind themselves to do nothing that would 'imply finally and irrevocably an adverse judgement upon the position of the Church of England in reference to the Gorham case', without giving two months' notice of their intention and seeking the counsel of others.[113]

But it was stillborn. Manning would not agree. He told Robert Wilberforce, who had favoured the idea, that he dreaded exceedingly 'the temptation to tamper with personal convictions and individual conscience and the support derived from numbers against our light before our Father which seeth in

---

[110] Gladstone to Manning, 18 June 1850, BL Add. MS 44248, f. 54 and the letter of the following day, ibid., f. 58 ff.
[111] Purcell, op. cit., 543.
[112] A. H. D. Acland, op. cit., 163.
[113] The full text can be found in BL Add. MS 44738, ff. 173–4.

secret'.[114] Without Manning's support Gladstone felt unable to proceed.[115]

There was little now to hold Manning back. At first Gladstone had been sanguine. When Samuel Wilberforce told him, towards the end of April, he feared that Manning might forsake the Church, he had disagreed. He admitted that since Manning's illness in 1847 this same idea had come to him at intervals. But he had been reassured by a letter received from him only a fortnight before. The whole spirit of it 'negatives the idea of a formed intuition, I would even say of any intention, to take the step to which you adverted'. It would be, he told Wilberforce, a step 'more ruinous (in my mind) than any other, except one, namely the abandonment of an article of the Christian faith'.[116]

By the end of July he had become more apprehensive. 'Manning has been with me today: looking better, and talking with much interest about me, travel and my position in politics,' he wrote to his wife. 'As to Church matters I am not less well pleased with his present frame than I was.' But he confessed that Manning's letter to the Bishop of Chichester seemed very strong and 'has more of the aspect of an intention to move'.[117]

By early September his fears had grown. In another letter to Samuel Wilberforce, recalling their earlier conversation, he confessed he was no longer convinced that Manning could be saved: 'It seems to me likely that he shall go.' Even now, however, he refused to despair. Manning's mind had fluctuated much, 'his almost unrivalled intellect giving to each momentary phase all the semblance of completeness and solidarity'. He might yet be kept if the Church would adopt a less equivocal and hesitating attitude, if there was 'a hope of a resolute movement, if not corporate, yet at least combined'.[118]

[114] Purcell, op. cit., 538–9. Manning to Gladstone, 22 and 24 May 1850, Chapeau, op. cit.; Gladstone to Manning, 9, 20, 23 May, BL Add. MS 44248, ff. 43–51.

[115] Gladstone to Manning, 23 May 1850, BL Add. MS 44248, f. 51.

[116] Gladstone to Wilberforce, 28 Apr. 1850, Wilberforce MSS cf. Newsome, op. cit., 363.

[117] Gladstone to his wife, 21 July 1850, Hawn. P.

[118] Gladstone to Wilberforce, 8 Sept. 1850, Wilberforce MSS; cf. Newsome, ibid. See also his letter to Wilberforce, 17 Sept. 1850, ibid.

But of such a movement there seemed little prospect. Only personal influence remained. Before leaving Fasque, where he had spent the summer as usual, Gladstone was visited by James Hope. He was not really certain where Hope stood now. 'All his old doubts and dispositions have revived,' he wrote in his diary, 'but he seems disposed to think and act steadily.'[119]

There was, however, little time. Gladstone had resolved to take his wife to Italy for the winter. Besides the pressure of political and ecclesiastical events he was still deeply depressed by the sudden and painful death of his little daughter Jessy in April.

He hoped to see Manning before he left. He had received a letter from Upton Richards, the priest at the Margaret Chapel, telling him that Manning was more than ever disheartened about things, especially the poor response to his circular. 'He scarcely takes any step without first consulting you,' Richards wrote.[120]

They met for four hours in the evening of 1 October and again the following evening for another four hours. 'His conversation on these two evenings opens to me a still darkening prospect,' Gladstone recorded in his diary. 'Alas for what lies before us: for my deserts it cannot indeed be gloomy enough: but for the sheep and lambs of Christ!'[121] On 18 October he left for Italy.

Manning's secession was now merely a matter of time. He had really been lost three or four years before. The Gorham Judgement had simply convinced him that the Erastianism of the Church of England, and the inconsistencies of its theology, were unalterable. He had been misguided ever to think otherwise.

His differences with Gladstone were now irreconcilable. 'I saw Gladstone twice in London,' he wrote to Hope, 'and had two jarring and useless conversations. We seemed at last to ascertain our differences to lie at the very idea of the Church and

---

[119] *Diary*, iv, 22 Sept. 1850.

[120] Upton Richards to Gladstone, 18 Sept. 1850, BL Add. MS 44369, f. 394. Richard Cavendish felt much the same; Cavendish to Gladstone, 3 Sept. 1850, BL Add. MS 44124, f. 259.

[121] *Diary*, iv, 3 Oct. 1850. For the conversation itself see his letter to Manning, 6 Oct. 1850, *Lathbury*, i. 117–18.

its functions. This made me feel that all hope of our keeping together was at an end.'[122]

Early in November Manning received a final appeal from Gladstone. Writing from Genoa, Gladstone reminded him of their conversation, in the summer of 1848, on Manning's return from Italy and

that you most fervently declared to me, how beyond expression solemn and firm was your assurance, brought from the region you had then been treading, not of the mercy of God to those in invincible ignorance, a mercy reaching to every religious profession, and to *none*, but of the unmoved and immovable title of the Church of England to her share in the one divine and catholic inheritance. Have you *really* unlearned those lessons?[123]

But it was no good. The protestant frenzy over the 'Papal Aggression' in November forced Manning to a decision. His fellow clergy asked him as archdeacon to convene a meeting of protest. He could not do so. On 12 November he saw the Bishop of Chichester and tendered his resignation.

He left Lavington on 3 December. Eight days later he wrote to Hope that he felt everything was now complete. He intended to go to Italy to see Gladstone before the final act and to let two or three months pass, 'not wishing to go hastily from one Altar to another'. It would give him great happiness, he told Hope, if they could act together.[124]

In fact the journey to Italy was abandoned. Manning decided to remain in England and prepare his relatives and friends for what was to come. Gladstone was deeply disappointed. He wrote from Naples at the end of December, pleading that Manning reconsider, begging that he acknowledge his former convictions as exercising a higher authority over his conduct in this hour of trial.[125] While well meant, it was a foolish insensitive tactic. Manning was beyond argument. Gladstone seemed merely to be hectoring. Hope felt so and Manning agreed. To him Gladstone appeared: 'not to confront the evidence nor to attempt any constructive proof—but only to object and embar-

---

[122] Manning to Hope, 23 Nov. 1850, Hope-Scott MS 3675, f. 92 ff.; partially quoted in Ornsby, op. cit., ii. 81–2.
[123] 5 Nov. 1850, Purcell, op. cit., i. 580–1.
[124] Manning to Hope, 11 Dec. 1850, Hope-Scott MS 3675, f. 98 ff.; partially quoted in Ornsby, op. cit., ii. 83.
[125] 20 Dec. 1850, Purcell, op. cit., i. 581–2.

rass which may be done by a Deist against all revelation'. This, at least, was the principle if not the intention of his argument.[126]

Gladstone returned at the end of February. Manning wrote asking to see him. Gladstone agreed but admitted he did not feel up to it either intellectually or morally.[127] Three days before they met Gladstone had a sad conversation with James Hope. He told Gladstone: 'Manning's mind I think is made up: I am not very far from the same.' 'What piercing words,' Gladstone wrote in his diary, 'We argued for two hours, but what am I for such high work?'[128]

The meeting with Manning was unsatisfactory. It could scarcely have been otherwise. They argued for three hours, but Gladstone found Manning's mind fixed. The following Sunday they met again; and again the following Sunday. On 30 March Manning met Gladstone at the York St. Chapel, his final service in the Church of England. He told Gladstone he was now on the brink, and Hope too.[129] Three days later they met for the last time as Anglicans.[130]

On 6 April the deed was done. Quietly and unobtrusively Manning and Hope were together received into the Roman Catholic Church. 'A day of pain! Manning and Hope!', Gladstone wrote in his diary.[131] The gulf had now been fixed. Gladstone felt emotionally drained. 'They were my two props. Their going may be to me a sign that my work is done', he wrote the day after.[132]

The old intimacy had ceased. On 8 April Gladstone added a codicil to his will striking out Hope as executor.[133] On 17 June he sent him a copy of his newly published translation of Farini's *History of the Roman State*.[134] He received a touching reply. Gladstone recalled it as 'the epitaph of our friendship, which

---

[126] Manning to Hope, 9 Jan. 1851, Hope-Scott MS 3675, f. 103. Manning changed his mind early in January and decided to join Gladstone in Naples, but by this time Gladstone was on his homeward journey.

[127] Gladstone to Manning, 5 Mar. 1851, BL Add. MS 44248, f. 122.

[128] *Diary*, iv. 6 Mar. 1851.

[129] The parting recalled in Purcell, op. cit., i. 617.

[130] *Diary*, iv, 2 Apr. 1851.

[131] *Diary*, iv, 6 Apr. 1851.

[132] *Diary*, iv, 7 Apr. 1851.

[133] *Diary*, iv, 8 Apr. 1851.

[134] Farini's history was written from an anti-papal standpoint.

continued to live, but only, or almost only, as it lives between those who inhabit separate worlds'.[135]

For Manning his shock and grief went deeper. What Manning later described as a 'quarrel', had been for Gladstone 'a death'.[136] 'I felt as if he had murdered my mother by mistake,' Gladstone told a friend.[137] For twelve years they did not meet and in 1862 they returned each other's letters.

To Robert Wilberforce he summed up his feelings:

I do indeed feel the loss of Manning, if and as far as I am capable of feeling anything. It comes to me cumulated, and doubled with that of James Hope. Nothing like it can happen to me again. Arrived now at middle life, I never can *form* I suppose with any other two men the habits and communication, counsel and dependence, in which I have now from fifteen to eighteen years lived with them both.[138]

The loss of Manning and Hope was a personal tragedy. But Gladstone also regarded it as a tragedy for the Church. 'It has been a sad year', he wrote in his diary at the end of December, a year that had seen 'the rending and sapping of the Church, the loss of its gems, the darkening of its prospects'.[139]

The blame he attached primarily to the bishops. It was their behaviour that was inexcusable. From the moment the Judgement had been announced he had looked to them for a decisive lead, for a resolute stand repudiating its consequences, for some action that showed they would not acquiesce in what had taken place. He was convinced that had they done so, it would have held Manning and others back. Their hesitancy and seeming lack of concern appalled him. After the rejection of Blomfield's second bill, on 3 June 1850, he had written to Robert Wilberforce lamenting the absence of Archbishop Sumner: 'Canterbury was absent!!! Why, Cranmer opposed the Act for the Six Articles. But Cranmer's weakest moments were heroism

---

[135] Ornsby, op. cit., ii. 286.

[136] Gladstone to Manning, 23 June 1891, BL Add. MS 44250, f. 321.

[137] Purcell, op. cit., i. 627.

[138] 11 Apr. 1851; quoted in *Morley*, i. 387. Cf. Manning's remarks to Robert Wilberforce, 28 Aug. 1851, 'I seem to have reached the end of life for I do not know what more to desire than "Fungi sacerdotio et offere Illi incensum odoris". I seem to have entered into the substance and reality of all my long visions of many years and nothing now remains'; a letter in the custody of the Priory of Our Lady of the Angels, Fernham nr. Faringdon. I owe this reference to the kindness of Dr Sheridan Gilley.

[139] *Diary*, iv, 31 Dec. 1851.

itself and ideal glory compared with the present shame and degradation which carries that honoured name.'[140]

No less shrill were his remarks to his wife three months later. He talked of the Church of England quietly sitting down 'under the abominations that had been practised', and the 'perpetrators and abettors . . . from the Archbishop of Canterbury downwards'.[141] To Sir Walter James he lamented 'the hopelessly continued silence' of the Church on a vital point of Catholic Doctrine. If only even a minority of the bishops remained steadfast and fearless 'they may achieve great things for us and for Christendom'.[142]

The Bishop of Exeter's letter to the Churchwardens of Brampford Speke, his effective acceptance of Gorham's induction as a *fait accompli*, deeply distressed him.[143] It was a 'sad omen', he told James. 'I am totally at a loss to reconcile it either with his principles, his professions, or his former proceedings.'[144] In January 1851 he received a letter from Phillpotts requesting a meeting on his return from Italy. 'How can I tell him in most decorous language,' Gladstone asked Phillimore, 'that the battle of which he speaks was decided, and decided by his own turning tail, when he wrote to the Churchwardens of Brampford Speke.'[145]

To Samuel Wilberforce, one of the few bishops for whom Gladstone had both respect and admiration and who was now a close friend, he sent a number of letters that reveal the depth of his outrage. The Episcopal Bench were losing respect, he told Wilberforce in May 1851. 'Anglicans upheld vigorously and unitedly on its negative side, and on its positive, by many denied—by many more just endured—by individuals taught in varying degrees of warmth—this is the picture, which tells its own story.'[146]

At the end of 1851 he expressed himself with a lack of restraint he later regretted. He did not want to criticize the conduct of the

[140] Gladstone to R. Wilberforce, 4 June 1850, R. Wilberforce MSS.
[141] Gladstone to his wife, 17 Sept. 1850, Hawn. P.
[142] Gladstone to James, 29 Sept. 1850, BL Add. 44264, f. 156.
[143] See Chadwick, op. cit., 269.
[144] Gladstone to James, ibid.
[145] Gladstone to Phillimore, 23 Jan. 1851, BL Add. MS 44276, f. 229.
[146] Gladstone to Wilberforce, 24 May 1851, Wilberforce MSS, Bodleian Library.

bishops in their dioceses. But it was their conduct as representatives of the Church and guardians of the deposit of Faith that filled him with the gloomiest apprehension. It was becoming increasingly difficult to place any confidence in any given number of them. Too many refused to do anything. They were merely lookers-on, men with no opinions, prepared to state doctrine for themselves but 'to abide patiently under a law which cuts away the whole foundation of dogmatic teaching'. They would rally against the Pope and pray for legislative protection, while postponing any attempt to protect the faith. Whatever they said in their charges, and however they acted in their dioceses, they stood before the world as men acquiescing in a system that seemed to him fatal to the Church, prepared to sacrifice their own standing ground 'in order to maintain the show of a make-believe unity with men from whom they vitally differ'.[147]

It could be, however, that this intense emotion and sense of betrayal, had its origin in an unconscious feeling of guilt. Had Gladstone himself done enough to defend the Church in its time of trial? There is certainly a problem here. Although Gladstone had realized since Maynooth, and certainly since the removal of Jewish disabilities, that the Church needed greater liberty and could no longer rely upon its national position or cling to its temporalities, he seems to have done little positively to help it gain that freedom. He was loath to initiate any moves in that direction; prepared only to act when a conflict actually rose. Even then what he said was not always backed up by definite action. Only in relation to the establishment of colonial bishoprics, and more particularly in the emancipation of colonial sees from metropolitan control, can he be said to have actually initiated measures that gave the Church a greater measure of freedom.[148]

Perhaps he was merely being realistic. From his position within parliament he saw, as the more radical High Church clergy often did not, what was possible in the actual circumst-

---

[147] Gladstone to Wilberforce, 31 Dec. 1851, Wilberforce MSS, Bodleian Library. Gladstone would not allow this letter to be published in the life of Samuel Wilberforce: R. G. Wilberforce, *Life of Samuel Wilberforce* (1881), ii. 130. See also *Lathbury*, i. 88.

[148] To this end he introduced a series of private bills, none of which were passed in the form he intended. See *Diary*, iii, Introduction, xxxv.

ances. It may have been that he had greater insight and realized that to gain liberty prematurely, without the necessary doctrinal cohesion, would simply lead to the disintegration of the Church into warring factions. He did not conceive of liberty as the opposite of authority, discipline or order. 'To obtain liberty for the Church is the object for which I should think it the highest, almost the only honour and delight to spend and be spent,' Gladstone wrote to Manning in July 1849. But he added: 'by this I understand liberty in the English sense, liberty under rule, and the whole question is what rule is admissible or desirable, what freedom will tend to or is required for the real development of your religious system.' [149] Perhaps also, while aware of the deficiencies of undogmatic folk religion, he saw that in England at least, it would remain a powerful and conserving force. In his *Chapter of Autobiography* he wrote that although what might be called the 'dogmatic allegiance of the State' had been greatly relaxed, during the last thirty years, its consciousness of moral duty had quickened and enhanced; 'We are still a Christian people,' he could declare in 1868. [150]

Yet the tensions between his religious self and his political self were very real and his behaviour at the time of the Gorham Judgement not entirely unequivocal. His decision not to sign Manning's declaration and instead to organize a principally lay and parliamentary address has already been discussed. It is perhaps curious that he did not attempt to do more in the parliamentary arena. He refused, for example, to introduce Blomfield's bill into the Commons.

He undoubtedly realized that action of this sort would damage his parliamentary career. But though he braced himself for this eventuality, he drew back from precipitating it. He looked to others outside parliament. When, for example, Lyttelton wrote to him in September 1850 asking his views on the demand by some High-Churchmen for the recall of Convocation, he replied that he looked on them 'as breaking up the ground, and helping onwards the natural development of events'. But he did little himself. It was 'the proper instrument for out door work. It is therefore no work for me: but I do not

---

[149] Gladstone to Manning, 6 July 1849, *Lathbury*, ii. 282.
[150] *Gleanings*, vii. 150.

deny that it may be work for others only I am slow and reluctant to be an adviser where having a common interest and feeling I do not mean to be a partner too.'[151] Yet High-Churchmen did look to him for a lead. As Richard Cavendish wrote, lamenting Gladstone's departure for Italy in such anxious and troubled times, 'to you I think great numbers are looking for guidance because they know that while your whole heart is with the English Church, you do not shut your eyes to the extreme peril in which she is now involved'.[152] In his desire to do nothing that would impede his usefulness in parliament, Gladstone left himself open in some High-Churchmen's eyes, to the charge that he had not done enough.[153]

One final matter remains to be discussed. Why was Gladstone so convinced of the essential rightness of the Anglican position? What were the crucial issues between him, Manning and Hope that made them go their separate ways?

The day after their conversion, Gladstone wrote in his diary: 'One blessing I have: total freedom from doubts. These dismal events have smitten but not shaken.'[154] His intellect deliberately rejected the grounds on which Manning had proceeded, he wrote to Robert Wilberforce four days later. Indeed, so definite was this rejection that his confidence in the healthiness and soundness of Manning's own intellect had almost been destroyed.[155]

Four areas of disagreement stand out: a difference of attitude to the devotional system of the Roman Church; differences rooted in history and doctrine; philosophical differences; and what can best be described as differences over the vocation of Anglicanism.

Their difference of attitude to Roman Catholic devotional practices can be dealt with swiftly. Gladstone's hostility to some aspects of the Roman Catholic cultus, mariolatry and com-

---

[151] Gladstone to Lyttelton, 29 Sept. 1850, Hawn. P.

[152] Richard Cavendish to Gladstone, 3 Sept. 1850, BL Add. MS 44124, f. 259.

[153] Early in 1850 he received a letter from Phillimore telling him that George Denison and others 'of more reasonable stamp' had complained to him that they had received less support from Gladstone in Church matters than they had expected. Phillimore to Gladstone, undated but probably early 1850, BL Add. MS 44275, f. 168. He did not attend the meeting on 23 July 1850 at St. Martin's Hall.

[154] *Diary*, iv, 7 Apr. 1851.

[155] *Morley*, i. 387.

pulsory confession in particular, have already been commented upon. While the reverence and sacramentalism of Catholic worship at its best had an obvious appeal, he could never overcome his antipathy to certain practices or reconcile himself to the abuses evident in much popular piety and preaching. His visits to Italy afforded ample opportunity of studying these at first hand and his diary records many instances of shock and horror at the more egregious examples of erroneous teaching in sermons or liturgical and devotional practice that seemed, to Gladstone, bordering on the idolatrous.[156]

For Manning, however, as his journey to Rome in the winter of 1847/8 showed, the ethos of Catholicism was something deeply compelling. The deficiencies of Anglicanism, its lack of many devotional practices that seemed to him necessary, made questionable its claim to Catholicity. 'There seems about the Church of England a want of antiquity, system, fullness, intelligence, order, strength, unity,' he had written in his journal in May 1846 as his confidence in the Church of England was beginning to weaken.[157] Whereas Gladstone saw evidence of corruption and idolatry, Manning was spellbound; 'for majesty and beauty, simplicity and severity, I have seen and heard nothing like it', was his comment to Henry Wilberforce after Holy Week spent in Rome in 1848.[158]

More fundamental, however, was Gladstone's unshakeable conviction that the Anglican position was justified by the appeal to history. He felt, he wrote to Robert Wilberforce in 1854: 'every day more and more the value of history—that it is so vain—and yet that it is the secure ground on which to build all testimony—and that it is a ground off which purely polemical theology and ecclesiastical questions tend constantly to lead us.[159] History, he believed, vindicated the Church of England's claim to Catholicity.

He did not believe that communion with the see of Rome and acknowledgement of the Pope's jurisdiction made a church Catholic. How could it when popes themselves had fallen into

---

[156] See e.g., of many possible examples, his description of the sermon in Naples, *Diary*, ii, 2 Nov. 1838.

[157] Purcell, op. cit., i. 484.

[158] Newsome, op. cit., 326.

[159] Gladstone to R. Wilberforce, 13 Sept. 1854, BL Add. MS 44382, f. 123.

error? 'Nothing ever so much made me Anglican *versus* Roman as reading in Döllinger over forty years ago, the history of the fourth century and Athanasius *contra mundum*,' Gladstone wrote to A. W. Hutton, one of Manning's first biographers, in 1888.[160] The existence of the Eastern Churches was living proof that the papal claims were unjustified. If the Church of England had ceased to be Catholic by renouncing the papal jurisdiction, then by the same token the Eastern Churches were not Catholic either. Newman's ignoring of the Eastern Church was, he told T. W. Allies in 1846, 'one of the boldest pieces of tactic in the history of controversy'.[161]

Gladstone remained convinced of the soundness of Manning's pamphlet *The Unity of the Church*, the importance of which, he told A. W. Hutton, 'lay in the principle that the essence of the Church is not conditioned by the intercommunion of its parts'.[162] Because of this he could not believe the Reformation had altered the status of the Church of England. Although it had cast off the papal jurisdiction and acknowledged the supremacy of the Crown neither of these things meant the forfeiture of its catholic title. It retained a material identity with the pre-

---

[160] Gladstone to Hutton, BL Add. MS 44215, f. 70. Gladstone met Döllinger in the same week that Newman was received into the Church of Rome (and that Renan left the seminary of St. Sulpice and the Catholic Church). It was the beginning of a lifelong friendship. See *Diary*, iii, 30 Oct. 1845 and BL Add. MS 44140, ff. 264–7. Gladstone's account of their discussion during this first visit is in BL Add. MS 44735, ff. 77–92. Döllinger's influence on Gladstone was profound. In 1888 he wrote that their first meeting was 'a great stage in my religious education'. BL Add. MS 447231 f. 54. Hutton wrote to Gladstone on 23 June 1891 as follows: 'Oddly enough too it was your intimacy with the greatest living Roman Catholic theologian that taught you you could not become a Roman Catholic with a good historical conscience.' He then went on to say that he once thought Gladstone had been inconsistent in not going over with Hope and Manning but added: 'No doubt there is a rough and ready consistency in bowing blindly to the principle of authority; but when one is clear (as you seem to have been) of certain historical facts irreconcilable with the teachings of authority, the position is changed.'

[161] 23 June 1846, T. W. Allies, *A Life's Decision* (1880), 91. Gladstone's remark is, in fact, rather stronger as he describes this tactic as Newman's *non ragionam di lor, ma guarda e passa* (Let us not speak of these; but look and pass), *Inferno III*. 51, Dante talking of the damned.

[162] Gladstone to Hutton, 21 Apr. 1892, BL Add. MS 44215, f. 1892. This letter gives an interesting insight in Gladstone's attitude to Manning in old age including the following: 'In one matter (their conversation in 1848?) I have to take an objection almost too strong for propriety. On the other hand he fought the battle for sixty years against the world and the flesh with such constancy, courage, and self-sacrifice that his plane is immeasurably above mine and I cannot be his critic or his judge.'

Reformation Church and therefore remained the Catholic Church of the realm.

Nor had the Church of England separated itself from Catholic Christendom by the adoption of doctrines at variance with those of the Catholic faith. Pre-Tridentine Catholicism was far more doctrinally heterogeneous than was often realized. Many of the tenets condemned by the English Church at the Reformation had never been asserted dogmatically by the Roman Church itself, still less by an Ecumenical Council. Doctrine had been held in the Church of Rome before the Reformation which had not been allowed since. The Henrician bishops, Gardiner and Tunstall, had both written against the supremacy of the Pope and the scholastic theologians had held a broad range of opinion concerning the Real Presence. Many of the doctrines rejected by the English Church at the Reformation were not held by the Eastern Church. In his own reading of authorized books of Orthodox teaching Gladstone had found nothing of importance that seemed incompatible with the doctrine of Anglicanism.[163]

The most important area of disagreement between him and Manning, however, was as much philosophical as doctrinal. In the end it was Manning's conviction that the Church, under divine guidance, was infallible in expounding the Faith and deciding controversies that forced him to abandon the Church of England. The whole concept precluded the notion of a divided unity. The Church must be one, visible and perpetual; a divided unity was nothing less than a form of ecclesiological Arianism. 'I entirely feel what you say of the alternatives,' he wrote to James Hope in December 1850. 'It is either Rome or licence of thought and will.'[164]

Gladstone, as a student of Bishop Butler, could not accept either the concept of infallibility or unbridled licence of thought. In his first book he had dealt with the relation of private judgement to Catholic consent and shown that probability made the latter more reasonable than the former, while not

---

[163] Gladstone discussed all these matters fully in a most interesting series of letters to E. L. Badeley between October 1851 and July 1852 which has been preserved in the Hope-Scott MSS 3678, ff. 171–3 and 3679, ff. 50–71. See also H. C. G. Matthew, 'Gladstone, Vaticanism and the question of the East' in D. Baker, ed., *Studies in Church History* (1978), 425 ff.

[164] Manning to Hope, 11 Dec. 1850, Ornsby, op. cit., ii. 83.

denying private judgement a place where the Church had left matters open. 'Bishop Butler was not a controversialist,' he told the Hon. Maud Stanley, a would-be Roman convert in 1856, 'but his works are more fruitful in sound principles applicable to the mode of Providential government in the Church as well as in the world than almost any others.'[165]

Finally, unlike Manning, Gladstone never lost his faith in the unique vocation of Anglicanism. Throughout their relationship Manning had always taken a darker view of the prospects before them. Every setback, every defeat made more questionable the Anglican claims. More and more its theology seemed in chaos, its unity disintegrating, its devotional life deficient. By 1846 it seemed to him to be 'diseased'; where it seemed healthy was where it approximated to Rome.[166] By the late 1840s he had come to see the Reformation as a fatal divide. The Church of England had become national instead of universal and Protestant instead of Catholic.[167] The Reformation settlement had been carried by violence and upheld by political power. Now that the State was divorcing the Church, Anglicanism was dissolving.[168] It was 'but Episcopal Protestantism, a human society with human opinions', he told Robert Wilberforce.[169] It had only one vocation: to cease to be national and Protestant and to become Catholic again by returning to the unity and authority of the universal Church.[170]

Gladstone's views could hardly have been more different. With an unshakeable belief in the validity of the Church of England on both historical and doctrinal grounds, he saw before it a great Providential mission. Although he abandoned his ideas on Church and State he retained a strong sense of religious nationality. The Church of England was the divinely appointed means of bringing Christianity to the English nation. If it was not the Catholic Church of the land, it was nothing. Moreover,

[165] Gladstone to the Hon. Maud Stanley, 27 Jan. 1856, *Lathbury*, ii. 30. The entire letter and the one preceding it provides a clear and interesting account of Gladstone's understanding of Anglicanism and a discussion of probability in relation to ecclesiastical controversy.

[166] Purcell, op. cit., i. 483–4.

[167] Purcell, op. cit., i. 623. Against this statement Gladstone had pencilled 'NB. *and.*'

[168] Purcell, op. cit., i. 556.

[169] 28 Sept. 1851, Purcell, op. cit., i. 637.

[170] Purcell, op. cit., i. 623.

it alone could convey to the English people Catholic principles. This was why he so much deplored 'the continual rain-dropping of proselytes into the Church of Rome'.[171] It was a process essentially retrogressive, which widened and continued the chasm between the English people and the Catholic Church. 'With my whole soul', he told Manning in June 1850, 'I am convinced that, if the Roman system is incapable of being powerfully modified in spirit, it never can be the instrument of the work of God among us; the faults and virtues of England are alike against it.'[172]

He refused to be disheartened. He rode out every crisis sustained by an unquenchable optimism. 'I am scathed, torn and strained by the tempest, but my roots are where and as they are,' he wrote to E. L. Badeley.[173] Ultimately it was this that kept him within the Anglican fold.[174]

But the more affliction and peril grow within the Church of England, the more do I feel that a noble work for God and for Christendom is to be done within her: aye and that it will be done, and that though Moses be cut off from one cause and Aaron from another some Joshua will be found to do it. For that which goes on within her is surely a marvellous phenomenon. That truth should prosper against the discountenance of the powers of this world, is not extraordinary: but that it should stubbornly and obstinately grow, and every year be stronger there than it was the year before, when the men who have been its captains and its generals drop off like a falling sickness, this as a fact appreciably by common sense, demands deep attention though I quite feel it is only the vestibule to other facts, which sustain and account for it: and which, with me form the great practical counterpart to the historical and ecclesiastical argument concerning the Church of England.[175]

[171] Gladstone to Manning, 23 June 1850, *Lathbury*, i. 104.
[172] Ibid.
[173] Gladstone to Badeley, 18 July 1851, Hope-Scott MS 3679, f. 68.
[174] It is, of course, unthinkable that Gladstone would ever have converted to Roman Catholicism. Had he found it impossible to remain within the Church of England he would probably have joined the episcopalian communion in Scotland, with whom he worshipped when in Scotland and in whose affairs he took a profound interest. Samuel Wilberforce suggested this course of action for his brother Robert in 1854, see Newsome, op. cit., 400.
[175] Gladstone to Badeley, 9 Nov. 1851, Hope-Scott MS 3679, f. 50.

# CONCLUSION

In this study of Gladstone's religious development two events have pivotal significance. The first, the Reform Bill crisis, made him a politician committed to the service of the Church and to the christianizing of the social and political order through the agency of the Tory party.[1] The second, the Maynooth crisis, showed him this was impractical and forced him to modify his view of the State and accept the principle of religious liberty.

He began his parliamentary career the defender of an exclusive Anglican establishment. The purgative experiences of the 1840s and early 1850s left him convinced that an ecclesiastical establishment could be justified only on utilitarian grounds. Social justice had become the principle of his political action and his commitment to the Church was no longer a commitment to preserving her exclusive claims or privileged position, but to work towards her emancipation from the State as circumstances demanded, in order that the Catholic truth to which she witnessed might be preserved intact. He had travelled a long and tortuous path from a belief in a Christian commonwealth towards the liberal ideal of a free Church in a free State.

Gladstone's experience was unique. Yet its complexity and fascination should not blind us to the fact that it was an experience he shared with other churchmen, not only in England but in Europe as well. For Gladstone's experience was the reaction of one man in a particular set of circumstances to a phenomenon as much European as English: the demise of the Confessional State and the emergence of what, in France, came to be called indifferentism and *l'état laïque*.

The crisis of Gladstone's life was the fate of his book published in 1838. It was the realization that his ideal was no longer

---

[1] 'Many men's political "proclivities" underwent curious transmutations in and about 1832.' G. A. Denison, *Notes of My Life* (1878), 68. cf. *Autobiographica*, 36–7, 38, 40.

possible which, with the disintegration of the Tory party, forced him to seek a *modus vivendi* between the catholic tradition and the liberal principles of the nineteenth century.

It is in this that his religious significance lies. For by accepting the principle of religious liberty and treading the path towards political liberalism Gladstone showed that High-Churchmanship need no longer be synonymous with defence of the Establishment and allegiance to the Tory party, or that it was necessarily hostile to the movement for political and social change. In so doing he forced many churchmen to reappraise their position and those who travelled with him, or followed after him, helped create a High-Churchmanship different from that which had existed before.[2]

By the late 1850s, Gladstone's position could be described as a liberal Catholicism, no less worthy of that name for having its origin in the context of England and Anglicanism. He had reached it as a result of a profound political and ecclesiastical readjustment accompanied by not inconsiderable emotional upheaval. It is this transition from Tory High-Churchman to Liberal Catholic that has formed the core of this study.

To combine liberalism and catholicism, however, was to combine two things which many believed irreconcilable. For Gladstone such a combination was not merely intellectually desirable, it was a personal necessity; on it hinged his vocation as a politician committed to serving the Church.

In old age he believed the path he had taken was the right one. But if we survey the later part of his career we should, perhaps, ask whether he ever managed effectively to translate this liberal catholicism into political terms or political action. Was it ultimately possible to reconcile the dogmatic nature of catholicism with the sort of religious liberty and free play of opinion implied by indifferentism? There remained a body of High-Churchmen like Archdeacon Denison, William Palmer and Charles and Christopher Wordsworth, loyal to the ideal of a Confessional State, who believed that it was not.

Gladstone never worked out an alternative theory of the relations between Church and State and this is surely significant. Many elements were to make up his political Liberalism. But it is not clear which aspects of it might be described as religious, or still more, as catholic. Did he in later life see himself simply working 'the lower ends' of government, recognizing that in the political conditions of the nineteenth century it was no longer possible for government to fulfil its 'higher ends'?

If this is the case then Gladstone, by abandoning his Ideal, put a gulf between his political and his religious self, however he justified his continuing in politics on the ground that he was working for the constitutional liberation of the Church.

What he achieved, therefore, was certainly no easy synthesis of liberalism and catholicism. It is almost as if he held these two, almost contradictory, impulses together in tension. It was this tension, perhaps, that provides an understanding of his political development. Perhaps it was also the source of his personal power.[3]

[2] See W. R. Ward, 'Oxford and the Origins of Liberal Catholicism in the Church of England', in *Studies in Church History* (1964), i. 233–52.

[3] See the remarks of M. D. Stephen, 'Liberty, Church and State: Gladstone's Relations with Manning and Acton, 1832–70', *Journal of Religious History*, i (1960–1), 217.

# BIBLIOGRAPHY

A. Primary Sources (manuscript)
B. Primary Sources (printed)
C. Secondary Sources
    (i)   Works by W. E. Gladstone
    (ii)  General
    (iii)  Articles
D. Theses (published and unpublished)

*A. Primary Sources*

Gladstone Papers; British Library Add. MSS 44086–44835.
Gladstone-Glynne MSS; housed at St. Deiniols Library, Hawarden. (Hawn. P.).
    From this collection I have used the correspondence of W. E. Gladstone with the following:
        Sir John Gladstone Bt., Mrs A. Gladstone, Sir Thomas Gladstone Bt., Robertson Gladstone, John Neilson Gladstone, Anne Gladstone, Helen Jane Gladstone, George Lyttelton.
Hope-Scott MSS; National Library of Scotland.
    3672   Gladstone to Hope-Scott, 1837–42
    3673   Gladstone to Hope-Scott, 1843–73
    3674   Hope-Scott to Gladstone, 1837–71
    3675   Manning and Pusey to Hope-Scott, 1836–72
    3678   Hope-Scott to E. L. Badeley
    3679   Miscellaneous.
Pusey MSS; Pusey House, Oxford.
    Letters of Gladstone to E. B. Pusey.
Churton MSS; Pusey House, Oxford.
Wilberforce MSS; Bodleian Library, Oxford.
    Letters of Gladstone to S. Wilberforce.
MS Eng. lett. d.89; Bodleian Library, Oxford.
    Letters of Gladstone to T. D. Acland.
MS Eng. lett. c.297; Bodleian Library, Oxford.
    Letters of Gladstone to Lord A. C. Hervey.
Hawkins MSS; Oriel College, Oxford.
    Letters of Gladstone to the Revd E. Hawkins.
Keble MSS; Keble College, Oxford.
    Letters of J. H. Newman and W. E. Gladstone.
R. Wilberforce MSS; owned by Miss Irene Wilberforce and kept at 2 York House, Church Street, Kensington.
    Letters of Gladstone to R. I. Wilberforce.

Hawarden Papers; St. Deiniol's Library, Hawarden.
Oratory MSS; Oratory, Edgbaston, Birmingham.
    Letters of Gladstone to J. H. Newman.
Manners MSS; Belvoir Castle, Leicestershire.
    Letters of Gladstone to Lord John Manners.
Houghton MSS; Trinity College, Cambridge.
    Letters of Gladstone to R. Monckton-Milnes.
Lincoln MSS; University of Nottingham Library.
    Letters of Gladstone to Lord Lincoln, 5th Duke of Newcastle.


*B. Primary Sources (printed)*
BROOKE, JOHN, and SORENSEN, MARY, eds., *The Prime Ministers' Papers: W.
    E. Gladstone I: Autobiographica II: Autobiographical Memoranda*, (1971–2).
CHAPEAU, A. Letters of H. E. Manning to W. E. Gladstone (1955). University
    of Paris thesis on microfilm.
FOOT, M. R. D. and MATTHEW, H. C. G., eds., *The Gladstone Diaries
    (1825–1868)*, 6 v. (1968–78).
*Hansard's Parliamentary Debates*, third series.
LATHBURY, D. C., ed., *Correspondence on Church and Religion of W. E. Gladstone*, 2
    v. (1910).


*C. Secondary Sources*
(i)
GLADSTONE, W. E., *The State in its relations with the Church* (1839).
—— —— *The State in its relations with the Church*, 4th ed., 2 v. (1841).
—— —— *Church Principles considered in their results* (1840).
—— —— *The Inaugural Address delivered at the opening of the Collegiate Institution,
    Liverpool* (1843).
—— —— *A Manual of Prayers from the Liturgy arranged for family use* (1845).
—— —— *Substance of a speech for the second reading of the Maynooth College bill, April
    11th 1845* (1845).
—— —— *Substance of a speech on the motion of Lord John Russell for a committee of the
    whole house, with a view to the removal of the remaining Jewish disabilities,
    delivered December 16th 1847·* (1848).
—— —— *Ecclesiastical Titles assumption bill. Speech of the Rt. Hon. W. E. Gladstone in
    the House of Commons, on the 25th of March 1851.* (1851).
—— —— *Gleanings of past years, 1843–1878*, 7 v. (1879).
—— —— *Later Gleanings, a new series of Gleanings of past years* (1898).
—— —— *The works of Joseph Butler*, 2 v. (1896).
—— —— *Studies subsidiary to the works of Bishop Butler* (1896).


(ii)
ACLAND, A. H. D. (ed.), *Memoir and Letters of Sir Thomas Dyke Acland* (1902).
ARNOLD, T., *Principles of Church Reform* (1833), ed. M. J. Jackson and J. Rogan
    (1962).
ASHWELL, A. R. and WILBERFORCE, R. G., *The Life of Samuel Wilberforce*, 3 v.
    (1880–2).

BASTABLE, J. (ed.), *Newman and Gladstone: Centennial Essays* (Dublin, 1978).
BATTISCOMBE, G., *John Keble. A Study in Limitations* (1963).
BENSON, A. C., *Fasti Etonenses* (1899).
BEST, G. F. A., *Temporal Pillars* (1964).
BOWE, M. C., *François Rio, sa place dans le renouveau catholique en Europe, 1797–1874* (Paris, 1938).
BRILIOTH, Y., *The Anglican Revival, Studies in the Oxford Movement* (1925).
BROSE, O. J., *Church and Parliament. The Reshaping of the Church of England, 1826–1860* (1959).
BUNSEN, F., *A Memoir of Baron Bunsen*, 2 v. (1868).
CHADWICK, O., *The Victorian Church* (1966).
CHALMERS, T., *Lectures on the Establishment and Extension of National Churches* (1838).
CHAVCHAVADZE, M., *Man's concern with Holiness* (1972).
CHECKLAND, S. G., *The Gladstones. A Family Biography, 1764–1851* (1971).
CHURCH, R. W., *The Oxford Movement. Twelve Years, 1833–1845* (1891).
*Church Quarterly Review*, cxv, 1904.
CHURTON, E., *Letters of a Reformed Catholic* (1838).
COCKSHUT, A. O. J., *Anglican Attitudes* (1959).
—— *Truth to Life, the art of biography in the nineteenth century* (1974).
COLERIDGE, S. T., *On the Constitution of Church and State according to the Idea of Each*, 3 ed. (1839).
DAWSON, C. H., *The Spirit of the Oxford Movement* (1933).
DENISON, G. A., *Notes of My Life* (1878).
DOYLE, F., *Reminiscences and opinions of Sir Francis Hastings Doyle, 1813–1885* (1886).
FEUCHTWANGER, E. J., *Gladstone* (1975).
FITZSIMONS, J. (ed.), *Manning: Anglican and Catholic* (1951).
FOWLER, J., *Richard Waldo Sibthorp, a biography* (1880).
GASH, N., *Reaction and Reconstruction in English Politics, 1832–1852* (1964).
—— *Mr. Secretary Peel, the life of Sir Robert Peel to 1830* (1964).
—— *Sir Robert Peel, the life of Sir Robert Peel after 1830* (1972).
GASKELL, C. M. (ed.), *An Eton Boy. Being the letters of James Milnes Gaskell from Eton and Oxford, 1820–1830* (1939).
GLOYN, C. K., *The Church in the Social Order* (Oregon, 1942).
HALDANE, A., *Memoir of the Lives of R. Haldane, of Airthrey, and his Brother J. A. Haldane* (1852).
HAMER, D. A., *John Morley, liberal intellectual in politics* (1968).
HAMPDEN, H., *Memorials of Bishop Hampden* (1871).
HEALY, J., *Maynooth College. Its Centenary History* (1895).
HODDER, E., *The Life and Work of the Seventh Earl of Shaftesbury, K. G.*, 3 v. (1886).
HYDE, F. E., *Gladstone at the Board of Trade* (1934).
KENNY, J., *The Political Thought of John Henry Newman* (1957).
LANG, A., *Life of Stafford Northcote* (1890).
LASKI, H. J., *Studies in the problem of Sovereignty* (1917).
LATHBURY, D. C., *Mr. Gladstone* (1907).

LAWSON, J. P., *History of the Scottish Episcopalian Church* (1843).
LESLIE, S., *Henry Edward Manning. His Life and Labours* (1921).
LIDDON, H. P., *Life of E. B. Pusey*, 4 v. (1894).
MACHIN, G. I. T., *Politics and the Churches in Great Britain 1832 to 1868* (1977).
MAGNUS, P. M., *Gladstone: a biography* (1954).
MARTINEAU, J., *Life of Henry Pelham, Fifth Duke of Newcastle, 1811-1864* (1908).
MORLEY, J., *Life of William Ewart Gladstone*, 3 v. (1903).
MORRELL, W. P., *British Colonial policy in the age of Peel and Gladstone* (1930).
MOZLEY, A. (ed.), *Letters of J. B. Mozley D.D.* (1885).
— — *Letters and Correspondence of John Henry Newman*, 2 v, (1891).
NEWMAN, J. H., *Correspondence of John Henry Newman with John Keble and others, 1839-1845*, edited by members of the Oratory (1911).
NEWSOME, D., *The Parting of Friends* (1966).
NIAS, J. C. S., *Gorham and the Bishop of Exeter* (1951).
OLDCASTLE, J., *Memorials of Cardinal Manning* (1892).
ORNSBY, R., *Memoir of James Robert Hope-Scott*, 2 v. (1884).
PALMER, W., *A Treatise on the Church of Christ*, 2 v. (1838).
— — *A Narrative of Events connected with the publication of the Tracts for the Times* (1883).
PARKER, C. S. (ed.), *Sir Robert Peel from his private papers*, 3 v. (1891–9).
PREVOST, G. (ed.), *The Autobiography of Isaac Williams* (1892).
PURCELL, E. S., *The Life of Cardinal Manning*, 2 v. (1896).
REARDON, B. M. G., *From Coleridge to Gore* (1971).
REID, T. W., *The Life, letters and friendships of Richard Monckton Milnes, first Lord Houghton*, 2 v. (1890).
— — *Life of William Ewart Gladstone* (1899).
ROE, W. G., *Lammenais and England* (1966).
RUSSELL, G. W. E., *William Ewart Gladstone* (1906).
— — *Mr. Gladstone's religious development: a paper read in Christ Church May 5, 1899* (1899).
SMYTH, C. H. E., *Simeon and Church Order, a study in the origins of the Evangelical Revival in Cambridge in the 18th Century* (1940).
SOLOWAY, R. A., *Prelates and People, Ecclesiastical Social Thought in England, 1783-1852* (1969).
SPECK, E. J., *Church Pastoral-Aid Society: Sketch of its Origins and Progress* (1881).
STANLEY, A. P., *The life and correspondence of Thomas Arnold*, 2 v. (1845).
STANMORE, LORD, *Sidney Herbert, A Memoir*, 2 v. (1906).
STEPHEN, L., *Hours in a Library* (1877).
STEWART, R. M., *The Politics of Protection, Lord Derby and the Protectionist Party, 1841-1852* (1971).
SVAGLIC, M. J. (ed.), *J. H. Newman, Apologia pro vita sua* (1967).
TEIGNMOUTH, LORD, *Reminiscences of many years*, 2 v. (1878).
VIDLER, A. R., *The Orb and the Cross* (1945).
VOLL, D., *Catholic Evangelicalism* (1963).
WALKER, W., *Life of Rt. Rev. Alexander Jolly, D.D., Bishop of Moray* (1878).
WARD, W., *W. G. Ward and the Oxford Movement* (1889).
WARD, W. R., *Victorian Oxford* (1965).

240 BIBLIOGRAPHY

WHITWORTH, W. A., *Quam Dilecta* (1891).
WORDSWORTH, C., *Annals of My Early Life, 1806–1846* (1891).

(iii)

ALLEN, L., 'Gladstone et Montalembert', *Revue de Littérature Comparée*, xxx, January 1956.
BEST, G. F. A., 'The Constitutional Revolution 1828–32 and its consequences for the Established Church', *Theology*, lxii, June 1959.
—— 'The Whigs and the Church Establishment in an Age of Grey and Holland', *History*, 1960.
CAHILL, G. A., 'The Protestant Association and the anti-Maynooth agitation of 1845', *Catholic Historical Review*, xliii, October 1957.
—— 'Irish Catholicism and English Toryism', *Review of Politics*, xix, January 1957.
CHADWICK, O., 'Young Gladstone and Italy', *Journal of Ecclesiastical History*, xxx, April 1979.
CONACHER, J. B., 'Mr. Gladstone seeks a seat', *Canadian Historical Association Report* 1962.
FOOT, M. R. D., 'Morley's Gladstone: A Reappraisal', *Bulletin of the John Rylands Library*, LI, 1968–69.
GREAVES, R. W., 'The Jerusalem Bishopric, 1841', *English Historical Review*, lxix, July 1949.
LYNCH, M. J., 'Was Gladstone a Tractarian? W. E. Gladstone and the Oxford Movement, 1833–45', *Journal of Religious History*, viii (1975).
MACHIN, G. I. T., 'Lord John Russell and the Prelude to the Ecclesiastical Titles Bill, 1846–51', *Journal of Ecclesiastical History*, xxv, 1974.
MATTHEW, H. C. G., 'Gladstone, Vaticanism, and the Question of the East', *Studies in Church History*, xv, 1978.
NICHOLLS, D., 'Gladstone on Liberty and Democracy', *The Review of Politics*, xxiii, 1961.
NORMAN, E. R., 'The Maynooth Question of 1845', *Irish Historical Studies*, xlv, 1967.
STEPHEN, M. D., 'Liberty, Church and State: Gladstone's Relations with Manning and Acton, 1832–70', *Journal of Religious History*, i, 1960–61.
—— 'Gladstone and the Composition of the Final Court of Ecclesiastical Causes, 1850–73', *Historical Journal*, ix, 1966.
WALSH, J. D., 'Joseph Milner's Evangelical Church History', *Journal of Ecclesiastical History*, x, 1959.
WARD, W. R., 'Oxford and the Origins of Liberal Catholicism in the Church of England', *Studies in Church History*, i, 1964.
ZAMICK, M., 'Unpublished letters of Arthur Henry Hallam from Eton, now in the John Rylands Library', *Bulletin of the John Rylands Library*, xviii, 1934.

*D. Theses*
FARNSWORTH, S. H., 'Gladstone's policy towards the Colonies, 1833–1855' (1977), unpublished B.Litt. thesis in the Bodleian Library, Oxford.
FORRESTER, D. W., 'The Intellectual Development of E. B. Pusey 1800–1850' (1967), unpublished D.Phil. thesis in the Bodleian Library, Oxford.

GREENFIELD, R. H., 'The Attitude of the Tractarians to the Roman Catholic Church 1833–1850' (1956), unpublished D.Phil. thesis in the Bodleian Library, Oxford.

HEUSS-BURCKHARDT, U., 'Gladstone und das Problem der Staatskirche' (1957), Dr. Phil. thesis, University of Zurich.

# INDEX